C0-DAO-044

Seek First
HIS
Kingdom

Seek First HIS Kingdom

An Autobiography

By Nathan Krupp
With input from Joanne

Written for their children, grandchildren,
and great-grandchildren.

Copyright 2014 - Nathan Krupp

This book may not be reproduced without
prior permission of the author.

Front Cover: An original portrait of Jesus, the Son of GOD.
Designed by my grandson - Alexander Jason Krupp
(Alex graduated as an art major from Indiana Wesleyan
University in Marion, IN, in April 2013.)

Are Jesus' hands outstretched in worship, preaching,
or welcoming us? Or all three!

Unless otherwise noted, all Scripture quotations are from either -
The New American Standard Bible, Lockman Foundation,
La Habra, CA.
or
The English Standard Version Bible, Good News Publishers, Wheaton, IL.

Printed by CreateSpace,
An Amazon.com Company
Charleston, SC
eStore address:
www.CreateSpace.com/1656411

ISBN: 1497577209
EAN: 978-1497577206

Library of Congress Number
2014906936

Printed in the United States of America

DEDICATION

This book is dedicated to all those who have

encouraged us along the way -

with your friendship,

encouraging words,

prayers,

and financial support -

you and GOD know who you are!

SCRIPTURES IMPORTANT
TO NATE KRUPP

The following are some of the key Scriptures that have guided my life.

Seek first the Kingdom of GOD
and His righteousness, and all these things will be given to you as well. - Matthew 6:33 (NIV version)

Not everyone who says to me, "Lord, Lord," will enter the kingdom of heaven, but the one who **does the will of my father** *who is in heaven. - Matthew 7:21*

That I may know Him, *and the power of His resurrection, and the fellowship of His sufferings. - Philippians 3:10*

Delight yourself in the Lord, *and He will give you the desires of your heart. - Psalm 37:4*

Bless the Lord, O my soul, and **forget not all His benefits,** *Who forgives all your iniquity, Who heals all your diseases. - Psalm 103:2-3*

He who **dwells** *in the shelter of the Most High will abide in the shadow of the Almighty. - Ps. 91:1*

Before I formed you in the womb I knew you, and before you were born I consecrated you;

I appointed you a **prophet** *to the nations . . . all to whom I send you, you shall go, and whatever I command you, you shall speak. - Jeremiah 1:5, 7*

i

*This I call to my mind, and therefore I have hope.
The steadfast love of the Lord never ceases;
His mercies never come to an end;
they are new every morning;*
Great is Your faithfulness.
- Lamentations 3:21-23

Man shall not live on bread alone, but on **every word** *that proceeds out of the mouth of GOD.*
- Matthew 4:4

You shall **love the Lord your GOD with all your heart** *and with all your soul and with all your mind. This is the first and greatest commandment. And the second most important commandment is to* **love your neighbor as you love yourself.**
- Matthew 22:37-39 (combined versions)

Jesus said, "Follow Me, and I will make you fishers of men."
- Matthew 4:19

Jesus said to them, **"Go** *into all the world and* **proclaim the Good News to every person."**
- Mark 16:15 (combined versions)

Ask of Me, and I will surely give **the nations** *as your inheritance, and the ends of the earth as your possession. - Psalm 2: 8*

CONTENTS

Appendices

INTRODUCTION

The Lord began to speak to me about writing the story of my life in 1994 through Psalm 145:4-7. In the following years He spoke further to me through Exodus 10:2, 17:14, 33:2; Joshua 4:22, 1 Chronicles 16:12, Psalms 9:1, 11, 40:10, 71:17-18, 73:28, 78:4, 89:1, 118:17, 145:4; Isaiah 30:8, 63:7; and Jeremiah 30:2, 36:2.

I started on this project in 1995 and finished it in 2014. It is the story of GOD's grace and faithfulness to a nobody from a little town in Ohio who tried to obey GOD in all that He spoke to him over a period of more than fifty years. The credit for anything that has been accomplished all goes to GOD - I have tried only to obey His leading.

It has been a great encouragement to me as I have reviewed my life to see the overwhelming goodness and faithfulness of GOD. As it says in Philippians 3:10, we have come to "know Him, the power of His resurrection, and the fellowship of His sufferings."

Writing this Biography was made possible because I kept a Journal since 1961. Entries from my Journal will be noted by "Je." Throughout the book many Scripture references are listed - these are verses that the Holy Spirit has made real to me, spoken to me through.

There are many details in the Autobiography that will not interest everyone, but I have tried to present a complete account of my life. You may want to skip over some of these details. Likewise, you may want to skip over some of my radical views about GOD's plan for His Church.

I am deeply grateful to my wife for her wisdom and much encouragement to me throughout our years together. Her input and editorial assistance in this writing project have been very helpful and extremely significant.

It is my prayer that this writing will be a blessing to my children, my grandchildren, and great-grandchildren, to the fourth generation (Psalms 78:5-7, Isaiah 59:21, 2 Timothy 2:2). I am very proud of each one of you! May each of you spend your life seeking first GOD's Kingdom, knowing that if you do, He will abundantly provide everything you need in this life, and in the life to come - Matthew 6:33.

I pray that this writing will likewise be a blessing to others who might be led to read it.

To GOD be the glory!

Nate Krupp
Salem, Oregon, USA
August 2014

CHAPTER 1 - GROWING UP

(Family, World War 2, Boy Scouts, Presbyterian Church, first jobs)

Fostoria Ohio - 1935 - 1953

My life began on September 7, 1935, but my beginning moments in this world were not without concern to my parents. I was born two months premature and was a "blue baby," a term given to a baby whose heart is not functioning properly giving the baby a bluish color. I guess it was touch and go for a short time before the doctors got my blood flowing normally. Some blue babies don't make it. I did - I guess GOD had a purpose for my living. I've had no further problems with my heart.

I was named Nathan George after my great, great grandfather, Nathan Joseph Babcock, who served in the Civil War, and my two grandfathers, George Krupp and George Allis.

The Krupp name was made famous by the Krupp dynasty and industry in Germany, which provided armament for both sides in wars from the 1500s onward, including the supply to Hitler during WW2. This is all chronicled in the book *The Arms of Krupp*.

My first seventeen years, until I went to college, were spent in Fostoria, Ohio, a town of about 18,000, in northwestern Ohio, USA. Fostoria is known for its Fostoria glassware, which originated there, but is now located in West Virginia. It is also known for its railroad trains - there were more trains passing through Fostoria than any other city in the world for the size of town. And it was known for having so many factories for a town that size, although some have moved away.

3

My father, Paul Howard Krupp, was born in Fostoria on May 8, 1905, and lived his entire life there. His father died of tuberculosis when Dad was only three. In fact, his father was on a trip West looking for a cure when he died, and is buried somewhere in Colorado. His mother worked in a garment factory to provide for the family, which consisted of older sister, Ruth, Dad, and younger sister, Virginia (Ginny). They were a poor family, living near the railroad tracks. One of Dad's early recollections was pulling his little wagon along the railroad tracks picking up pieces of coal, that had fallen off the coal cars, to heat their small home.

Grandma died on April 28, 1947. Ruth was a Christian and went home to be with the Lord on January 14, 1970. I had the privilege of leading Aunt Ginny to Jesus in a nursing home in Fostoria in the final months of her life and she died on March 4, 1991. Aunt Ginny's husband, Al, left her in the early years of their marriage for another woman. Her life was not easy, although she was very creative, writing music and painting. She wrote the theme song for the city of Dearborn, Michigan, where she and her son, my cousin, Alan, lived.

Dad started selling newspapers and writing articles for the *Fostoria Review* newspaper while in high school. Upon graduation from high school he wanted to attend Wooster College in Wooster, Ohio, and prepare for the Presbyterian ministry. Instead, he felt he needed to go to work to help support his mother and two sisters. He worked for over fifteen years at the *Review* newspaper, doing a variety of jobs, starting with getting stories by visiting the downtown stores, to finally doing the paper layout.

In March 1941, he went to work in the sales department of Fostoria Pressed Steel, a company that made fluorescent lights. During the war they also manufactured other war-related products. In time he became sales manager.

He took a trip by train about once a year to New York or Philadelphia to meet with leading Pressed Steel sales reps. It was a big occasion to go as a family to see him off at the train station. I went with him to New York City one time and another time to Chicago.

After retiring in 1970, Dad returned to his first love - the newspaper - and from 1977 to 1989 he wrote a weekly column called *Potluck* on some aspect of Fostoria's history. He always ended his column with a section called *Heeding GOD's Word* where he would quote from the Bible, with appropriate comments. He finally had his "ministry" - we were sure proud of him! Everyone in town looked forward to reading his columns. He was known as a committed Christian and considered by many to be the town's unofficial historian.

Dad once told me that Fostoria had given me much and I owed something back. GOD used that conversation later in my life to lead me to work on putting his columns into book form as my gift back to Fostoria. From 1996 to 2002 I worked with a number of people in Fostoria to put the best of his columns into two books, *Images of America - Fostoria, Ohio, Volumes I and II*. That group included Ray Dell, Norman Gibat, George Gray, and David Krupp, with help from Clarence Pennington, Harry MacDonald, Mel Murray, Leonard Skonecki, Ben Pohman, Nancy Slaymaker, the Fostoria Library staff, and others. Arcadia Publishers published it: *Volume One* came out in 2001 and *Volume Two* in 2002.

My mother, Cleo May (Allis) Krupp, was born in Tiffin, Ohio, a town thirteen miles east of Fostoria, on May 20, 1909. Her mother, Cleo, died in the influenza epidemic when Mom was only nine years old. Her Dad, my Grandpa, remarried to Ella from Tennessee, who had three daughters. Mom had to move out and went to live with her Uncle Roy and Aunt Laila Hoffman in Fostoria when she was sixteen. She took a commercial business course at the Fostoria High School.

(I'm sure that rejection of having to leave her home was terribly wounding to Mom.) After graduating from high school Mom went to work at the local J.C. Penney clothing store. She later did office work at National Carbon and then the *Fostoria Review* newspaper.

Grandpa Allis was the custodian at the Tiffin High School. He was a champion ice skater. We saw him about once a year, either in Tiffin or Fostoria. When I was about ten he bought me a pair of roller skates - I had quite a time standing up, but finally got the hang of it.

On Mother's dad's side she had three aunts, Lula, Emma, and Kate. Aunt Lula was married to Uncle Taylor. They had an adopted daughter, Kathryn. They lived in several country homes near Tiffin, Ohio, where we often visited. I remember one place where there was no inside toilet - only an outhouse. When Grandpa died Uncle Taylor and Aunt Lula moved to Grandpa's home in Tiffin. Aunt Lula put out a garden each year and lived to be 104. Uncle Taylor did deliveries for an egg company. I remember going with him once.

Aunt Emma was married to Uncle Roy and lived in Lancaster, in Southern Ohio. They had a small grocery attached to their home. We visited them once when I was a boy and also saw Old Man's Cave. They had one daughter, Helen, who taught at a business school in Pittsburgh. Aunt Emma lived to be 95 and Helen 100. There was also an Aunt Kate, but we didn't have much contact with her.

On Mother's mother's side of the family she had three aunts - Aunt Laila, married to Uncle Roy Hoffman, lived in Fostoria; Aunt Avilda, married to Ray Apger, lived in Toledo; and Aunt Clara was a widow who lived in Fresno, California. The Hoffmans had three daughters, Aileen, Lucille, and Royetta, all of whom lived in Fostoria. The Apgers had two children, Maxine, who lived in Toledo, and Harold, who lived in California.

Aunt Clara came by train to Fostoria to visit every few years. One year she brought me a cowboy outfit of chaps and a gun belt and pistol. I would run around the yard playing cowboy and singing Gene Autry's song, *I'm Back in the Saddle Again.* The only cousin on Mom's side that I am still close to is Gary McPherson, Aileen's son.

Mom and Dad met when they were both working at the *Fostoria Review* newspaper. They were married in a simple wedding on July 11, 1931. They first lived with Dad's mother, and then rented their first home on West Center Street, across from the post office. When I was just a baby the folks purchased their first home and we moved to 727 North Countyline Street. We lived there until I finished my sophomore year in high school, when we moved to 927 North Main Street. The Countyline home was on the edge of the city and during hunting season the pheasants would come into our back yard to be safe from the hunters. How the pheasants knew when hunting season began, where the city limits were, and where they could be safe is beyond me.

We had an outside porch off of one of the bedrooms on the second floor. One time, when I was about ten, I jumped off of the porch, using an umbrella as a parachute!

Dad went home to be with his Lord on January 26, 1999, at the age of 93. He was a GOD-fearing Presbyterian - and very patriotic. (The other Krupps in Fostoria were Catholic and we hardly knew them.) Mom died on December 18, 2001, at the age of 91. Dad didn't make it to the new century, but Mom did.

I have a brother, David, called "Dave," born May 19, 1940. When he was about five he developed epilepsy. This was of great concern to my parents, especially Mom. I was given the responsibility of keeping an eye on him. I clearly remember one time running out into busy Countyline Street to retrieve him when he had wandered out there.

I had the privilege of leading my brother to Jesus at the Navigators center, called Glen Eyrie, in Colorado Springs, Colorado, in the summer of 1960 when he, Mom, and Dad were visiting me there. He is a deeply committed Christian, spending several hours each morning studying his Bible.

Through my Mom's cousin, Maxine Godsey, we learned of Mr. Heugle, a faith healer, in Toledo. We all began going to him, especially Dave when he had one of his seizures.

I have a sister, Janet, called "Jan," who was eleven years younger than I, born May 11, 1946. She was only six when I went away to college so I wasn't around her much in her growing-up years. I do remember carrying her on my back up the stairs to her bedroom at night. She married her high school sweetheart, Kenny McCarley, in 1964. They had three daughters, a stillborn named Lisa, Amie, and Lorie.

Their marriage ended in 1975. Janet lived in Florida for a number of years but is now back in Fostoria. Amie is married to Allan Ashby and has two daughters, Amber and Alyssa.

After living in Florida for many years, Amie and Allan have also moved to Fostoria. Lorie lives in Florida, was married in 1997 to Johnny Stevenson, and has a son named Devin.

We attended the Presbyterian Church as a family. That included Sunday School and the Sunday morning service. Dad taught the adult Sunday School class for several years. I never remember the Gospel being preached. At age twelve I attended the membership class and after the completion of the class I stood up in front of the elders and said, "I accept Jesus Christ as my Savior." I must not have fully understood what that meant because there was no change in my life. But my involvement at church did lay a foundation for what GOD later did in my life (see Chapter 2).

I was active in Boy Scouts, first as a Cub Scout, and then as a Boy Scout. The Cub Scout meetings were held at David Spooner's home. The Boy Scout meetings were in the basement of the Presbyterian Church. I became one of the leaders of our Boy Scout troop and received the Eagle Scout award, with a bronze leaf, and the GOD and Country award. I was on the area camp staff in the summer of 1950 at Camp Berry, near Findlay, Ohio. Dad made me a wooden box about 2'x3'x2' to keep my belongings in while on the camp staff. My son, Gerry, now has that box.

Dad and I went to Philmont Scout Ranch together with a local group of about forty in the summer of 1951. Dad took his two-week summer vacation for this venture. The group traveled in a school bus from Findlay, Ohio, to Cimarron, in northeastern New Mexico. The Missouri and Mississippi rivers had just flooded badly, so we had to detour several times to get across these rivers on the way out.

At Philmont we hiked or rode horse by day and camped by night. The scenery was beautiful!

Dad and I held the distinction of being two of a very few who could shinny up a hanging rope at one campsite! This trip was quite an adventure and such a privilege to be with Dad for two weeks.

We always had a large garden when I was a boy. This was during the Second World War, and just about everybody had a "Victory Garden." Everyone was encouraged to raise their own food so that there would be more of the food supply that could go to the troops. As I got older, the garden became more and more my responsibility. This meant carrying buckets of water to it in the evening and keeping the garden weeded. I always enjoyed my garden work - and still do today.

With regard to the war, I can remember several things:
- I remember the Sunday afternoon we were taking a family automobile drive when the announcement came over the car radio that Pearl Harbor had just been bombed.
- We could not take any long trips during the war because gasoline was rationed. And no new cars were manufactured during the war because all industry was making war equipment.
- When we got our ration coupons for bananas, and somehow Mom knew that A & P was going to have them, I was sent on my bicycle to get some.
- Dad kept getting older just enough to stay ahead of the draft, which we considered such a blessing as a family.
- German prisoners-of-war could be seen doing road work on Hwy 199 (now 23) north of Fostoria.
- The war was often discussed at our dinner table.
- The war in Europe ended on May 8, 1945, which was also Dad's 40th birthday.
- After the war was over in Europe I can remember large squadrons of bombers flying overhead, very high, going west from Europe to the war in the Pacific.
- I was almost 10 and remember well the day the war totally ended on August 15, 1945. Sirens blew, church bells rang, and everyone was so joyous. There was a large edition of the local newspaper and Dad brought a copy home for me to keep.

Work was part of my growing-up years. My first job was at home carrying the ashes from our coal-burning furnace out to the back alley. There was also the garden work in the summers. And it was my job to paint the white picket fences that separated our backyard from our neighbors on both sides. I hated that job! I still don't like to paint! When I was old enough to start making money, I began by mowing lawns. And in the seventh grade, I worked a couple hours on Saturday mornings at a little grocery store on South Street near Countyline, run by a friend of my Mom's.

Dad and Mom never went to college and they instilled in me the need to save up money so that I could go to college in order to have a better job career. They taught me to divide my money: 50 percent was saved for college; 10 percent was given to our church; 20 percent was set aside for buying clothes; and I could spend the remaining 20 percent. I had about $2,000 saved up when it was time to go to college. That was a lot of money in those days!

When I was in the eighth grade I got a paper route, carrying *The Toledo Blade*. My route was about 75 customers on Perry, Summit, and Elm streets. After school each day, I went to the paper office uptown, folded my papers, and then delivered them. But on the way to the paper office I would stop at a drug store for pie ala mode, a milk shake, or an ice cream sundae, or at the hamburger joint for a burger - never spending more than 15 cents a day! Saturday was spent collecting what was owed to me by my customers. Christmas was always a fun time - with the tips my customers gave me I bought power tools each year: a jig saw, table saw, and planer.

When I became a sophomore in high school I began working at Kroger Grocery store. First I worked at the old store on South Street. Then I helped open the new store on Perry Street. I started out sacking and carrying out groceries. Then I began working late two nights a week stocking groceries when the trucks came in. Later I began working in produce, setting up and waiting on customers.

I also went in early each day before school and helped set up the produce department. One summer I managed the produce department for a month while the produce manager was on vacation. I enjoy purchasing the produce for Jo and me to this day. Back then bread was 10 cents a loaf, a can of tomato soup was also 10 cents, a large can of canned fruit was 25 cents, and gasoline was 19 cents a gallon. Oh, what inflation has done to the value of our money!

An enjoyable event two different summers was going as a family on a week's fishing trip to northern Michigan, near Cedarville. Mom did not enjoy these trips because she still had to work, cooking for the rest of us. Between my sophomore and junior year we moved from Countyline Street to a three-bedroom home at 927 North Main Street. Dave and I shared a nice-sized room, and Janet was finally able to have a room of her own.

Thanksgiving Day we usually spent with Uncle Dewey and Aunt Ruth, my Dad's sister, and their children, Barb, Paul, Carol, and Loren, who was just a few years older than I. Some years they came to our home and some years we went to theirs in Upper Sandusky, Ohio. We always stuffed ourselves! A couple of years my other cousin, Alan, and Aunt Ginny were also able to join us from Detroit.

Barb married Dan Reed, who served in WW2; they lived their entire lives in Upper Sandusky, and had two sons, John and Tom. Paul married Annie and they had a son, Dick. Paul died in 1961 from a bad heart. Carol married Chuck Bixler, lived in Fremont, and had three daughters, Gwen, Gail, and Greta. Loren married Lois, lived in Upper; they had two children, Steve and Sue, and had an auto dealership in Upper.

One fun thing I did when growing up and on through college was to go fishing in the summer with Uncle Dewey in his boat on Lake Erie. After retiring from running Upper Auto Parts he and Aunt Ruth purchased a cottage on the lake and lived their retirement years there. Also, one summer I spent a few days in Upper with Loren. Another summer I spent a few days with Paul and Annie at their home in the country.

We were not a family with much means. I remember my first bike was an old, used, skinny-tire one my Dad bought from a neighbor for $5.00. It was painted black and I was embarrassed to ride it because the other neighbor boys had new bikes.

12

My folks set aside money each week for Christmas and tried to bless us kids. One year I got an electric train. I was quite young (4 or 5) and Dad played with it for several years before it was turned over to me! Another year I got a new Flyer sled. It was a terrific sled and I could usually out-distance everyone else on the favorite town hill at Gray's Park. Another year I got a pair of ice skates and became quite a good ice skater at the city reservoir in the winter.

My neighborhood friends were Jack Smith, Norman Knisley, Melvin Leedy, and Norman Gibat. Jack Smith became an insurance agent and moved to Montana. Norman Knisely married Shirley Mansfield, moved to Tiffin, and was in sales for a meat company.

Melvin Leedy was killed in an auto accident in his early twenties, but had become a Christian a short time before his death. Norman Gibat had a computer business in Fostoria.

I took the college preparatory courses in high school including chemistry, physics, algebra, geometry, trigonometry, Spanish, and typing. I was not very studious during those years. I could get B's without studying or taking homework home, so why study? I was so lazy that I reported on the same Hardy Boys book at book report time each year for three years. I remember taking homework home only one time during high school. This all changed when I met the Lord in 1957 - He gave me an unquenchable thirst for knowledge, which has been evidenced by a life of acquiring and reading books.

I played the bassoon in the high school concert band and orchestra and the base drum and cymbals in the marching band. I also had taken piano lessons for several years from Miss Marjorie Newhouse. I could play fairly well, but hated to practice! My favorite pop singer was Perry Como and I still enjoy listening to his recordings, especially *When I Fall in Love* and *It's Impossible*.

Helen Widener, my Mom's cousin, wanted to give me an accordion, but I turned it down. (Boy, do I wish I would have taken it. I love accordion music.)

In sports I was pretty good at football, softball, and basketball, but I was best at running the mile. However, I was too busy working to go out for any varsity teams.

I went by Nathan until my sophomore year in high school when one of my classmates, a Jewish lad named Jerry Steinman, began to call me Nate. It caught on and I have gone by Nate ever since, although some of my relatives still call me Nathan.

I felt left out in high school because Mom would not let me hang out with the "fast crowd." But I did have girlfriends: Ethel Kranz from the eighth grade through my junior year and Judy Shiflet starting in my senior year. My youth Sunday School class was quite small, so there was no real fellowship there.

I did run around some with the guys at Krogers - Doug Boster and Ron Griffin. They both attended the Church of the Nazarene. Ron seemed like a nice guy. I started drinking with Doug after we finished work at Krogers at night. He later was soundly converted.

All through my teen years, I knew there was a void in my life - something was missing. Church didn't fill the void. "Being good" didn't fill the void. Being successful in Boy Scouts didn't fill the void. Working hard didn't fill the void. Having girlfriends didn't fill the void. What was I looking for - and how could I find it?

CHAPTER 2 - AWAY TO COLLEGE

(Engineering, Naval ROTC, Student Government,
Becoming a follower of Jesus Christ)

Purdue University: 1953 - 1957

The idea had been instilled in me quite early in my life that I needed to go to college and get a good education in order to get a good paying job. Thus I would not have to "struggle" financially as the folks had had to do. We were not poor, I would say we were of middle income, but we did live quite frugally. Their frugal lifestyle also stemmed from their coming out of the Depression of the early 1930s. Most everyone lived more simply in those days.

In the fall of my senior year of high school Dad took me to Chicago for a series of tests that tell you what your basic talents/abilities are - those given by GOD. He combined the trip with Pressed Steel business. We stayed in a hotel and ate in restaurants - I thought it was quite a deal! The tests showed that I was very high in three-dimensional visualization, and, therefore, should be either a surgeon or a structural engineer. I couldn't stand the sight of blood so decided to become an engineer. Not knowing the Lord, I knew nothing about asking Him what His plan for me was.

Dad arranged for me to meet Ira Cadwalder, a businessman in Fostoria, who had graduated from Purdue University. Ira very strongly encouraged me to attend Purdue as the best place one could go for engineering. My senior year I sent away for information from several engineering schools: Purdue, Ohio State, University of Cincinnati, Carnegie in Pittsburgh, Case in Cleveland, and MIT. I decided on Purdue because it was only a four-year school. Some of the engineering schools took five years and I thought I didn't have an extra year to waste!

15

Purdue also was not too far from home - yet far enough to be on my own. Sometimes I would hitchhike back and forth and sometimes Dad would take or get me, which gave me some quality time with him. (It was much easier to hitchhike in those days than it is today.)

During the summer after graduating from high school, Dad and I took a trip to West Lafayette, Indiana, to see Purdue. While there we saw a sign on a building about Naval ROTC. I knew that I would have to have ROTC and preferred Navy to Army. Upon inquiring we discovered that it was not too late to apply. When I had my interview they were especially impressed with the fact that I was an Eagle Scout. Some weeks later I received word that I had been accepted.

In early September 1953, Dad took me to Purdue, where I would spend the next four years. I lived on the second floor of the southeast wing of Cary Hall, a men's residence hall. At many colleges, most of the students live in fraternities and sororities, but at Purdue the majority of students live in residence halls. Cary was the oldest men's hall, but very nice, very close to campus, and the dining hall served good food.

My roommate my freshman year was Al Lang from Youngstown, Ohio. He became a member of the famous Purdue Glee Club and joined a fraternity. My roommate my sophomore year was Larry Axsom from Indianapolis. He and his family were members of the Christian Church. My junior year my roommate was from Toledo, Ohio. His father had an engineering company and wanted his son to take it over some day, which he didn't really want to do.

The first day in the fall of 1953 I stood in long lines at the armory to register for various basic engineering courses. I started out in Civil Engineering, but my counselors suggested that there was more flexibility in application by studying Mechanical Engineering, so I switched.

16

Then I became quite interested in time study and in organizational charts and opted toward Industrial Engineering. Purdue did not have a School of Industrial Engineering at that time but one could get a degree in Mechanical Engineering, with an Industrial option, which is what I did.

Since I did not need to study very hard in high school, at Purdue I had to learn quickly how to study. The end of my first semester most of my grades were on the border between A and B or between B and C. I needed to get as high grades as possible in order to qualify for a scholarship for the second semester. I had only $2,000 saved up toward college and that would go quickly. So the week of final exams at the end of the first semester I did not sleep the whole week, from Sunday night until Saturday night! I went to class and took a test, then came home and studied all night for the test the next day. That was repeated all week long. After finishing the final test on Saturday morning, I came home, went to bed, and did not wake up until Monday morning! I slept right through Sunday! I did get the higher grade in most of the courses - and I did get scholarship assistance - for the rest of my years at Purdue.

Shortly after the year started, my Naval ROTC instructor told me that the Executive Officer wanted to see me in his office. He was a thirty-year career officer - and he asked me if I was really interested in "the program." I said, "Yes, Sir!" He then asked why I had not gone to the Naval Armory to pick up my rifle? And why had I not seen my name on the two message bulletin boards? Somehow I missed the announcement in class to go check out a rifle. And I was not aware of the bulletin boards for special messages - I had missed that announcement, too. So it looked like I was not too sharp or not very interested. The XO said he would give me one more chance to "get with the program" or be dropped from NROTC. Well, I assured him that I would follow through on this.

I went immediately to the armory and told the Marine sergeant there that I had come to get my "gun."

You don't call a rifle a gun when talking with a Marine drill sergeant! After a thorough lecture, I was given my rifle. So I almost got dropped from NROTC.

Three years later, my junior year, I was nominated for the NROTC honorary, Quarterdeck Society, by Gene Cernan, later an astronaut. And I was chosen by the Navy officer instructors to be the Battalion Executive Officer my senior year, number two in command of all of the NROTC troops. I had gotten with the program!

Each spring on Armed Forces Day at Purdue, we had a big parade and review of the troops. Our NROTC student commanding officer, Ray Traxler, was selected to head all of the troops, Navy, Army, and Air Force. This meant that I, as second in command of the Navy, had the privilege of leading all the Navy battalion in the parade. There were awards given out that day and I was awarded the "Outstanding Midshipman of the Year" award - quite an honor - for a guy who was almost dropped from the program!

Toward the end of my freshman year, Bob Seifert, who had a room down the hall in Cary Hall, asked me to run for Sophomore Class President on the same ticket with him. He was an older guy, an Army vet, was about to enter his senior year, and was going to run for Student Body President. He was tired of the fraternity and sorority people having all of the positions on campus and decided it was time for those in the residence halls to become more active. So he was putting together an entire ticket of people from residence halls. He seemed to like me and must have thought I would be a good student leader.

I can't remember if the entire ticket won or not, but I do know that Bob, and the candidate for speaker of the Senate, Dick Eykamp, and I, all won. So my sophomore year I was class president.

This meant that I was a member of the student government senate, which met about once a month. It was an interesting experience and gave me contact with the other key campus leaders. But I was so nervous before each meeting that I lost my dinner on the way to the meetings. I may have been a student leader on the outside, but I was very insecure on the inside.

At the end of my sophomore year I was encouraged to run for Speaker of the Senate - and was elected. Then at the end of my junior year, everyone expected me to run for Student Body President. I wasn't sure whether I was up to that or not. I remember counseling with my Presbyterian minister at home about it. He encouraged me to go for it, and, in fact, felt it was my GOD-given responsibility. I did run. And won.

So my senior year I was Student Body President. This gave me the privilege of working closely with the Dean of Men and Dean of Women on various projects - and to meet other administration officials including Dr. Fred Hovde, the president. As SBP I had the privilege of speaking to the incoming freshmen at the big, famous Purdue Music Hall. Two of our big projects while I was SBP were working with the administration in initiating a campus-wide student health insurance program and adding a judicial branch to the Student Government.

I remember speaking at one Friday-evening, all-campus rally before a big football game the next day. This was at the time when Len Dawson, with whom I was acquainted, was the quarterback. He went on to play pro ball. It was a long-held tradition that whoever won the civil war game between Purdue and Indiana University got to keep what was called the "Old Oaken Bucket" until the next civil war game. And as Student Body President, I had the honor of carrying the Old Oaken Bucket out on the field at the halftime of the Purdue-IU football game that year.

I spent the summers working. Between my freshman and sophomore years and between my sophomore and junior years I worked in the Engineering Department as a draftsman and junior engineer at National Machinery in Tiffin. I rode to work from Fostoria to Tiffin each day with Tony Ward, a neighbor down the street from us. One week, when Tony was on vacation, I rode with Reverend Wilcox, a Wesleyan Methodist preacher. He told me about all of the things that that church believed one should not do - wear make-up, smoke, drink, go to movies, dance, wear jewelry, etc., but he never told me about the salvation and abundant life that was available through Jesus.

Between my junior and senior years I worked for a short time in the Quality Control department at National Carbon in Fostoria. I also had a six-week training cruise with the Navy. I was stationed aboard a destroyer, the USS Purdy, DD-732. We were part of a fleet of ships that went from Norfolk, VA, to New Orleans; down and through the Panama Canal to Panama City; back to Guantanamo Bay, Cuba; and back to Norfolk. Because I had already been chosen to be Battalion Executive Officer for my senior year at Purdue, the officers aboard the destroyer chose me to be the student commanding officer of the NROTC student battalion on the ship for the first two weeks. The next two weeks I was the commander of one of the companies. One day I found two students from the South who were not willing to clean the toilets. They said that their culture did not allow them to do that. I told them, "In this man's Navy you will clean the toilets!" And they did! The last two weeks I was just one of the troops and found myself spending those weeks in the hot, steamy engine room.

Between the Panama Canal and Gitmo we were skirting a hurricane. The ship was listing 30 degrees to port, then starboard. I was not able to sleep in my bunk so went topside to the deck to sleep. I could have easily rolled off the deck and been lost at sea. GOD was watching over me!

That summer I also went to Minneapolis to a national gathering of student body presidents from around the nation. During part of that trip I sat on a bus with a leader from a university in Texas. He was planning to be a missionary upon graduation and his life and witness found lodging in my heart.

At the end of the summer I also had a special two-week course at Purdue on welding and casting.

I continued drinking from high school days - and began drinking more - especially my senior year. I would study until 10 or 11 - then head across town with a carload of guys to Lafayette because West Lafayette, where Purdue was located, was dry. Each of us would drink a pitcher of beer, and then be back at the dorm by 12 or 1.

My years at Purdue were very busy, between difficult engineering studies, Naval ROTC responsibilities, and Student Government responsibilities. I learned to make every minute count. Most of my friends were those connected with my engineering classes, NROTC, and Student Government. Across the hall, though, was my closest friend, Ron Hayden, who was a year ahead of me. I got his single room my senior year. My responsibilities were such my senior year that I decided it would be best to have my own room - so I paid a little more and got Ron's - it was a good decision. I haven't seen Ron since he graduated, but we did recently reconnect by e-mail and phone.

My senior year I returned to Purdue a few days early to speak to the incoming freshmen class and for other Student Body President responsibilities. While I was in my room unpacking, a knock came on the door. He was a foreign-looking student who introduced himself as Abraham Zion David. He had a single room right next to mine. I learned that Abraham was from Israel, was Jewish, and had attended the American University in Beirut, Lebanon, before coming to Purdue.

21

He also had one year at a religious college, Marion College, in Marion, Indiana. He was at Purdue to get a masters degree in Agricultural Economics to prepare to help developing nations. He actually had planned to go to Rice University in North Carolina, but changed his plans at the last minute. When he arrived at Purdue there were no rooms in the dorms so he spent his first week living in the college infirmary. One day a room opened up - right next to mine!

We became close friends. David (he went by David rather than Abraham or Abe) stopped by often to see if we could go to the dining room and have our meal together. He always bowed his head and prayed before he ate. We did that in my home as a boy once a year on Thanksgiving - he did it every meal!

Abe seemed different. He was happy and peaceful and seemed to know where he was going with his life. I questioned him on this. He said it had not always been that way, but that things changed one day when he turned his life over to "the Lord." I didn't know that "the Lord" was Jesus - and I had never heard of turning one's life over to Him - or that things could change "in a day."

Sometimes when I came back from drinking I was pretty much out-of-it. In fact, sometimes they had to carry me to my room. David was always there to help me get to bed. What a guy! One time he came into my room to shine my shoes before an important date. I had started smoking a pipe my senior year (big man on campus!), drank, and listened to Doris Day records. Abraham never said anything negative about my bad habits - he just befriended me, loved me, and served me.

One Saturday in March he came into my room and said that Nate Scharff, the businessman from Dayton, Ohio, who was sponsoring him in the United States, was going to speak the next day at the little church David attended in Lafayette, called Wesleyan Methodist.

22

David wanted to know if I would go with him. I had attended with him once in the fall, but didn't feel comfortable because the folks would spontaneously say "Amen" as the preacher delivered his sermon.

I usually attended the Presbyterian Church, which was right next to the Purdue campus. I had heard of Nate Scharff from David and wanted to meet someone with the same first name as mine - Nathan or Nate - so decided to go.

At the morning service Nate told his life story - how he had as his goal in life to be a millionaire by the age of thirty - and had achieved it by developing a chain of clothing stores in western Ohio. But he was not happy - and his marriage to a Gentile lady, Mary, was not going well. One day Nate tried to blow his brains out, but the gun would not go off. He told how his life changed when he met Jesus one Sunday evening in a Wesleyan Methodist Church in Dayton, Ohio. For years, the pastor of the church, John Woodhouse, had come to Nate's main store and talked to him about Jesus. Sometimes Nate physically threw him out of the store.

The Monday morning after Nate was converted he stood in front of his store giving away socks and telling people that Jesus had something better to give them. Nate became a very zealous witness for his Messiah, speaking at CBMC (Christian Business Men's Committee) meetings; traveling to Israel to talk to the Jewish people, including the prime minister, David Ben-Gurion; and conducting citywide evangelistic crusades.

After the service I met Nate Scharff and he invited me to come back to the church in the afternoon to see slides he had taken on trips to Israel. I had an important meeting to go to as Student Body President, but felt strangely compelled to send Bud Smith, my Speaker of the Senate, to the meeting, and returned to see the slides.

23

After the slide presentation, Nate and Abraham invited me to have a bite of supper with them. I said yes and we went to a student hangout called "The Big Wheel." It was packed with students since everyone was on his own for the Sunday evening meal.

On the way there Nate asked me what I was going to do now that I was about ready to graduate. (It was now March 17, 1957, just a few months before graduation.) I said, "I don't know. I believe GOD has a plan for everyone's life (good Presbyterian theology!), but I don't know what His plan is for mine." Nate said, "Well are you the Lord's? I can't tell my neighbor's servants what to do - just my own - and the Lord can't tell you what to do until you become His. You must turn your life over to Him." This was only the second time I had ever heard anything like this - Abraham's was the first.

By now we were in the restaurant eating. Nate said, "You know there is only one person keeping you from turning your life over to the Lord." To my own surprise, I said, "Yes, me." He then said, "You know you could turn your life over to the Lord today if you want to." Again, to my own surprise, the words just popped out of my mouth, and I said, "That's right - and I want to." Nate bowed his head and began praying out loud right there in the restaurant! He asked me to follow him in a prayer. I don't know exactly what I prayed - but I do know that with all of my heart I turned my whole life over to "the Lord" as I prayed. When I finished I felt so different - so clean inside, and so full of peace, and joy, and love. (I didn't yet have any understanding that I had just been "born again.")

After we finished the meal, they invited me back to church again, for the evening service - three times in one day! That was a record for me. Everyone was so excited that I had "turned my life over to the Lord." The only other thing I remember was singing *What a Friend We Have in Jesus*. I had sung it in our Presbyterian Church as a boy, it never meant much to me, but this time it had tremendous meaning.

After the service, we (Nate, David, and I) went over to the pastor's home to have a snack. That was the beginning of a friendship with Rev. and Mrs. Hoover.

After the snack, Abe and I took Nate to Logansport to catch a train back to Ohio. On the way there, Nate encouraged me to do three things - start the day reading the Bible, beginning in *John's Gospel*, and praying, and then telling people about "the Lord" as I went through the day.

When we got back to the dorm about midnight, I was very zealous and began going from room to room telling my fellow students about how I had "turned my life over to the Lord" that day. I still wasn't sure whom "the Lord" was - but that night as I lay in my bed drifting off to sleep, I saw a picture of the face of Jesus on the ceiling of my room - and I knew whom "the Lord" was! I'm not sure how I knew that it was the face of Jesus, but I did.

I found out later that other Christians at Purdue and at Marion College had been praying all year for me.

As a follower of Jesus I immediately discovered that my desire to get drunk was gone, as was my profanity (I use to swear every other sentence). In the years to come the Lord continued to change my life, taking away the bad and adding the good.

The next day Abe gave me an olive wood covered Bible from Israel. In the front he wrote: *To Nate Krupp with all my prayers that He would perfect the thing which He has started within you. May your life so shine for Him and tell of His great story, that people might know that you have been with Jesus. Accept this as a token of love because of His love - Your friend, His servant, A. Z. David.* He also listed three verses - 1 Samuel 12:23, Isaiah 58:9, and Isaiah 60:1.

I had been around Christians all of my life, but no one told me about how Jesus could change my life. For me, GOD had to save a Jew in Lebanon, bring him to the United States, change his college plans and bring him to Purdue, and put him in the room next to mine, so that I could hear the Good News. Oh, the lack of obedience of many Christians! - And, Oh, the faithfulness of GOD!!

From the eighth grade on I had had a string of girlfriends - Ethel, Judy, Barb, Ginny, Sue, Joanne (not my wife). I was looking for love. Now I had found it - GOD's love!

During my senior year I had the opportunity to teach a drafting course to freshman and also to work a few hours a week at the Purdue Engineering Department.

I also began interviewing companies for employment upon graduation. Purdue had quite a placement program, where company executives would come to campus to interview senior students. With B average grades and all of my leadership responsibilities I could have had about any job I wanted. I took a trip to the East during the Christmas break to visit Babcock and Wilcox in New York City, DuPont in Delaware, an aircraft company in Connecticut, and IBM in New York State. I also had a letter from a Boeing vice president, who had grown up in Fostoria, inviting me to come to Seattle for an interview.

Because of NROTC, I had a two-year commitment with the Navy after graduation, but companies were eager to sign up graduates to come to work for them after their military duty. I decided to not take any job since I did not know what the future held - now that I had turned my life over to Jesus. The Lord had already begun to impress upon me that Mark 16:15 was to be an important part of my life: *"Go into all the world and preach the Gospel to the whole creation."*

On June 1, 1957, I was commissioned an officer in the United States Navy's Civil Engineer Corps. And on June 2, I graduated with a Bachelor of Science degree in Mechanical Engineering (Industrial Option).

Here are a few incidental memories of my Purdue days: During my sophomore year I had a speech class. On the first day of class we were each to stand at our seat and give our name and hometown. I was so petrified that I stood and promptly forgot both! But my senior year I was inducted into the speech honorary.

I had an accounting class my senior year just after lunch. It was not my favorite subject, and after a bountiful lunch, I had a seat in the back of the class, and slept through most of the classes, but did get a C for the course.

Ginny Son and I were named *Outstanding Independent* our senior year by the fraternity and sorority leaders.

Also, during my senior year, I purchased a set of golf clubs from Sears and began playing golf in my spare time. This was part of being BMOC (Big Man On Campus)!

One interesting thing about Purdue: There is a central heating plant and the heat is sent through ducts under the sidewalks to the various buildings. In this way the snow melts on the sidewalks during the winter. Designed by a Purdue engineer I'm sure!

An unusual event that year was my meeting Louie Armstrong. He and his band had performed at our senior dance. After I took my date home I stopped at a coffee shop for a snack. And there seated at one of the booths was Louie. I went over and introduced myself and he invited me to sit down with him. I probably spent twenty minutes with him - he was so easy and natural to be with. So I spent 20 minutes with Louie Armstrong! - What an interesting opportunity!

27

Most of the early astronauts were from Purdue. It was my privilege to meet Neil Armstrong and to know fairly well Roger Chaffee and Gene Cernan. Roger and I had NROTC and engineering classes together and I knew Gene through a mutual friend, Dick Pletcher. Chaffee, along with Gus Grissom and Ed White, died when fire swept through the capsule of Apollo I.

CHAPTER 3
DISCOVERING LIFE AS A FOLLOWER
OF JESUS CHRIST

(US Navy Civil Engineer Corps officer)

Port Hueneme, CA; Kingsville, TX: 1957 - 1959

After graduating from Purdue I went home to Fostoria, Ohio, for a few weeks until I had to report for active duty in the Navy. I was so tired from all of the study and other responsibilities at Purdue that I spent much of the time sleeping.

Frank Judy (yes, that was his last name), a fellow Navy ROTC graduate, from Kentucky, was given a new car for graduation by his parents. He picked me up and we headed for Port Hueneme, in Southern California. We were going to camp out and cook out along the way (mainly my idea), but after a couple of cold nights in South Dakota and Utah, we stayed a night or two in motels. It was an interesting time, seeing sights I had never seen before - Mt. Rushmore, Bryce Canyon, Zion Canyon, then over to California. We stayed one night with my Aunt Clara in Fresno, California. She put on quite a breakfast the next morning! Then we drove through San Francisco and on to Port Hueneme. We arrived at the Civil Engineer Corps Officers' School in mid-July for a six-week course for newly commissioned Civil Engineer Corps officers.

I had applied for the CEC during my senior year at Purdue. With my engineering degree it was a natural - and I was having increasing doubts about being able to kill people as a line officer on a ship. There were about thirty of us at CECOS from all over the United States.

Each afternoon when class was over we headed for the beautiful California beaches near Oxnard.

One week of our training was at Camp Pendleton Marine Corps Base. We had to strip and reassemble an M-1 rifle blindfolded; crawl under live machine gun fire; target practice, at which I happened to have been the top marksman; and an all-night field problem.

One Sunday evening I had an urge to attend church so I went out through the base gate and just started walking. Within a few blocks I found a little Baptist Church and the service was just about to begin. After the service I got acquainted with the pastor - and also a Navy commander, who was attending. I went back a time or two to their mid-week prayer meeting. It was mainly the pastor, his son, and I. I asked him the question I had about killing people and he encouraged me to read the Bible to find an answer (what wisdom!). So I started reading the Bible - and haven't stopped! I also occasionally attended an evangelical Presbyterian Church in Oxnard, a larger town near Port Hueneme.

One evening I was in Oxnard walking down the street when I saw a sign on a door that said "Christian Servicemen's Center." I decided to investigate since I was now a Christian and a serviceman. Opening the door I climbed a flight of stairs to the center. A fellow who said his name was Mert Martin met me. We talked some and he gave me a little packet of memory cards called "B-Rations" that were produced by a Christian ministry called The Navigators. On these cards were the Bible verses 1 John 5:11-12 - the assurance of salvation, 1 John 1:9 - the assurance of forgiveness, John 16:24 - the assurance of answered prayer, and 1 Corinthians 10:13 - the assurance of victory. I began to memorize them.

During our six-week course there was an Admiral's Ball, a dance to honor us students. I took a good-looking blonde that I had met on the beach one day. She was from Long Island and was spending the summer with her sister-in-law while her brother was on special assignment as a CEC officer in Alaska.

I spent our time dancing talking to her about the Lord. She said someone back at college had also been sharing about Him with her.

Also, during our CECOS course we were interviewed by an officer from the Navy Bureau of Personnel in Washington, DC, as to what kind of assignment we preferred. There are three types of duty for CEC officers: an officer with the Seabees, doing military construction for the Navy overseas; a Public Works Officer, being responsible for base maintenance at an established base; or Resident Officer in Charge of Construction, overseeing construction being done at a base by a private contractor. We could request one of these three types of duty. We could also request where we would prefer to be assigned.

When my orders arrived I did not get either the type of duty nor the location I had requested. But I knew that I had received orders for what GOD wanted for me because before I met with the Bureau person I had asked GOD to give me the duty He wanted me to have. According to John 16:24, which I had just memorized, that is exactly what I would get. John 16:24 says, *"Until now you have asked for nothing in My name; ask, and you will receive, that your joy may be made full."*

Shortly before graduating from CECOS I bought my first automobile - a used 1949 Chrysler - at a used car lot in Oxnard for $119. Upon graduation in late August 1957, I was on my way to my assigned duty in Kingsville, Texas, driving my "new" 1949 Chrysler. On Saturday I spent the day with Jamie Jamieson and his wife, Sue, in San Diego.

I had known Jamie through student government at Purdue, and he also was a Navy officer. They gave me a copy of *The Man Called Peter,* the life story of Peter Marshall. As I read this book over the next weeks, GOD spoke to me that his life-verse, Matthew 6:33, was to be mine also. It says: *"But seek first His kingdom and His righteousness; and all these things shall be added to you."* The Lord said to me that, if I would absolutely put Him first in my life, He would provide everything else I needed in life. He surely has done that! And you can see where I got the title for this biography.

En route to Texas, I stopped along the way to see a distant cousin in Tucson, Arizona, where I got a good night's sleep. I discovered that the auto heated up driving in the hot August daytime sun across the Southwest desert so I had to drive at night and sleep in the daytime. After several days I arrived in Kingsville, south of Corpus Christi, in Southeastern Texas.

For the next 21 months (from September, 1957, through May, 1959) I lived at the Bachelor Officers' Quarters on the Naval Auxiliary Air Station at Kingsville, Texas. I was the junior officer of two in the Resident Officer in Charge of Construction office. I was an ensign and George Peevy was a lieutenant, junior grade. In addition to the two of us there was a secretary, and four or five inspectors who spent their time right on the various construction projects to make sure that everything was done properly. We reported to Commander (later Captain) Robert (Bob) E. Sparks. We called him "Commander Sparks" or "Sir."

They were making the base into a permanent installation, with two airfields for advanced pilot training, so there was a lot of construction going on. Private contractors were doing this construction and our office was responsible to coordinate all of it. The basic training for pilots was at Pensacola, Florida. Then the student pilots would come to Corpus Christi, Kingsville, or Beeville, TX, for their advanced training.

32

During my time there we coordinated the construction of a new Officers' Club; a new Bachelor Officers' Quarters; a new, multimillion dollar airplane maintenance hangar; two new enlisted men's barracks; a new enlisted men's mess (dining facility), and more. I spent about three-fourths of my time in the office, looking over paper work and spending some time doing Bible studies. I also drove a Navy pickup truck around and visited each job every day, touching base with the inspectors.

Commander Sparks was a deeply dedicated Christian, but he was a tough officer to work for. Our office was allowed to see him once a week, on Friday afternoon, for no more than 30 minutes. We (usually Peevy, but sometimes I) could not take in any problems on the various construction projects. We couldn't even take in the solutions. We had to take in a one-paragraph letter for Commander Sparks to sign that would initiate action to solve whatever problems had arisen. I learned from him much about efficient administration and saying things with as few words as possible.

In the Public Works Office, also under CDR Sparks was Lt. Fred Coople. I went to his home one evening and attempted to give him the Plan of Salvation and lead him to Christ. It was the first time I had ever done this and I gave him far too many verses. He was not ready, but some months later he told me that he had gotten down on his knees by his bed one evening and did accept Jesus as his Savior. I was sure excited! We have kept in touch for many years and he continues to walk with the Lord and be active in a Church of Christ in Michigan.

I would eat my meals at the Officers' Club. I was the only one who bowed his head and thanked the Lord for his food before eating. At Friday dinner, after most of the "fly boys" had been drinking too much at the "happy hour," they often made fun of me. I was beginning to learn some of what was involved in being a follower of Jesus Christ

Shortly after arriving at Kingsville I received a letter from Nate Scharff encouraging me to make a full surrender of my life to Jesus, based on Romans 12:1-2. This letter really spoke to me, and I spent all day Saturday in my room, reading the entire book of *Matthew*, and giving my life more fully to the Lord.

One Saturday I was in my BOQ room reading my Bible. When I came across 2 Corinthians 6:17, which says, *"Therefore, come out from their midst and be separate," says the Lord. "And do not touch what is unclean:"* The Lord spoke to me that I should quit smoking my pipe since it was "an unclean thing." I immediately took my pipe and can of tobacco and dropped them in the wastebasket. That was the last time I ever smoked anything.

Although GOD took getting drunk away from me during my final days at Purdue after my conversion, he had not yet convicted me of social drinking. But during my time at Kingsville He did. And I was so busy witnessing that I no longer had time for dancing or watching movies at the base theater.

After work each day I would come to my BOQ room and listen to radio evangelist Lester Roloff. He was an independent Baptist and quite a well-known preacher in Texas. One time Oral Roberts was on the radio - and I was not feeling well - he encouraged folks to touch the radio as a point of contact - I did, and was healed. Later I heard he was having a tent revival in Corpus Christi so I went one evening. This was my first contact with Pentecostals.

I heard of a Bible study conducted at the base chapel, one evening a week, so I went to check it out. At the study I met Paul Jackson, an enlisted man of many years. He invited me to become part of the base Sunday School and I was soon teaching the junior high school boys' class.

I had the privilege of leading many of them to the Lord after class was over. One day at lunch, an old, salty Marine Colonel said, "Krupp, I understand you have my boy in Sunday School. I don't know what you've been doing, but keep it up. He's a different boy." I hadn't done anything except lead him to Jesus!

Paul Jackson also told me about an on-fire church in town, Calvary Baptist Church. So I started attending. The first time I went was on a Sunday evening and Bob Clement, the preacher, was preaching on being "born again." As he spoke, the Holy Spirit showed me that that was what had happened to me in the restaurant near Purdue on March 17, 1957!

I became quite active in that church for the remainder of my time at Kingsville - the Sunday morning service, after the base Sunday School responsibilities; Sunday evening, Wednesday night, and jail preaching and home visitation on Saturday morning. Also, during my two years there, a larger church building was being erected with much of the work being done by the men of the church. I helped some and got to know the head deacon, Brother Chism, who was a wonderful, godly gentleman. Another blessing at the church was listening to Doyle, one of the men in the church, sing *When the Roll is Called Up Yonder, I'll be There* in his beautiful tenor voice.

Another blessing during this time in Kingsville was meeting Lydia Beltran. She was the daughter of a Baptist pastor in Spain, where he had experienced much persecution since Spain was strongly Catholic. The Sparks had gotten to know Lydia during his previous assignment, which was in Spain. When they came back to the states, Lydia came with them to attend Baylor University in Waco, Texas. I met her when invited to the Sparks' home for Thanksgiving dinner during my first year at Kingsville and she became like a big sister to me, mentoring me in the things of GOD.

During these years I began to pass out tracts. Because of my inferiority complex I started by putting them in empty phone booths!

GOD began to use me on the base leading others to Christ. I met with a group of Christian sailors early one morning a week for Bible study and prayer. As an officer, I should not have been fraternizing that closely with enlisted men, but GOD had told me to do it. The Lord spoke to us as a group that we should blanket the base with Gospel literature every six months, which was when there was a turnover of student pilots. We divided the base up so that every building was someone's responsibility. We used the leaflet *God's Simple Plan of Salvation* by Ford Porter.

Between midnight and four in the morning we each got up, went to our area, and put a leaflet on each desk, under each door, on each bunk, and on each auto windshield. The next morning as everyone got up, or drove to the base from town, the entire base was covered with Gospel literature. We saw men get saved through this. One of the converts was a student pilot. After he completed his training he was transferred to a carrier in the Mediterranean - he and I kept in touch for a while - he was leading others to Christ there. Sunday afternoon was a favorite time of mine to do personal evangelism throughout the base. I saw many people saved.

After doing the Gospel literature blitz twice, Commander Sparks called me into his office one day. He said the base Commanding Officer, Captain Sullivan, had learned that I was behind this Gospel outreach, and he wanted it stopped. The next time I met with the sailors we prayed about the matter. A few weeks later Captain Sullivan was mysteriously transferred to another base!

A few weeks after the new skipper arrived on the base he came to the Officers' Club to have breakfast with those of us who ate there.

I sat across the table from him. Somehow I began to share with him the story of my coming to Christ. The other officers left for their duty assignments and the skipper stayed to intently listen as I finished my testimony. I saw him one other time, when I was checking out of the Navy, and had opportunity to share with him further about Christ.

After being there about six months I bought a new car, a Renault. With this nice car, I started another Gospel outreach. I would pick up sailors, who were at the base gate waiting for a bus to go to town, and tell them about Jesus all the way to town. After dropping one off in town, I would return to the base and pick up another one, etc. What a way to spend an evening! I also put the following in big red letters on my car bumpers: "JESUS SAVES" on one and "CHRIST IS THE ANSWER" on the other.

With this new car I was able to go home to Ohio for two weeks leave in the summer of 1958. As I traveled I listened to radio preachers Charles E. Fuller, who founded Fuller Theological Seminary, and C. M. Ward, an Assembly of God evangelist.

I spent most of the time with my family in Fostoria, but I did spend a couple days with Nate Scharff at his home in Dayton, Ohio. I saw the building in downtown Dayton where Nate had Psalms 34:6 painted on an outside wall, *"This poor man cried, and the Lord heard him, and saved him out of all his troubles."*

While I was at home I went downtown to the Kresge five-and-ten store and made restitution for some fishing tackle I had stolen as a teenager. The manager didn't know what to say!

One Sunday evening the message at the Baptist Church in Texas was based on Matthew 4:19-20, where Jesus said, *"Follow Me, and I will make you fishers of men."* And it says, *"They immediately left the nets, and followed Him."*

I had been struggling with a call to full-time Christian service because I didn't want to give up my engineering, a degree I had worked so hard to obtain. That night the "immediately" really convicted me. When the message was over, I went forward and surrendered my life to the Lord for full-time service. The Baptists called it being "called to preach." That was in the summer of 1958.

I started preaching at some of the little country Baptist churches that were scattered around that part of Texas. My first opportunity to preach at Calvary Baptist, as one of several "preacher boys" in the church, was at a New Year's Eve service, December 31, 1958. I spoke on 2 Timothy 4:7-8, *"I have fought the good fight, I have finished the course, I have kept the faith; in the future there is laid up for me the crown of righteousness, which the Lord, the righteous Judge, will award to me on that day; and not only to me, but also to all who have loved His appearing."*

One time I went to a revival meeting at a Southern Baptist church in the Rio Grande Valley and heard R. G. Lee give his famous message, *Pay-Day Someday,* about heaven and hell. It has been said that it was the most preached, most famous sermon of the 20th Century.

"Rusty" Reynolds, a chief petty officer, and his family were a great blessing to me during my Navy time. They were active at Calvary Baptist Church and sometimes would invite me home for a snack after the Sunday evening service. They were like an older brother and sister to me. When I left Kingsville, I left my uniform and sword with them to sell - and give the money to missions. He later retired to San Antonio, Texas.

Another person of great blessing to me during those days was Jim Knutz. He was also a chief petty officer. We used to meet for prayer in a small room at the base chapel - the Lord would often meet with us in a very precious way. I have often wondered what happened to Jim. I have not seen or heard of him since I left Kingsville.

After I finished memorizing the four verses that Mert Martin had given me in Oxnard, I wrote The Navigators for more study material. I started going through all of their Bible study booklets. They sent my name to the Nav representative for Texas, Hal Ward. Hal came to Kingsville, looked me up, and taught me how to have a Quiet Time. (Hal developed cancer and went home to be with the Lord in September 2011. We talked on the phone only every few years, but I really feel a void in my life with his passing.)

I was encouraged by the Navy to stay in for 20 years and make it my career. I really wanted to do that, but GOD spoke to me through Ecclesiastes 2:11: *"Thus I considered all my activities which my hands had done and the labor which I had exerted, and behold all was vanity and striving after wind and there was no profit under the sun."* He said to me that all of my work in the Navy - and so it would be in the coming years if I stayed in - were unimportant compared to the work He had for me to do.

My tour of duty was to have been for two years, but I was given an opportunity to get out two months early, at the end of May 1959. The Navigators had invited me to come to their headquarters, Glen Eyrie, in Colorado Springs, Colorado, for the summer of 1959 for further Christian discipling. So I took the offer to get out of the Navy early and went to Colorado.

What a change! When I left Purdue I had planned to go to Harvard and get a Masters in Business Administration (MBA) after I got out of the Navy. I then planned to have a career in industrial management, and hoped to someday be president of General Motors, live in a big house in the Crosse Pointe area, and have a sailboat on Lake St. Clair. Instead, I was on my way to be discipled by a Christian ministry and become a fisher of men.

CHAPTER 4
DISCOVERING LIFE AS A FOLLOWER
OF JESUS CHRIST (Continued)

The Navigators: Colorado Springs, CO - 1959 - 1960

The Navigators had invited me to come to their headquarters, Glen Eyrie, in Colorado Springs, Colorado, for the summer of 1959 for further Christian discipling. So I took the offer to get out of the Navy two months early and went.

I was part of a summer trainee program at Glen Eyrie during the summer of 1959. There were about twenty-five of us - mostly single guys and gals - mostly in our early twenties - mostly fairly young Christians - who meant business with GOD and wanted further discipling. We were housed with older Nav staff. I spent the summer living in "the Barn." This was a building, part of which was used as a barn for horses, and part of it had been converted into housing, i.e., sleeping space. We were all single guys - some trainees and a staff person.

I thought I was going to spend the summer attending Bible conference meetings. I was in for a big surprise! We would all put in a full day working at the headquarters. I was assigned to the maintenance department. Within a few weeks of being on the maintenance department, the main sewer line coming from the main building, the Castle, broke. I spent the next week digging - dirt - then sewage - until we found the break and fixed it. I dug during the daytime. I dug through the evening while others walked by on their way to the Conference meetings. I dug all day Saturday. I dug until the hole was as deep as I was tall. I dug until we found the problem - by now I was standing in sewage. I fixed it. Then I shoveled some more - filling the hole back in.

41

The next week a water line broke. The following week another water line broke. Shortly thereafter another water line broke. I spent all summer digging ditches - and fixing broken sewer and water lines. I hated it! But I finally came to the place one day when I prayed, "Lord, I'll be a ditch digger the rest of my life if that is what You want!"

My boss at the maintenance department was Clyde Lawson, then Hal Hannibal. One week I was part of a crew that did some work at Eagle Lake, a campground the Navs owned up in the mountains west of Glen Eyrie. While there I recited all of the verses of the TMS to Clyde. The Topical Memory System was 108 Scripture verses - 3 verses each for 36 topics - that the Navs had developed. Every trainee was expected to memorize them during their time at Glen Eyrie. After completing the TMS I continued to memorize other passages that the Lord made "real" to me.

The very next week after I prayed my "ditch digger prayer" I was told to report to the main headquarters office where I was informed that the top leaders had decided to put me in charge of a new construction program. I was to coordinate the architects, engineers, utility companies, construction personnel, and Nav leadership for the erection of two new dormitory buildings to be used for people coming to the Glen to attend conferences. No one knew the prayer I had prayed the previous week - but GOD did! - And He directed them to give me a new assignment - once I had passed the test!

This new assignment was over my head! I had a degree in engineering, but little practical experience. In the next week or so I sought GOD much about this. One day in my morning quiet time he spoke to me through Exodus 31:3: *"And I have filled him with the Spirit of God in wisdom, in understanding, in knowledge, and in all kinds of craftsmanship."* GOD assured me that He would equip me for the task.

Over the next several months (spring and summer of 1960), I worked with two wonderful Christian architects at the Air Force Academy. They had designed the academy, which had just been built, and now were drawing up plans for the two new buildings for the Navigators. I worked with the utility companies to have proper telephone and electricity for the buildings. And once construction began, I coordinated all of this with the on-site foreman.

We had an interesting development during the early days of construction. The on-site foreman, who had been brought into the picture from town (Colorado Springs), decided to build the buildings differently - drastically different! - than the plans showed. This resulted in a big meeting with the top brass - Lorne Sanny, Bob Foster, Jim Downing, the foreman, the assistant foreman, who was an old-time Nav guy, and me. The conclusion of the meetings was that the buildings were to be built according to the plans - and I was given more authority to make sure things were done right!

During that summer the Nav staff was gathered together from around the world. I was asked to tell them about the building program - it was quite an honor for me and they applauded when I finished.

One morning when I reported to the maintenance office for work I was told to report to the Pink House, where Lorne Sanny and his family lived. When I got there I was asked to help Cliff Barrows and his wife with their suitcases. Mr. Barrows was Billy Graham's song leader and had taught the entire Glen family the previous evening to sing *How Great Thou Art*. So I had the privilege of carrying Cliff Barrows' suitcase!

Our evenings were free to be spent as we chose - most of us spent the time studying our Bibles or attending the evening Conference meetings. One early morning a week we had a housing Bible study group.

I remember our going through 1 John as one of the first books we studied. Then 1 Thessalonians. Then Philippians. *The Amplified New Testament* had just been published and most of us were using it in our studies. I learned much about how to study the Bible during those months - and I spent as much time as I could find studying my Bible. They also taught us to keep a journal, which I began to do.

I often skipped lunch - packed a sandwich at breakfast - so I could have more time to read, study, and pray during lunchtime. Most of us scrounged around and found a quiet place to have a study. Mine was under the Castle in an area I shared with the rats! As part of our daily life at the Glen we were often discussing Bible matters. I remember some of us deciding that Christ's Return would certainly be before the year 2000!

During the Philippians study, GOD spoke to me through 3:7-8: *"But whatever things were gain to me, those things I have counted as loss for the sake of Christ. More than that, I count all things to be loss in view of the surpassing value of knowing Christ Jesus my Lord, for whom I have suffered the loss of all things, and count them but rubbish in order that I may gain Christ."* He led me to get rid of all of my earthly possessions. One of them was a set of golf clubs from Purdue days. I gave them to Bob Foster. I saw him many years later - in the mid - 1980s - he was still using the clubs. I was now free to go anywhere, and do anything GOD led me to do, unencumbered by "things."

My Renault car was beginning to give me some trouble. Another trainee said we should overhaul it. So we began. We just got it torn down when he said it was time for him to leave the Glen - and I could put it back together! I tried - and had a couple parts left over! I tried to drive it and the engine blew up. They finally hauled it off for junk! Another "rubbish" (Philippians 3:8) was gone!

I had planned to take a trip back to see my family at the end of that summer (1959). Without the car it became questionable. Another trainee was going to hitchhike back to Wisconsin for college, so we decided to go together. It was illegal to hitchhike in Colorado, so we took a bus to Cheyenne, Wyoming. From there we started hitchhiking east on Route 30 and Interstate 80 where it had been completed. One of our rides was a Pentecostal preacher - he talked to us about the baptism of the Holy Spirit and speaking in tongues.

Clint had to get to Wisconsin on a certain date for college so we decided that we would pool our funds and get him there if we didn't get rides quickly enough. But GOD was faithful - we got really good rides all the way to Illinois. Clint and I said good-by - he headed north to Wisconsin - and I took a train the rest of the way to Fostoria.

I was home about two weeks. While there I borrowed the family car and visited Purdue, Howard Noggle at Marion College, and a Billy Graham Crusade in Indianapolis. I stayed overnight one night with Howard and Marie Noggle. Before I went to bed Brother Noggle asked me to place my shoes outside my bedroom door. The next morning I discovered that my shoes had been shined - what saints they were! Howard gave me several books to read on the subject of sanctification, or the Spirit-filled life. I read the books over the next months and became hungry for a deeper relationship with GOD.

In March 1960, Nate Scharff came to the Glen at Chuck Farah's invitation to speak about the Jewish roots of Christianity. On Sunday afternoon Nate and I were spending some time in prayer. As we did, the Spirit of God fell upon me - I was literally filled with the Spirit. (This was without the speaking in tongues aspect, which is so prevalent today. GOD did give that to me later.)

45

What a change it made in my life - new levels of victorious living, new boldness in witnessing, and a greater hunger for GOD's Word and prayer.

One Saturday morning, during the summer of 1960, Chuck Farah, who was the director of trainees, was speaking to all of us trainees from Jeremiah 33:3 - about believing God for BIG THINGS! Later that day I climbed one of the hills on the property, found a quiet place, and asked GOD for a ministry on every continent by the age of thirty! Quite a prayer for a young Christian from a little town in Ohio. Do you know what - GOD answered that prayer! Fewer than two years after leaving Glen Eyrie the Lord led me to write a textbook on personal evangelism, *You Can be a Soul Winner - Here's How.* Without any advertising, the book began to be used around the world. We started getting letters from one continent after another. Just before my thirtieth birthday, we heard from the last continent. Through that book GOD had used me on every continent by the age of thirty! He is so faithful!

One memorable thing that took place while I was at the Glen was when Mrs. Pearl Goode came to share with us. She lived in Pasadena, CA, and during Billy Graham's first crusade, in Los Angeles, the Lord told Mrs. Goode that He was going to use Billy around the world, and that she was to go wherever he was having a crusade, rent a hotel room, and spend the time praying for him. She shared all of this with a group of us and spent time in prayer with us - it was a great privilege and inspiration.

Another memorable thing that took place was meeting Hubert Mitchell. He had come to Glen Eyrie to spend a few days in prayer with Lorne Sanny. Hubert would play a big part in my life in the years to come. (This is told in later chapters.)

A couple times Ford Madison took me with him on Wednesday evenings when he did visitation evangelism from First Presbyterian Church, an evangelical church. Ford was the owner of a dairy in the Springs. He used C.S. Lovett's *Soul Winning Made Easy* approach and presentation. One time there was a milk price war between Ford and his two competitors. He met separately with each of them to discuss the situation. They did not settle the price war, but he led each of them to Christ. I learned much from Ford.

I began to disciple Duane Redeker in evangelism. I had met him at the Southern Baptist church that I was attending. Some Sundays we would skip Sunday School and go to the city park and witness and pass out Christian literature. Then we would return to the church for the Sunday service. I have often wondered whatever happened to Duane since we have had no contact since I left the Glen.

One time the Navs assigned me to teach a church youth group how to do a book study on 1 Thessalonians. I felt greatly honored to have been given that assignment - and I really enjoyed it.

In the fall of 1959 I was transferred from the Barn to the Greenhouse, a building that had been a greenhouse, but had been converted into permanent housing for staff and student.

By the end of the summer of 1960 I was getting anxious to move on. Several had spoken to me about attending the Graduate School of Missions at Columbia Bible College in Columbia, South Carolina. So I packed my belongings and sent them with others to South Carolina. Before I left the Glen, the guys at the Greenhouse took me out to dinner and gave me verses for my future. The most memorable one was Job 23:10, *"But He knows the way I take; when He has tried me, I shall come forth as gold."* - after much processing, someday I would be a vessel of gold. GOD is still working on that project!

47

Before leaving the Lord spoke to me Isaiah 55:12, *"For you shall go out in joy and be led forth in peace; the mountains and the hills before you shall break forth into singing, and all the trees of the field shall clap their hands."* He also spoke to me Isaiah 30:15, *" . . . in quietness and in trust shall be your strength."*

I headed for Indiana. Another trainee the second summer at the Glen had invited me to be part of an evangelistic team with Ed Gregory from Fuller Theological Seminary. They were to conduct a crusade at New Middletown, a little town in Southern Indiana. I gave my testimony one night - and helped out in other ways.

While in Indiana I also went to Winona Lake to spend a week with Nate Scharff during the annual staff conference of the American Association for Jewish Evangelism. It was wonderful to be with him - and to meet other Jewish Christians including Hyman Appleman, the famous Jewish evangelist. One evening I was part of a small group with Nate that prayed for Dr. Appleman just before he was to speak.

I also dropped by Marion to see Howard Noggle. He encouraged me to come to Marion College instead of going to Columbia. I went to Chicago, also, to see Hubert Mitchell, whom I had met at Glen Eyrie when he was there once to spend a few days in prayer with Lorne Sanny, the Navigator president. I also visited Pacific Garden Mission with Nate Scharff and we had lunch with Herb Jauchen of *Christian Life Magazine*. This was to be the first of many visits I would make to Pacific Garden Mission where I preached to the men in the main auditorium and did personal work in the counseling rooms and out on the streets.

During that trip to Chicago I spent some time one day praying about Howard's invitation - and sensed GOD speaking to me through Genesis 24:27, Isaiah 42:16, and Acts 16:9 that I was to go to Marion College rather than Columbia Bible College. How greatly our lives are often influenced by what seem to be small forks in the road!

CHAPTER 5
COURTSHIP AND MARRIAGE

(Marion College, Joanne Sheets Brannon and Gerry, the Wesleyan Methodist Church)

Marion, IN: 1960 - 1961

<u>*1960*</u>

As previously mentioned I had planned to attend Columbia Bible College's Graduate School of Missions in preparation for being a missionary. My few belongings were already there. But Nate Scharff was encouraging me to go to Marion College. He said it would be more theologically compatible since I no longer believed in eternal security. And Howard Noggle was extending a warm welcome - and financial assistance. They would make me a dorm counselor on the west end of the second floor of Williams Hall, which would pay for my room. And they would also extend a scholarship to cover my tuition. That sure sounded good because the day I arrived I didn't even have money for a haircut! The time in Chicago, when GOD spoke to me through Genesis 24: 27, Isaiah 42:16, and Acts 16:9, settled it - it would be Marion College, not Columbia Bible College. I had my few belongings sent back from South Carolina to Indiana.

During the first days there Dr. Leo Cox, the main theology professor, interviewed me. He was a very godly man. He encouraged me to go to Asbury Theological Seminary in Wilmore, Kentucky, rather than Marion since I already had an undergraduate degree (in engineering). But I told him that GOD had directed me to Marion College - so Marion College it would be.

The Lord also worked it out for my brother, Dave, to attend that year - and be my roommate. But he had several bad epilepsy seizures and had to drop out before the end of the first semester. If I remember correctly they never gave me another roommate so I finished out the year with my own private room!

I had my meals the first semester at the campus dining room in the basement of Teter Hall with all of the other students. But I was short on funds the second semester so I didn't get a meal ticket. I lived on popcorn and soup, which I fixed myself, and an occasional meal at a South Marion restaurant. No wonder I weighed only 130 lbs when we got married!

I was at Marion to get further grounded in the faith and to prepare for ministry so I took courses in theology with Dr. Cox, Bible with Professor Clarence Huffman, Logic with Dr. Duane Thompson, and Speech with Professor Laura Emerson. They were all very wonderful Christian teachers.

I signed up to be on a Gospel team. These were groups of about five who would go to various churches on the weekends to preach, sing, etc. I lasted only one or two weekends. The others on the team didn't impress me as being too serious with the Lord, so I dropped out.

Instead, I started going to Chicago on the weekends and working at Pacific Garden Mission. These were great times - witnessing on the streets and preaching and doing personal work at the services. Various students would go with me from time to time. My folks had given me their second car, a 1955 Plymouth, so that's how I got to Chicago. My times in Chicago also often included spending time with Hubert Mitchell, who had a ministry of starting prayer groups with businessmen in their offices.

He was also strong on memorizing Scripture - chapters and entire books. He could quote *John, Romans,* and *Revelation,* along with some of the shorter *New Testament books.* He challenged me to memorize that way rather than just individual verses as the Navigators had taught, so I learned *Psalms 1, 15, 19, 23, 46, 63, 91, 139, 145, Isaiah 53, Matthew 5-7, 1 Corinthians 13, the Book of Philippians, and Hebrews 1 and 11.*

I also started going to downtown Marion on Friday evenings to witness in the vicinity of the Court House. Other students started going with me. One of them was Dave Castro, a student leader on campus. We became close friends and he was best man at our wedding. The professor at Marion who taught a course on personal evangelism, Dr. Elliott, heard about my work and invited me to share with his class once.

One of my big goals for that year at Marion College was to find out what GOD's plan was for my life. I knew that He had called me to some type of ministry - and I knew it had something to do with the evangelization of the world (Mark 16:15). In September, the Lord spoke to me through Hosea 6:3, *"Then shall we know, if we follow on to know the Lord."* He said that if I wanted to know His will, I needed to get to know Him better. So I started spending all afternoon each day reading through my Bible. I had classes in the morning and I studied in the evening, but the afternoon was for getting to know GOD. I needed a quiet place to do this and found that place in an empty Sunday school room in the basement of the College Church. These were wonderful times - reading through the Bible and praying about my future. At this point, all I knew was that it had to do with evangelizing the world.

Increasingly, I became convinced that the missing ingredient to world evangelization was personal evangelism. Missionaries took the Gospel to new lands and started churches. Evangelists like Billy Graham preached to those who would come to the meeting.

But who would reach those who would not come to the meeting? Only Spirit-led lay witnesses -- everyday people, who would reach their neighbors and business associates for Christ, could do that. What was GOD saying to me about this?

It was during these afternoon times with the Lord that I believe He commissioned me to be a prophet, based on Jeremiah, Chapter 1, *"Before I formed you in the womb I knew you, and before you were born I consecrated you; I appointed you a prophet to the nations. Do not say, 'I am only a youth'; for to all to whom I send you, you shall go, and whatever I command you, you shall speak"* (Jeremiah 1:5-7).

The Lord also made it clear to me that I was to keep my mouth shut unless He gave me something to say. I have not always followed that edict perfectly, but I have tried to speak only when GOD has given me something to say. This was also a time of waiting on GOD rather than bearing fruit (Habakkuk 3:17-18).

In August, through Nate Scharff, Herb Jauchan of *Christian Life Magazine* had become interested in publishing my testimony in tract form. So one of my projects that fall was to get it written. Through his efforts it was published the next year by American Tract Society, entitled *I Met Christ on the Campus.* It went through several printings and was used around the world. I still print copies from an original and give them out here and there when appropriate.

I had decided, based on 1 Corinthians, Chapter 7, that I was not to marry. However on December 7, 1960, God spoke to me twice during my quiet time, through Genesis 24: 7, *"The Lord, the God of heaven, who took me from my father's house and from the land of my birth, and who spoke to me, and who swore to me, saying, 'To your descendants I will give this land,' He will send His angel before you, and you will take a wife for my son from there."*

And verse 27, *"And he said, 'Blessed be the Lord, the God of my master Abraham, who has not forsaken His loving-kindness and His truth toward my master; as for me, the Lord has guided me in the way to the house of my master's brothers.' "* I sensed that He was saying that He was soon going to provide me with a wife. So I had to do some "tall" praying about this whole matter. Was I to marry after all? And whom was GOD going to provide? It had to be someone from among the Wesleyans ("the house of my master's brothers"), to whom He had led me through Nate Scharff and Abraham David.

In late August, when I visited Marion College to check things out, Howard Noggle had introduced me to a young widow, Joanne Sheets Brannon. In late October, another couple, Dick and Toby Durkop, had twisted my arm to invite Joanne out for a Coke with them after church one Sunday evening. I enjoyed the time and in early November invited her to go to a missions conference at Taylor University, in the nearby town of Upland, Indiana, where Dr. Norman Grubb was speaking. We had a good time, but got into a theological debate on the way home and the evening didn't end too well. I had had a date or two with two other girls that fall - walked them home after church, etc. After GOD spoke on December 7, I started doing some serious praying through the month of December - who was this "one" that GOD was going to provide.

1961

Increasingly I came to the conclusion that the one that GOD had for me was this young widow lady. I didn't know what to think about marrying a widow who had a young son. But GOD assured me that it was His will.

Joanne was born on February 5, 1936, in Ottawa, Kansas, and named Joanne Elizabeth Sheets. She had two older sisters, Arlene and Evelyn.

Her father, Harold, grew up in Kansas and was the oldest of seven - Harold, Frances, Ralph, Marie, Vernon, Orville, and Warren. Her mother, Miriam, grew up in Pennsylvania and was the youngest of five - Jacob, Howard, Paul, Cyrus, and Miriam. They met at the Brethren in Christ School in Grantham, Pennsylvania. Both had been raised in the Brethren In Christ Church, but just prior to Joanne's birth they had felt led to leave that denomination (mainly due to the strict dress code that they did not find in the Bible) and join the Wesleyan Methodist Church. They were pastoring a Wesleyan Methodist church in Ottawa, Kansas, when Joanne was born.

Because Harold and Miriam already had two girls, when Joanne was on the way they were hoping for a boy and were going to name him John. But, lo and behold, that boy turned out to be a girl so they named her Joanne. They originally spelled her name Joan, but people were calling her Joan rather than Jo-anne, so they added the extra "ne" to the spelling.

Since Harold had no boys, Joanne sort of became his "boy" and would often be called upon to help him with "boy-type" projects as she was growing up. He nicknamed her "Joey." One time she even had to crawl inside of the huge furnace down in the basement of a rental her Dad owned to give it a good cleaning. She hated it. She was a bit of a tomboy as a girl, but through it all never lost her femininity.

In 1938, they moved to Enid, Oklahoma, where Harold was to pastor a Wesleyan Methodist church. In 1945, Joanne's father went into full-time denominational work, developing the Youth Department with the Wesleyan Methodists. The family moved to Marion, Indiana, where the headquarters for the Wesleyan Methodist Church was located, and also so the three girls could attend Marion College, which was also located in Marion.

Joanne had been taught about Jesus for as long as she can remember and there was never a time when she didn't love Him. She remembers going to an altar of prayer when she was about six or seven in the church her father was pastoring in Enid. However, she dates her true conversion to a night when she was twelve years old. The Lord woke her up with a heavy heart. She did not have the assurance that she was truly saved. So she got out of bed, went into her parents' bedroom and asked them to pray with her. Together they knelt beside their bed, a parent on either side of her, and supported Joanne while she gave her heart to the Lord. She has walked with Jesus ever since.

After Joanne's second year at Marion College, she was married to Gerald Gene Brannon on June 27, 1956. Gerry was attending Asbury Theological Seminary at the time so after their marriage she transferred to Asbury College and got her degree in Social Studies with elementary teaching requirements. Upon both of their graduations they moved to Waukesha, Wisconsin, to pioneer a new Wesleyan Methodist church.

On August 20, 1959, tragedy struck when Gerry drowned while they were on vacation in Minnesota. Joanne was seven months pregnant at the time and moved back home to live with her parents. On October 31, a son was born whom she named Gerald Gene, after his father. Her time of sorrow was greatly softened by his birth and she spent the next year taking care of her baby and recovering from the loss of her husband.

By August 1960, although she was not looking for another husband, she was ready to move on to the next chapter of her life, whatever that would be. Although she had grieved deeply, she had never doubted GOD's wisdom in taking Gerry and knew He still had a plan for her life.

But when Howard Noggle, who was known as the campus match-maker at Marion College, approached her in the College Church foyer and told her he had someone he wanted her to meet, and motioned in the direction of where I was standing, she instantly realized she was being directed to a young man. As they walked the width of the foyer to the place where I was standing, Joanne said to herself, "Oh no you don't, Howard Noggle, you're not doing this to me." But, in spite of that, two months later we did have the two dates previously mentioned.

Over Christmas vacation, Joanne went back to Kansas and Oklahoma to visit Brannon relatives and her sister and husband, Arlene and Bob Hughes. Her interest and even thoughts about me took a back seat. But, upon returning to Marion and resuming her usual routine, as she would see me at church, her interest in me began to be stirred. But I was not particularly paying any attention to her and when she saw me walk another girl home from church one Sunday evening in early January, she realized that jealousy was really setting in.

When she got home and had put Gerry to bed, she was sitting in the living room pondering the whole situation when GOD clearly spoke these words to her, "Joanne, if I want you to have Nate Krupp, nothing will keep you from having him. And if I don't want you to have Nate Krupp, then you don't want him anyway." That made so much sense to her that she got up, walked down to her bedroom, knelt by her bed and repeated those words back to the Lord. In so doing, she turned our relationship over to the Lord, got up from her knees and promptly forgot about me.

About that same time I began feeling it was time to get better acquainted with Joanne. Mayer David, the younger brother of Abraham David who had helped me come to the Lord at Purdue, was a student at Marion that year. He talked me into inviting Joanne to a Marion College basketball game.

58

After watching Purdue basketball, this was small-town stuff. But exactly four days after she and GOD had had their conversation, I did ask her, and she said, "Yes." We went with Mayer and his girlfriend, and later wife, Mable. Joanne was a bit apprehensive about going since it was her first time out in public in Marion with another man. It was a small college and she knew that our being together would be an attention getter and cause for "talk." But she decided that she had her own life to live and that she was going in spite of any talk, and have a good time. So we went - and did have a good time. That was January 21, 1961. After the game we went to Mable's apartment for pizza.

We began seeing each other quite frequently as our interest in each other had begun to deepen. On January 25, we went to see an educational movie on campus about Berlin, Germany. My journal entry, "The evening was one of the most enjoyable I've ever spent."

On January 27, my journal entry was - "My attitude has been that I could not marry until I knew specifically what the Lord wanted me to do. But this is wrong - this is not living by faith. If GOD brings together myself and another, gives us a love for each other, she fulfills most of the Scriptural qualifications of a wife, and is willing to go anywhere and do anything, anytime, with me for Jesus, then I should trust the Lord to lead us together."

One time during these months George Beverly Shea, Billy Graham's soloist, came to sing at chapel at Marion College. I was an usher and had the privilege of seating Joanne. This seemed significant to me and increased my interest in her even more.

One Saturday in February we had what proved to be a very interesting and eventful time together. I had wanted to take Joanne to Purdue and show her my alma mater, so we decided to go to see a Purdue basketball game.

We took her car, a 1956 Chevrolet, since it had a better heater (which turned out to be a wise decision) than my Plymouth. Before the game we went to an upscale, well-known steak house in Lafayette. After the game it was snowing when we started home. The farther we drove the more it snowed and the deeper the snow got.

Before long we realized we were in the midst of a huge snowstorm. We started getting stuck over and over. We finally made it to the town of Delphi and realized we would have to spend the night there since the roads to Marion were totally closed. Joanne's friend, Helen Heron, was taking care of little Gerry since her folks were out of town so we called her to let her know of our dilemma. We found the only hotel in Delphi and asked for separate rooms on different floors, not wanting to leave the wrong impression with anyone. But they gave us rooms across the hall from each other, and Joanne was glad to have me nearby as it was not the highest-class hotel and she didn't feel completely safe.

The next morning (Sunday) the highways began to be cleared so we started toward Marion. We stopped for breakfast - and spent the time discussing 1 Corinthians 7, about the subject of marriage. It took us until the afternoon to get home since we had to take a very roundabout way to find roads that were open.

February 14 Journal entry (hereafter designated Je) - "In the park today the Lord's presence was as real as I've ever known it. The greatest privilege of life is to be in the center of His will. My only needs for the future are GOD's provision (Philippians 4:19), His leading (Psalms 32:8), and His grace (2 Corinthians 12:9). I continue to look for further confirmation through the Word and prayer with regard to Joanne." I was truly beginning to fall for her and she for me. But she still would not let me hold her hand when we got near a street light! She didn't want to give anyone anything to talk about.

February 15 Je - "I continue to see that the biggest need today is for Spirit-filled engineers and businessmen who are soul winners. Will require a wonderful wife, hostess, helpmate, and secretary. Is this it? - Jo, engineering management . . . Saw Jo this evening - the Lord continues to draw our hearts together - I love her more each time we're together."

Feb. 20 Je - After a trip to Chicago - "Bob Foster's and Herb Jauchen's comments continue to show me that Jo is GOD's perfect choice."

Feb. 21 Je - "I continue to see that I should not get labeled denominationally, doctrinally, or being ordained . . . am continually convinced of (1) Jo and (2) working as a layman."

By this time I was head-over-heels in love with this beautiful lady GOD had sent into my life. I thought she looked like Doris Day. After being with her I would return to the dorm and sit down and swoon over her. Dave Castro, and his roommate, Chuck Kenworthy, got quite a kick out of this normally very serious guy who was totally "over the moon" for this woman. We joked that I was practicing pure religion by visiting a widow and orphan - James 1:27. On April 25 GOD spoke to me through Psalm 126:6 that Jo would be a soul winner.

In the spring I began doing yard work for Dr. Richard Davis, a well-known physician in the city, to have a few funds for dating Joanne, and to have an occasional meal other than popcorn and soup. They had a maid who was a deeply dedicated Christian and was quite a blessing to me.

On March 11, we were spending the evening together. It became a long evening and past midnight on March 12 I asked Joanne if she would marry me. She said, "Yes!" I was so excited! GOD was so faithful to lead me to the one He had promised! We made it public in the newspaper on May 7 and were married on September 16, 1961.

Joanne had been part of the Wesleyan Methodist Church all of her life and I had recently become a member. This was a very conservative group that frowned on wearing jewelry. So instead of an engagement ring we drove down to Indianapolis together one day and got her a watch at Goodman Jewelers for $65.45. We also got her a simple wedding ring band for $19.75 for a grand total of $85.20!

One of my joys that winter, spring, and summer was to get better acquainted with Jo's little son, Gerry. He was a year old when we started seeing each other and turned two shortly after our wedding. After Jo and I had had a few dates, when I would be standing at the door saying good night to her, Gerry would be down the hall in his bed, but not asleep. He would call out, "Nee, nigh." Then it progressed to "Nay, nigh." He never called me "Nate." He went from "Nay" to "Daddy" soon after we were married.

Shortly after we were married, Jo said to me, "Honey, how were you able to marry someone who already had a child and be willing to raise him?" My answer to her was, "Well that wasn't hard, I just had two people to fall in love with." And I surely had fallen in love with little Gerry. At the same time, I felt a very heavy responsibility in raising him, even more than if he had been my own biological son. He was an easy son to raise. Gerry has been a pastor in the Wesleyan Church denomination, pastoring in New Jersey, Indiana, and Wisconsin. His last assignment was in Mukwonago, Wisconsin, near Waukesha, where his mother and biological father were pioneering a church at the time of his death. He and Wenda are now part of a missional community in Mukwonago.

In the spring, Dr. Wilber Dayton from Asbury Seminary visited Marion College and encouraged me to consider coming to Asbury for further training. As I prayed about it GOD spoke to me through 1 John 2:27 that the Holy Spirit would be my teacher - and He certainly has!

The Lord also spoke to me through Isaiah 30:21, 52:12; and Psalm 37:23 that He was going to clearly lead us regarding our future.

June 7 Je - "In looking back over the time at Marion the Lord has fulfilled Ephesians 3:20 for me - *'Now to Him who is able to do far more abundantly than all that we ask or think.'* In these nine months the Lord has -
1   Given me doctrinal answers.
2   Given me a wife and son.
3   Given me a denomination.
4   Given me a calling for the coming year or so.
5   Given me a basic foundation of theology, upon which I can build.
6   Published the tract *I Met Christ on the Campus*.
7   Given more open doors to learn and serve than ever before."

On June 12, I went to Chicago to look for work. I had concluded that I should get an engineering job and become a lay evangelist in the engineering world. My Journal entry for the day read, "Left Marion with $11.57 and His presence, guidance, and promises. Witnessed to four and saw one come to the Lord. Wonderful day!"

I stayed at the Navigator home in Wheaton. I had not been there very long until I had a tremendous lack of peace and knew that I had missed it somewhere. My Journal entry on June 15 read, "The Lord, these past days has showed me -
1   I can never be happy doing engineering - must be in full-time Christian service.
2   Thrust of life must be evangelism.
3   No seminary or pastorate for the present.
4   My experience, burden, spiritual gifts, age, tract, and background would fit me for Campus Crusade for Christ work. Dr. Sheets, Herb Jauchen, and Nate Scharff agree.

63

5   There is no need to stay in Chicago - get back to Marion to discuss CCC with Jo, work and live there until the Lord opens doors, correspond with Bill Bright from there, and wait on the Lord."

The Lord spoke to me through Proverbs 20:24 that He was leading and knew what He was doing.

I returned to Marion to wait upon GOD. Joanne's father, Dr. Harold K. Sheets, owned several apartment rentals. They needed painting. So I spent the early summer painting. I hate to paint! I was also praying for personal revival based on Habakkuk 3:2. About this time Joanne began giving me my haircuts, which she is still doing!

In late June, Brother Bray, the District Superintendent of the Illinois District of the Wesleyan Methodist Church, offered us a church in Creve Coeur, a suburb of Peoria, Illinois. We drove over and spent a day there, but were not led to take the church.

On July 2, Joanne and I went to Winona Lake Christian Conference Center in Winona Lake, Indiana, to hear Dr. Bob Pierce, founder of World Vision, tell about his successful evangelistic crusade in Tokyo, Japan. We had lunch with Eldon Turnidge and his wife and discussed the possibility of our going to Haiti to work with a mission organization that he was affiliated with, the Oriental Missionary Society, or OMS. We also met Dr. Paul Petticord, president of Western Evangelical Seminary in Portland, Oregon, and John Woodhouse, who had brought Nate Scharff to the Lord.

Somehow we had heard about a new ministry called Campus Crusade for Christ that was strong on personal evangelism, and had a lay witness department. We called the appropriate phone number and talked to the director, Dr. Bill Bright.

He saw no reason why we could not be part of the lay witness department or start a CCC work at Purdue. He encouraged us to attend their three-week training time in Mound, Minnesota, in August. We did and it was a very enlightening time. But they believed in eternal security, which we did not believe was biblical. And increasingly I felt that what Campus Crusade and The Navigators were doing was what the local church should be doing. Joanne's sister, Evelyn, and her husband, Ron Rhoades, were pastoring a Wesleyan Methodist Church in Minneapolis so we also got to see them. And Gerry got his first barbershop haircut while we were there.

By this time, Joanne's father was a General Superintendent in The Wesleyan Methodist Church, and he felt the time might be ripe for someone to bring the challenge of personal evangelism to the Wesleyan churches. We increasingly felt that this was what GOD wanted us to do, so we left the Campus Crusade training a week early, and returned to Marion to see how it all would develop. Just before leaving Mound we met Gene Edwards, who was also getting involved in local-church-related personal evangelism training. During those weeks I was being further burdened for souls based on Psalm 57:7.

August 14 Je - "We have five doors open to us - Asbury Seminary, Western Evangelical Seminary, OMS, Wesleyans, Campus Crusade." GOD spoke Proverbs 16:33 to me, and in the next few days we felt clear that we were to walk through the door with the Wesleyan Methodists. GOD was going to do *"a new thing"* (Isaiah 43:19). He was promising through Isaiah 58:10-12 that I would *"raise up the foundations of many generations"* and *"be called the repairer of the breach, the restorer of streets to dwell in."*

The director of the Evangelism and Church Extension Department was Dr. Virgil Mitchell. He sent a letter out to all of the Wesleyan churches telling of our availability to come and teach personal evangelism.

65

The district president of the Dakota District, John Hunter, was especially interested in our ministry. He wanted us to come to their annual pastors' retreat in late September to present the challenge.

August 19 Je - "Have spent the day studying and preparing for the Soul Winning Clinic work.
Realize the job is 3-fold -
1   Get the people concerned - zeal.
2   Teach and show the people how - knowledge.
3   Provide a channel for their zeal and knowledge - a weekly visitation program geared to presenting the Gospel to every person in the community or church area. Can see the need of a mimeographed textbook for the work."

August 23 Je - "Our life in the coming months is committed to the Wesleyan work - the denominational officials are backing us, pastors and conference presidents are calling for us, and all agree that this is the need. We look to the Lord for a house trailer, auto, wedding and honeymoon plans, and especially wisdom as we plan the Clinic details and itinerary - James 1:5, Philippians 4:13, Luke 10:2, Ephesians 5:25."

So I spent late August and early September painting and writing a little booklet we would use in the local church training sessions. Because we would immediately be a family when we got married, we felt the need to have our own little home in order to develop our own family life, rather than living with the many pastors' families it would otherwise be necessary to do. So we started looking for a trailer we could pull from church to church and a car large enough to pull it. We found just the trailer at the Franklin Trailer Company in Nappanee, Indiana. And we found a 1959 Olds '88 - red and white! - in Gas City, Indiana, through a newspaper ad.

66

We were married on Saturday, September 16, 1961, at the new College Church in Marion, Indiana. At the reception we had Psalm 34:3 inscribed on our wedding cake: *"Oh, magnify the Lord with me, and let us exalt His Name together!"* In marrying Joanne (and Gerry) GOD was fulfilling His promise in Psalm 84:11 to me - *"No good thing does He withhold from those who walk uprightly."*

On September 16, GOD also spoke to me through Proverbs 19:14 that Jo would be a wise counselor. That has surely been the case - all through the years she has been a counselor to many others and me.

We drove the Olds to Washington, D.C., for a couple days of honeymoon and sightseeing. September 20 Je - " . . . have had good times of prayer together and been privileged to pass out many tracts."

CHAPTER 6
MOBILIZING CHURCHES
FOR PERSONAL EVANGELISM

(The Wesleyan Methodist Church;
Beth born; Lay Evangelism, Inc.)

Marion, IN; Wheaton, IL: 1961 – 1965

When we returned to Marion from our honeymoon we went up to Nappanee on Friday to get our travel trailer. On Saturday I took a bus to Madison, in Southern Indiana on the Ohio River, for my first Lay Evangelism Clinic while Joanne stayed in Marion to get the trailer ready for our first trip. I missed her terribly, phoned, and she and little Gerry drove down for the last few days of the week in Madison.

After returning from Madison to Marion we finished packing up our trailer and headed for South Dakota - for the annual Pastors' Retreat of the Dakota District of the Wesleyan Methodist Church. Joanne drove part of the way so that I could work on my messages. At the retreat, various ones scheduled us to come to their churches for a clinic. So after the retreat, we spent the fall traveling from church to church, bringing the challenge and practics of personal evangelism to these dear folks - in Garden City, Mitchell, Watertown, Aberdeen, Rapid City, Belle Fourche, Custer, Pierre, Brookings, Sioux Falls, Tolstoy, Huron, etc. It was a wonderful fall - much experience in preaching, teaching, taking people out into homes, and gaining more experience myself in witnessing, presenting the Gospel to those who were ready to hear, and leading to Christ those who were ready to respond.

I would preach on the Great Commission on Sunday morning. Sunday evening the message was on being filled with the Holy Spirit. We usually took Monday in the daytime off for family fun, but had a training session in the evening.

Then we would conduct training on the practics of soul winning Monday through Wednesday evenings. On Thursday and Friday evening we would go out witnessing, mainly to people on the fringe of the church who were not yet converted. Those who went out were a team of two, with a soul winner and a silent partner. The silent partner would babysit and pray while the soul winner presented the Gospel. Others stayed at the church building and prayed. Then we all gathered back at the church after the witnessing and soul winning and each team would tell of their experience - we would learn from each other plus teaching comments from me. On Saturday Joanne, Gerry, and I would travel to the next clinic location.

We began teaching C. S. Lovett's plan of salvation presentation. But the Lord soon showed me that it lacked an emphasis on repentance and the Lordship of Christ. For one to come to Christ, he must repent (turn from his sins) and receive Jesus as his Savior and Lord. I added Acts 3:19 to the presentation - and found that the converts were more genuine and truly converted.

At our first clinic location, Garden City, the pastor, Arnold LaRue, admitted that he could give an altar call, but did not know how to lead someone to Christ away from the altar. The clinic transformed his life and ministry.

Some Journal entries -
October 27 - "Garden City - 8 people found the Lord and 8 people completed the clinic."
November 3 - "Seven pairs out at Watertown - 5 find the Lord - the people are greatly encouraged."
November 18 - "Rapid City - best clinic yet."

The last clinic in the Dakotas was at a country church. It was so cold out that they placed bales of straw around our trailer to help keep it warm. When we left they partially paid us with dozens of eggs. For the next few weeks we had eggs cooked every way possible!

We were to be in the Dakotas through December 20, but when we learned that a blizzard was on its way, we headed south on December 17. The blizzard was only a few hours behind us all the way to Kansas, where we spent a couple of days with Joanne's Uncle Howard and Aunt Marie. (Aunt Marie was Joanne's father's sister.) Then we traveled on to Enid, Oklahoma, to have Christmas with Bob and Arlene Hughes, Joanne's sister and husband, who pastored a Wesleyan Methodist Church there.

December 31 Je - "1961 has been a wonderful year greatly blessed of the Lord. He has wondrously blessed me with a wife, a son, doctrinal answers, all material needs (home, car, clothes, food, books), an open door of ministry, a denomination of my liking, prospects of a wonderful future."

1962

I first met Gene Edwards at Mount, Minnesota, during our training time with Campus Crusade for Christ. I spent the first few days of 1962 with him at his home in Tyler, Texas, learning more about his approach to personal evangelism training.

January 6 Je - "Outlined Basic Ministry Plans for the future. Goal - To evangelize the world in this generation through personal evangelism by Christians completely evangelizing their 'world' as they work primarily through their church. Set up corporation 'Lay Evangelism.' " One reason we set up the corporation is because GOD had spoken to us through Luke 4:43 that we were to expand our ministry to help groups beyond the Wesleyan Methodists.

Before leaving Enid, we had a Lay Evangelism Crusade (we changed the name from clinic to crusade) with the Westside Wesleyan Church that Bob and Arlene pastored.

One interesting thing that happened at the Enid Crusade was this: On Wednesday evening we would pair the people up so that they could practice leading each other to Christ. When Joanne began to practice with one of the ladies she discovered that the lady did not know the Lord, so this was not "practice," she actually came to know the Lord as her personal Savior during that practice time.

We also had a crusade with the Wesleyan Church in Ponca City, Oklahoma. This was followed by a crusade in Topeka, Kansas, with the Brannons, Joanne's first husband's parents, and a crusade in Cedar Falls, Iowa. All four of these crusades were quite fruitful.

At one point during these weeks I took a quick plane trip back to Marion and drove with my father-in-law, Dr. Harold K. Sheets, to Houghton College in Houghton, New York. At the Houghton chapel service I gave my testimony of how a Jew loved me to Jesus and one-third of the student body responded to my invitation to become soul winners. I also taught for two days at one of the college classes.

In March we had two crusades in Michigan. March 23 Je - "Spent time in prayer this evening at the Lansing church. Earnestly asked the Lord to remove anything from my life causing me from being totally yielded to the task of taking the Gospel to the millions who yet have not heard."

With the expanding work to train people other than Wesleyans we felt the need to write a book on personal evangelism. From March through May I spent time writing the original edition of *You Can Be a Soul Winner - Here's How!*

Joanne was pregnant and not feeling well so I also spent time caring for her and Gerry. The book was printed by Wesley Press, with a Foreword by Dr. Virgil Mitchell, executive secretary of the Department of Evangelism and Church Extension, and paid for by some of Joanne's insurance money left from her first husband's death.

In the summer of 1962 we went to Tulsa, Oklahoma, to do survey work for a new Wesleyan Methodist church being started there. It was a work of faith. Our food supply got down to a can of beans, a box of corn bread mix, and a jar of mustard! I spoke at a Baptist Church one Sunday morning. After the service they did not give us an offering or even invite us out to eat! GOD was teaching us to trust Him. During my year at Marion College, I had read George Mueller's biography, so I understood a little about trusting GOD for our needs. So our Sunday dinner that day was corn bread and beans - we still had a jar of mustard!

A lady, Thelma Hickman, from Joanne's childhood, would bring vegetables by our trailer, and apologetically give them to us. Little did she know they were our provision for those weeks in Tulsa. I also spent much time praying about the coming fall - should we stay in the lay evangelism work, go to seminary, or take a pastorate? - And felt that we were to stay in the lay evangelism work at least for another year. Also, during my prayer times, the Lord again emphasized to me my call as a prophet - Jeremiah 1:7-10, 6:27; Ezekiel 37:10, and Zechariah 3:7. He also made it clear that we were to "camp" or "travel" at His command - Numbers 9:23.

From Oklahoma we headed to the Dakotas for more ministry there. But part way through the time I took Joanne and our travel trailer back to Indiana as she had become pregnant in February and was getting near her due date.

I then took the train to Minneapolis, and plane to Aberdeen, for further ministry in the Dakotas. I had boarded the train in Huntington, Indiana, the train was running a little late, and I informed the conductor of my connection in Chicago.

He got in touch with the connecting train and when I arrived in Chicago there was someone there to meet me, we ran across the terminal to the waiting train, I hopped on the caboose, the conductor waved his lantern, and the train pulled out. This second train had waited for me - GOD was in charge and wanted me to get to my next preaching appointment! When I arrived at the church in South Dakota the service had already begun, but I was there in time to bring my message, challenging the people to be soul winners.

Joanne and I were apart for more than seven weeks. During this time I also began praying about citywide crusades, having our own organization, working with all denominations, and having a home and office somewhere other than Marion, Indiana.

In late October I had gone to Bismarck, North Dakota, to check out a possible crusade and was en route by bus from North Dakota to Lincoln, Nebraska, for a crusade there when I received word in the Council Bluffs, Iowa, bus station that I was the father of a little baby girl. I had planned to be back in Marion after the Lincoln crusade for her birth, but she came two weeks early! So I called the Lincoln pastor, rescheduled the crusade, and hopped on a train for Marion. I had enough money to get to Chicago, where Dave Castro met me, and loaned me $20 for a flight to Marion (that's all it cost then!). A couple hours later I saw our little girl - she sure was little, weighing 5 pounds, 10 1/2 ounces. We named her Elizabeth Ann.

A few days before Beth was born, on October 29, the Lord had given me a promise for her life: Luke 1:15-17 - *"For he (she - Beth) will be great before the Lord. And she must not drink wine or strong drink, and she will be filled with the Holy Spirit, even from her mother's womb. And she will turn many of the children of Israel to the Lord their God, and she will go before him in the spirit and power of Elijah, to turn the hearts of the fathers to the children, and the disobedient to the wisdom of the just, to make ready for the Lord a people prepared."*

I was home for a few days after Jo and Beth came home from the hospital - then it was back to Lincoln for the crusade, which was ten days in length, and one of the best to that date.

During the bus trip from South Dakota to Council Bluffs the Lord began to speak to me about a book that would tell the story about contemporary soul-winning laymen. We later collected the information, Evelyn Stenbock of Kansas wrote the book, and Beacon Hill, the publishing house for the Church of the Nazarene, published it, entitled *Soul Winning Laymen.*

After the crusade in Lincoln, and a few days in Marion with Joanne, Gerry, and Beth, I was off to Taylor, Michigan, for a crusade with the Wesleyan Church where Bro. Zuber, a very precious man, was the pastor. I also counseled with Dr. Vick, pastor of a soul-winning Baptist church in Detroit, where 600 to 800 people are out in visitation evangelism each week, and with Dr. Paul Rees.

December 8 Je - "GOD gave me John 17:4 for a life goal - *'I glorified You on earth, having accomplished the work that You gave me to do.'* " And my journal entry of December 11 stated that I was to remain a layman based on 1 Corinthians 7:20.

1963

Je - "Goals for 1963 -
1   Deeper prayer life.
2   Greater depth in the Word.
3   Better family life.
4   Better able to cooperate with the Holy Spirit.
5   More answers:
    a.   How to do personal evangelism.
    b.   How to get a local church doing continuous personal evangelism.
    c.   How to mobilize the evangelical churches of North America.
6   Decision on organization through which to work.
7   Increasingly effective and enlarged ministry -
    a.   13-day crusades.
    b.   Openings with other denominations.
    c.   Book revised.
    d.   One citywide crusade.
    e.   Beginning of ministry training other 'specialists.'
    f.   A few churches experiencing a 'breakthrough' - continuous personal evangelism.
    g.   Greater prayer support.
    h.   More effective follow-up on churches after the crusade.
    i.   More answers on office, finances, and secretary.
    j.   Other books - *Crusade Guide, Soul Winning Laymen.*"

On January 1 we participated in the Wesleyan Methodist Conference on Evangelism in Indianapolis, which had been organized by Joanne's father.   It was a good window for our ministry, although some old-time conservatives questioned the idea of people being saved away from the church building.

On January 5 I spent time with Charles Kingsley, who emphasized personal evangelism in the Free Methodist denomination. He was very dedicated to his work of mobilizing FM men for evangelism. He wanted me to come and work with the Free Methodists. I never was led to do that, but I did have some very successful crusades with FM churches in Michigan, Ontario, and California. Kingsley and I would touch base a couple times each year and both received encouragement from our times together.

That winter we had ministry in Michigan and Ontario, Canada, with Free Methodist churches, Wesleyan churches, and one crusade with an Open Standard Church, a very conservative group. I had to take my necktie off to be acceptable to them! We greatly appreciated our time in Canada - Sarnia, Kitchener, Brantford, Hamilton, Toronto, Belleville, and Ottawa.

I always carried a tract carrier, filled with an assortment of tracts, with me to hand out wherever I went. One day in our trailer I was getting dressed. I did not yet have my tract carrier in my back pocket. Little Gerry, now four, saw it lying on the shelf, and got it and gave it to me. For my son, having my tract carrier was part of my being properly dressed!

In early February I read Robert Coleman's book, *The Master Plan of Evangelism* - it had a major impact on my life. I began to make it available wherever we went.

March 9 - Je - "Traveling by bus to Flint, Michigan - sat on the bus with an alcoholic - had prayer with him. Passed out twelve tracts at a lunch break in Ft. Wayne."

March 14 - After much prayer for many months, we made the decision to develop Lay Evangelism, Inc., rather than work with the Navigators, Campus Crusade, Wesleyans, Kingsley, or Christian Outreach. Live and have our office in Wheaton, Illinois, which is an evangelical center.

A number of Christian organizations were headquartered there - Youth for Christ, National Association of Evangelicals, Christian Life magazine, Pioneer Boys and Brigade Girls, TEAM, etc. And there was a good Wesleyan Church for our family and the Chicago O'Hare airport for my travels.

Journal entry - "God has called me to be a prophet to the Church. We must not get connected to any approach, denomination, and organization. We must be free to 1) call the Church back to her mission, and 2) provide training and materials."

Eventually our advisory board for LEI included some "big" names in evangelical Christianity including Robert E. Coleman, Dale Cryderman, Robert Ferm, Forrest Gearhart, Paul Little, Hubert Mitchell, Waylon Moore, Rosalind Rinker, Harold Sheets, Stanley Tam, Ward Williams, and Sam Wolgemuth.

We had a number of people who worked with us as associate evangelists including Mason Bailey, David Cunningham, Garland Darnes, James Davis, Jay Ferris, Leonard Harris, Hugh Hedges, Tom Johnston, George and Joanne Moser, Vic Munyer, Marion Noll, Phil Parks, Merlin Perrine, Arthur Prouty, Glenn Rader, Bill Ramsey, Paul Smith, James White, Glenn Wilcox, and Ron Wills.

Our Board of Directors was Mase Bailey, Glen Martin, Jim White, and Joanne and I. Our office and administrative staff at various times included Joy May, Debbye Ewick, Jean Schuler, Gary Miltenberger, Walter Simonds, Marvin Baker, and Dad Krupp.

Our original motto was "Mobilizing Laymen to Evangelize Their City" and was later changed to "Mobilizing Local Churches for Evangelism since 1961."

It had been on my heart to settle in Wheaton, Illinois, since the fall of 1962. I mentioned it to Jo in November and to Forrest Gearhart, pastor of the Wesleyan Church there, in December 1962. During a crusade in Cadillac, Michigan, the week of March 10-16, I spent much time praying about the future and GOD promised, through Joshua 21:45, to fulfill all that was on our hearts.

March 18 - Jo and I visit Wheaton.

April 10-17 - Spent further time in Wheaton. We were parked in the overnight lot at a trailer court. We were out of milk and Joanne's folks were traveling through and going to have breakfast with us the next morning. In my quiet time that morning I prayed that GOD would provide some milk. A few minutes later a knock came on the door. There stood a milkman who, noticing that we were new to the court, gave us a free quart of milk. Oh, the faithfulness of GOD!

During that week we saw a home at 312 E. Lincoln Avenue.
April 22 - loan company gave us a $20,000 mortgage offer.
April 27 - We made an offer of $26,500 + 500 verbally and the owner, Carl Cue, agreed.

May 17 - We are okayed by Wheaton College to have senior girls living with us for the next year. It was a large house; we lived on the first floor, built our offices in the basement, and had seven Wheaton College girls on the second floor. Their rent made our house payments.

May 19 Je - "Have laid our needs before the Lord and wait to see him faithfully supply. They include - down payment for Wheaton house, furniture, office equipment, washer and dryer, stove and refrigerator, summer house payments." (Added later - "all provided by late August!") May 27 - Down payment provided - our money plus Dad Sheets and Dad Krupp.

In April GOD spoke to me through 2 Samuel 7:12-13 that Gerry was to be greatly used by the Lord - and sometime later He gave me 1 Chronicles 28:5 for him, too.

We moved to Wheaton in June and I spent the summer waiting on the Lord and writing materials for LEI, including a new, revised edition of *You Can be a Soul Winner.*

In August I was invited by Bob Crandall to the Free Methodist Youth Advance at Winona Lake, Indiana, to train Free Methodist young people from all over the country. We took them into town to do door-to-door work. I met Dale Cryderman who was also at the Advance speaking to the youth. He later became an important person in my life, opening many doors for our ministry. In September we had a crusade with an interdenominational Bible church in Minneapolis - "one of the best yet." While there we spent time at Bethany Fellowship where we met the director, Ted Hegre, and spent time with Harold Brokkie, who later became director.

In October we had a crusade in Brantford, Ontario. Also, Silver Creek, New York. Je regarding the Silver Creek Crusade - "What a crusade! About 50 saved." It was a wonderful crusade - believers were being filled with the Spirit and sinners saved everywhere. Closest thing to the *Book of Acts* I have ever seen.

During the Silver Creek Crusade I was reading Edwin Orr's book, *Full Surrender* - what a book, on being fully surrendered to GOD.

In November we had a crusade with a group of Free Methodist Churches in Flint, Michigan. During that week President John F. Kennedy was assassinated on November 22. On Sunday morning I spoke in two churches and we got word over the car radio that was taking me from one church to the other that Lee Harvey Oswald had been shot.

December 6 Je - "Jesus wants a New Testament Bride here when He returns. The existing system will never become that Bride voluntarily because, to become New Testament, it would mean:

1   closing all denominational headquarters.
2   closing all church buildings.
3   firing all paid workers, except apostles.
4   stopping 'the program.'

The Holy Spirit will either <u>start over outside</u> of the Church, or bring it about <u>by persecution</u>."

1964

January 21, 1964 Je - "Spent the day with the Lord in Milan, Michigan - trusting God to give us a worldwide ministry."

February 6 Je - "Isaiah 54 - the Lord again confirms that (1) we should expand the work and (2) He will use us and the work around the world."

March 14 Je - "Am continually burdened for the foreign field."

March - Crusade with Wesleyan Churches in Gastonia, NC area - towns of Ragan, Shelby, Gastonia, Cherryville, McCaddenville, and Kings Mountain - one of our best united crusades to date - a number were saved. They were all together for the training sessions, and then I went around and worked with each church.

Spring and summer 1964 - I spent much time evaluating our work. We need to concentrate on citywide crusades. Also began reading about preparation for end-time persecution. I had contact with John Noble, who spent time in Soviet prisons, and John Hedlund, a Wesleyan Church pastor in St. Louis, who had a great interest in preparing for end-time persecution.

October - Crusades with Wesleyans and Free Methodists in northern Michigan.

The pressure of the work had given me an ulcer. I had to cancel some of our crusades and was on a milk diet and spent weeks in bed during this fall time. Hubert Mitchell invited me to be part of a men's prayer retreat in early December, Friday evening through Saturday.

On Friday evening the men noticed that I was not eating, asked why, and wanted to pray for me. When they did I felt the power of GOD touch my stomach and I believe that GOD healed me. The next morning I had bacon and eggs for breakfast! When I went back to the doctor the X-rays showed that the ulcer was completely healed. All the ungodly doctor could do was curse.

November 13 Je - "All nations to be blessed by our ministry - Genesis 22:18."

Nov. 17 Je - "Groups that the Lord is giving us a fruitful ministry with - Free Methodist, Wesleyan Methodist, Ohio Yearly Meeting of Friends, United Brethren in Christ, Brethren in Christ, Churches of Christ in Christian Union."

Nov. 25 Je - "Our call is the call of an apostle (in addition to prophet) - sent one, traveler."

December 1 Je - "I need to spend much time this next week meditating on the phrase, 'You produce what you are!' "

Dec. 2-3 - Many pages of journal entry regarding enlarging LEI staff, citywide crusade procedures, and renovation of Wheaton home basement.

Dec. 17 Je - "Lord, don't let me waste my life with things of secondary importance."

1965

January - Citywide crusade in Detroit, MI - sponsored by National Association of Evangelicals.

The entire city was divided into four sections - we had training in each section, which took four weeks. After a section was trained they went out to witness. The Detroit Crusade could have been a prototype for the other cities of the world - but GOD had another plan for my life. It was followed though by the "Evangelism Explosion" work of Dr. D. James Kennedy and the "I Found It" work of Dr. Bill Bright and Campus Crusade for Christ.

February 5 Je - "God's various revelations to me in the approximate order given:
1   Our supreme task - fulfilling the Great Commission.
2   The importance of the Word of God.
3   The importance of prayer.
4   The importance of the Holy Spirit.
5   The importance of the laymen.
6   The importance of personal evangelism.
7   The importance of the local church.
8   The importance of fasting.
9   The importance of pastors - leading their church into aggressive evangelism.
10   The place of united action."

Feb. 6 - I spent the entire day with the Lord. Je - "Numbers 11:1 - ' . . . *when the people complained, it displeased the Lord . . .*' - 'Lord help me to never again say anything that is critical, negative, or complaining in nature.' "

"Must discipline my time to:
1   Get 8 hours sleep each night.
2   Spend an hour in prayer and an hour in the Word the first thing, before breakfast.
3   Memorize a chapter of Scripture each month.

83

4   Pass out at least one tract each day.
5   Talk to at least one person daily about the Lord.
6   Have family worship each a.m. after breakfast.
7   Read and pray with Gerry each evening.
8   Review memory verses and pray with Jo each evening."

"With reference to the family:
1   I must be more of a buddy to Gerry and less of a disciplinarian.
2   I must be a real friend and give much love to Gerry and Bethie.
3   Do something special as a family each time I'm home and do something special with each individual each time that I am home."

"With reference to LEI:
The Lord Jesus has raised this work up to call and lead the Church back to New Testament purposes, power, and patterns. His blessing is upon it. He has not called us to start another organization, but to be a prophet and a servant to the existing."

Feb. 24 - Stan Hahn added to our staff to oversee the office and assist me in various ways.

March - Four weeks in Southern California for crusades with Free Methodist churches - very fruitful. While there I picked a box of citrus fruit and mailed it home.

On the way home from Southern California, when flying over Iowa, the pilot came on the speaker and said that O'Hare was socked in and we would circle over Iowa and see what might develop. I felt an urgency to get home and was led to pray that GOD would part the clouds so we could land. After circling over Iowa for about thirty minutes the pilot came back on the speaker and said we would make one pass over O'Hare. If we could land we would.

Otherwise we would fly on to Detroit. We made one pass over O'Hare, the clouds parted, and we and one other plane on our tail landed. Oh, the goodness and faithfulness of GOD!

April - Jackson, Michigan, citywide crusade.

Spring and summer - much time spent praying about enlarging LEI staff and work.

August 8 Je - "Lord, help me to wake up the time and burn out for Thee."

Just before my 30th birthday on September 7, 1965, we heard from the last continent that *You Can* had been used on every continent in answer to my prayer at Glen Eyrie, based on Jeremiah 33:3, that GOD would use me on every continent by the age of thirty.

August thru December - had many days of prayer - praying about how to best mobilize the Church for evangelism. Had five weeks of crusade work in the West.

I carried mail in Wheaton December 3, 1965, thru January 1, 1966, to help pay our bills.

CHAPTER 7
A NEW UNDERSTANDING ABOUT THE CHURCH

Wheaton, IL - 1966

In January 1966, I flew to Rochester, NY, to have a three-day seminar on personal evangelism with a group of Free Methodist pastors from around the Eastern part of the U.S. to be held in Webster, NY, with my Free Methodist pastor friend, Art Prouty. A snowstorm came in before anyone could arrive and we had to cancel the seminar.

Art and I discovered that we were both looking for answers - does God have a plan for His Church or not, and if He does, what is it? We decided, since we were stranded, that we would spend those several days fasting, searching the Scriptures, and praying about the matter.

After several days of study and prayer, on Friday, January 14, 1966, these were our conclusions -
1   The New Testament gives the total pattern for the Church of Jesus Christ until the end of the Age - 2 Timothy 3:16-17.
2   The Lord desires such a Church in every nation in the world today.

On Saturday, we further concluded -
1   It may be possible to reach some nations by an evangelical movement that centers its worship in buildings other than homes.
2   Many nations, and perhaps all nations, will be reached only by an evangelical movement that meets in homes.

3   It is doubtful that a man could raise up a true New Testament church in America today while remaining a part of, or through the structure of, the present evangelical movements as we know them.

4   If a pastor in an existing evangelical movement were to try to develop a church similar, as much as possible, to the New Testament church, he would probably -

a.   Eliminate all organizations (Sunday School, youth organization, etc.).

b.   Have an extended, informal Sunday worship service for the entire family where the gifts of the Spirit are in operation, the Lord's Supper is celebrated weekly, the Word discussed and applied to daily life, spontaneous singing, praise, prayer, testimony, reporting, and discussion of evangelism strategy.

c.   Endeavor to develop among its families a scriptural home and family life that places much greater responsibility upon the home and parents for discipline, fellowship, recreation, instruction in the Word and practical matters of life for the children than is currently practiced.

d.   Endeavor to involve its families in every strata of community life for Christian influence and evangelism.

e.   Have a corporate ministry of evangelism.

f.   Have its basic evangelism strategy the practice of every believer winning the "world" of his neighborhood, place of employment, and other natural contacts.

5   With the light that we now have relative to the New Testament church, as contrasted with the present evangelical movement, it is becoming increasingly evident that we must move to some city, find employment, and cooperatively search the Scriptures seeking to find the New Testament pattern of church life and strategy for world evangelization in order to see the Holy Spirit put these into effect in our midst and to the ends of the earth.

On January 10, the Lord spoke to me through Genesis 17:16 that Jo would be "a mother of nations." (I believe that is being fulfilled through her book, *WOMAN - God's Plan not Man's Tradition* that she wrote in 1991. It has been translated into several languages and used around the world and through those whom she, and we together, have discipled or influenced, including her CLU students and the Harvest of Jubilee Bible School students, who are serving the Lord in various nations around the world.)

On January 16, the Lord further spoke:
1   We will be judged by the Lord in accordance with His Word. He will judge our personal lives and our church life according to His Word.
2   Since the Lord laid out the whole thing, it all goes together.   So there probably cannot be New Testament Christians until there is a New Testament Church in every sense of the word.
3   It is becoming increasingly evident that I:
    a.   Cannot schedule any more LEI Crusades.
    b.   Can no longer attend a traditional, organized church.

January 19 Je - "I still feel very strongly:
1   That we are to soon move into Chicago to begin to develop New Testament churches.
2   That Prouty and Jones will come and be with us. (They never did.)
3   That the materials portion of LEI will continue.
4   That the Lord will arrange the next move - He will work out the details."

Jan. 25 Je - "The average evangelical pastor:
1   Is without vision and burden and passion.
2   Is spending as much time studying books, etc., as the Word of God.
3   Has been trained in the wrong things.
4   Is shackled by tradition and machinery.

89

5   Has his people shackled with tradition and machinery.
6   Is wrapped up in a building-centered, pulpit-centered, sermon-centered Christianity."

At this point it needs to be said that, although the Lord was giving me much new light about His plan for His Church, my attitude toward the existing church was not always right - I was disillusioned and bitter, of which I later repented.

In this dreadfully late hour, GOD is raising up His own men and women, those who:
1   Are prayer warriors (also fasting).
2   Are constant students of the Word.
3   Have a passion for souls.
4   Live sacrificial, disciplined, dedicated lives.
5   Are soul winners.
6   Are in touch with society.
7   Think big, but keep it simple.
8   Are filled, initially and continually, with the Holy Spirit.
9   Are revolutionary in their approach to world evangelization.
10   Are unshackled by church machinery, organization, buildings, tradition, and hierarchy.

"Lord, make me one of these, band me together with others of like mind, and use me to raise up thousands more."

Jan. 27 Je - "With the new book, *A World to Win*, published by Bethany Fellowship, with foreword by Clyde Taylor, coming out, it seems that the Lord is saying, 'You have been faithful to deliver your message about personal evangelism. You must now retire to the desert because I have new things for you to learn and to experience.'"

The present-day evangelical system by its nature:
1   Encourages trust in buildings, programs, man, headquarters, services, and the traditions of men, rather than in the living GOD.

2   Encourages that one be taught the Word of GOD by man, rather than by the Holy Spirit.

3   Does not teach people to: pray; study the Word; win souls; live a holy, sacrificial, disciplined, dedicated life; depend upon the Holy Spirit; believe GOD; fast; seek for New Testament patterns; seek for the gifts of the Holy Spirit.

4   Does teach people to: teach Sunday school classes; sit in the pew and listen; sing; and look to the pastor, rather than the Holy Spirit, for leadership.

February 1 Je - "We must tie in with a group that:

1   Believes in all of the gifts of the Spirit.

2   Meets in homes.

3   Longs to see the Great Commission fulfilled.

I know of no existing group like this - may the Holy Spirit bring it to pass."

Feb. 5 Je - "A New Testament church is self-governing, supporting, propagating, and disciplining."

Feb. 11 Je - "We continue to sense the Lord leading:

1   To merge LEI with another ministry.

2   Leave LEI, get into industry, move to the city (Chicago), and begin a home-centered ministry."

Feb. 12 Je - "The Holy Spirit in many ways continues to confirm the transition. I am available to do anything, go anywhere, that the Holy Spirit directs."

Feb. 20 Je - "I am believing GOD to soon baptize me with a true Holy Spirit baptism."

Feb. 21 Je - "What is the next step in our lives? I am not interested in further schooling or tying in with any existing Christian organization that I know of. I am interested in:

1   Being a part of New Testament Christianity.

2   Learning more about life.

3   Learning more about reaching my world.

4   The big cities.
5   Being a part of a group that really digs into the Word - is open - will take it at face value.
It would seem that the Lord is in the move to Chicago."

"Lord, I want your very best:
1   For my life.
2   For my family.
3   For the Church of Jesus Christ.
4   For a world that is yet to hear. For Jesus' sake. Amen."

Feb. 24 Je - "Truths that different groups have:
1   No church buildings - Two-by-Twos, Plymouth Brethren, Navigators.
2   Each church self-governing - Baptists, Congregational.
3   Gifts of the Spirit - Pentecostals, CMA.
4   No clergy - Plymouth Brethren, Navigators, Church of Christ.
5   Sanctification - Holiness, Keswick, CMA.
6   Lord's Supper weekly - Church of Christ, Christian Church.
7   Personal evangelism - Navigators, Campus Crusade.
8   Mass evangelism to the crowds - Open Air Campaigners, Pentecostals.
9   Small groups - Navigators, many in recent years.
10   Man-to-man training - Navigators.
11   Follow-up of converts - Navigators.
12   Apostles - Watchman Nee, Bakht Singh.
13   Father and home-centered training for children, recreation, and fellowship - Navigators.
14   Fulfillment of Great Commission - Navigators, Campus Crusade.
15   Every believer reaching his world - Navs, CC.
16   Fasting - some Pentecostals.
17   Students of the Word - Navs.
18   Live sacrificial, disciplined, dedicated lives - Navs.
19   Really in touch with society - ?
20   Revolutionary in pattern - Navs, CC.

21   Holy Spirit - Keswick, CMA, Pent'l, Holiness, Campus Crusade.
22   Prayer warriors - some Pentecostals, Holiness.
23   Foot washing - various Brethren groups."

Feb. 27 Je - "It's amazing how I've lost all burden for the established church. My whole burden and vision is now for something new (Isaiah 43:19) - a true New Testament movement in my day to reach the cities of the world.

I do not have peace about ever again attending the Wheaton Wesleyan Methodist Church. This was not an easy step, especially for Joanne who had been a Wesleyan all of her life. We soon began to meet on Sunday mornings with a small group in our home."

March 10 Je - "I seek:
1   To be baptized with the Holy Spirit.
2   To be part of a New Testament church pattern.
3   To be used for the evangelization of the world.
4   To be a soul winner and trainer of men."

March 12 Je - "God is calling us to reach the unreached multitudes of Chicago and the cities of the world by a revolutionary movement that gathers its converts into New Testament assemblies."

March 13 Je - "I increasingly believe that I may have the call of an apostle."

March 18 Je - "Today is the day of decision . . . I will accept a job today or Monday, as soon as hearing from Campbell's Soup, unless the Lord shows me differently in the meantime." (I did accept the job at Campbell's Soup Company and worked there for six weeks until the Lord very clearly showed me that I was not to work secularly, but trust Him solely for our support.)

March 28 Je - "What a challenge I have before me:
1   Build a Christian home.
2   Be a Christian husband and father.
3   Be a 'regular guy.'
4   Be a dedicated Christian.
5   Be a top-notch foreman.
6   Be a soul winner and trainer of men.
7   Be like Jesus.

I believe that the Lord is leading a group of us to band together in Chicago so that He can:
1   Teach us His Word.
2   Baptize us with the Holy Spirit.
3   Establish a New Testament movement in our midst.
4   Reach the multitudes of Chicago through us.
5   Fulfill His many promises to the ends of the earth.
We wait upon Him."

April 10 Je - "I am at the Grace Gospel Church at Waco, Texas. There are many things that seem to be very New Testament."

April 15 Je - "Today I counseled with Ted Hegre of Bethany Fellowship in Minneapolis about the baptism of the Holy Spirit. He shared how he experienced it, but speaking in tongues did not come to him until some time later."

May 2 Je - "I quit Campbell's Soup today. Spent the day working in the yard. I trust the Lord to raise up New Testament groups and supply our needs. During the six weeks that I worked at Campbell's Soup I felt increasingly that I was to quit, give myself to reaching Chicago, and live by faith." This was a very difficult and scary step for Joanne.

However, on the Monday morning that I went to work to resign, God proved Himself faithful. We were using powdered milk that we purchased in 50-lb bags from a neighbor in Wheaton who would make periodic trips to Chicago to pick up a supply for a number of us. However, when Joanne called her a few days earlier to see if she had a bag we could purchase, the neighbor told her she was completely out. Several days later, on the Monday morning that I went to work to resign and before I had time to return, this lady appeared at our door with a partial bag of powdered milk. She told Joanne, "I was having my quiet time this morning and the Lord told me to bring this to you." Immediately God spoke to Joanne and said, "See, Nate isn't even home yet from resigning and I'm already providing for you."

This began our lives of totally trusting GOD for all of our needs. We have lived that way from 1966 to the present (2014) and GOD has wondrously taken care of us. During the next few years, while we were still living in Wheaton, we saw GOD miraculously provide many times. Here are a few stories:

One time Joanne went to the store to buy our needed groceries. When she got to the checkout she discovered she did not have enough money, so she took a jar of pickles back. When she got home and was putting the groceries away, one of the Wheaton college girls who lived on our second floor came down to the kitchen and said to Joanne, "Could you use this jar of pickles? My boyfriend gave it to me as a joke and I don't have any use for it." So GOD even supplied a jar of pickles!

On another occasion Joanne had a grocery shopping list, but no money. I encouraged her to walk out the front door by faith. As she did the mailman was coming up the driveway and had a check that covered the groceries.

In December of 1966, we were low on funds and I was praying about carrying mail again over the Christmas period. We needed about $85 to cover some utility bills. I decided that, if the money did not come in by Monday, I would carry mail. On Monday we received a money order for $85 from a soldier serving in Viet Nam, someone we did not even know, and do not know to this day. We have no idea how he got our name and address! GOD is so faithful to provide, even in surprising ways.

During this year Gene Edwards gave me a copy of *The Normal Christian Church Life,* by Watchman Nee, who had had an apostolic ministry in China before and during the Communist takeover. This book simply confirmed many of the things that GOD had been showing me.

Especially significant was his understanding that there are two basic structures in GOD's plan for His Church: There is the local church, which he calls "the church," and there are those with an apostolic ministry, which he calls "the work."

Youth With A Mission calls these "the local church" and "the traveling church." Ralph Winter, founder of the US Center for World Mission, calls these "sodality" and "modality." The Roman Catholic Church uses the terms "the local parish" and "the orders." The early Protestant movement used the terms "the congregation" and "the missionary bands." So there are definitely two parts to GOD's plan for His Church, each to obey GOD and to serve the other.

CHAPTER 8 - MINISTRY IN CHICAGO

1966 (continued) - 1970

The Lord was calling me to evangelize in Chicago so I spent the summer of 1966 evangelizing in the parks and beaches. I would take the train or drive into Chicago and spend the day in Grant Park or the beach on the Northside witnessing, passing out Christian literature, and leading to the Lord those hungry ones who were ready. Some were even from other nations and I would take them to the Chicago Bible House and get them a Bible or New Testament in their language.

June 2 Je - "My only task in life is to let the Holy Spirit conform my life and ministry to the Word of GOD as I obey Him daily."

July 31 Je - "The Lord has definitely led us to:
1   Stay in Wheaton another year, continue to have Wheaton College girls upstairs, and fix up the house to sell.
2   Continue shipping LEI materials until He works out some transition.
3   Release *A World to Win*.
4   Concentrate solely on the Chicago area."

Summer - I began to speak in tongues. A copy of *They Speak With Other Tongues* by John Sherrill had been given to me by a couple during an LEI Crusade in Southern California. As I read this book I became hungry for the baptism of the Holy Spirit. One morning in my study in the basement of our home in Wheaton, I found myself worshipping the Lord in a language unknown to me.

August 1 Je - "Today we received the first copy of *A World to Win*. The publishers, Bethany Fellowship, have done an excellent job. We thank the Lord for the book and give Him all the credit. May it be an instrument in the hands of the Lord of the Harvest.

August 9 Je - "May the Lord use me to usher in New Testament Christianity in our day before He returns."

September 3-5 Je - "Have spent most of three days in prayer for Chicago. GOD has given me many promises for the work - Isaiah 43:4, 45:13-15, 60:15, 20-22; 61:4-6, 66:22; Jeremiah 30:19, 31:4, 31:8; Ezekiel 36:10-11, 33, 38; Zechariah 4:9.

I feel that I am to attack the city by wards and believe the Lord for a Bible study group of new converts in each of the 50 wards by the end of 1967." (This did not fully come to pass but was a great vision statement.)

September - I began the door-to-door work in Chicago - on the West side, south of Lake Street, between Cicero and Laramie streets. I would go door-to-door passing out Christian literature. I discovered that this was a multi-ethnic area so I had to have with me literature in English, Spanish, Italian, Polish, and Hebrew. As I knocked on the door and began to offer them literature in English, they would tell me if they spoke another language. My approach was to give out literature, discuss spiritual things with them as far as they were open to go, and discover who might be interested in a four-week group Bible study. After getting a list of the people interested in a study, I would go back around and see who would like to have us meet in their apartment the first week.

At the end of the first meeting I would ask who would like to have us meet in their apartment next week, and so forth. We used different study approaches, but most often went through the book of *1 John* using the easy-to-read *Today's English Version New Testament*. We would read a chapter and discuss it. Then we would pray for those who expressed some need. The study groups usually lasted more than four weeks and in time people gave their lives to Christ as a result of the study.

October 4 Je - "Projects for October:
1   Finish painting our house.
2   Spend as much time as possible with Gary Henley, Don Tomkinson, and Frank Foltz.
3   See all new converts at least once."

November - We met with others heading toward New Testament church life through Bro. Britain, who had a conference grounds in Missouri, and had come to Chicago to host a gathering of like-minded people. Through this meeting we learned of a group and began meeting with them at the Legion Hall in Oak Park on Sunday mornings as our regular, weekly church life. The group included the Willard Cummings family, the Willie Douglas family, the Earl McClure family, and us. I also went to Bro. Britain's annual conference in Missouri two summers.

December 31, 1966 Je - "Summary of 1966. This has been quite a different year - a year of transition. For five years our whole life was one of serving the organized church. It seems that we are now headed down a completely different road."

1967
Five-year goals - to be accomplished by September 7, 1970 (35th birthday) - Jeremiah 33:3!
1   Deeper prayer life.
2   Good grasp of the Word.
3   Basic understanding of New Testament Christianity.
4   Good family life.
5   Good grasp of how to win, train, and send men within the framework of N. T. Christianity and the big city.
6   A start in the apostolic ministry to which the Lord has called me.
7   A movement in Chicago sufficient that we can move elsewhere if the Lord so leads.

January 4 Je - "My primary task is to demonstrate the person and office of apostle. Set the pace in Bible reading, study, memory, application, sharing; prayer, love, faith, compassion, zeal, selflessness, Spirit-filled living, Christ-centered home - and in evangelism, follow-up, church planting, teaching foundational truths. The greatest need in America is a living example of an apostle. 'Lord, do it through me for Your glory.'"

Jan. 27 Je - "New Testament pattern in its simplest form includes:
1   Meeting in homes.
2   Open to any believer.
3   Body ministry - 1 Corinthians 14:26.
4   Baptism and gifts of the Spirit.
5   Evangelization of the multitudes."

March 26 Je - "Today I was baptized in the Name of the Lord Jesus at Herrick Lake. I was sprinkled as a baby in the Presbyterian Church; immersed in the Name of the Father, Son, and Holy Spirit at Calvary Baptist Church in Kingsville, TX, in 1958; but had now received additional light on being baptized in Jesus' Name." (I have since concluded that the exact wording spoken over one is not that important. What is important is one's whole-hearted commitment to Jesus.)

April 10 - "Bill Oberg ministered deliverance to me this date." (Bill was on the staff at Wheaton College, had experienced the baptism of the Holy Spirit, had a weekly meeting in his home, and had a ministry of deliverance.)

April 21 Je - "Today I had the experience of rebuking a tornado storm and seeing it miss Wheaton. I was coming up the stairs from my study in the basement of our home. When I reached the back door landing, I could see how black it was outside. Something in me (the Holy Spirit) led me to pray against this storm and that Wheaton would be protected."

"We found out later that a tornado was headed straight for Wheaton but lifted when it got to the edge of the city. GOD is faithful! (Others may have been praying, too.)"

May 8 Je - "The Lord has been speaking to me about being a servant. I should expect nothing from anyone. I am here on earth to (1) love, obey, and serve God, and (2) love and serve my neighbor. True love loves at all times regardless of the situation or response.

The price that must be paid by those whom God will use in the Last Days will be tremendous. Those who are not willing to pay it will be shelved or taken home."

May 10 Je - "Today I got rid of my library in obedience to the Lord. His Word is sufficient - 2 Timothy 3:16-17."

May 27 Je - "GOD spoke to me through Revelation 10:11 that I would prophesy again. I took that to mean that I would someday again have a traveling, trumpet-blowing ministry, like I did with personal evangelism." (I believe that was fulfilled being a voice for extraordinary prayer, 1981-90; and for simple church, 1991-97. See Chapters 13 through 16.)

June 14 Je - "Many Scriptures about moving to Chicago."

July 22 Je - "We finished fixing up the house and put the 'For Sale' sign out today."

"Signed a contract with Salstrands on September 7, but they later backed out. We will be in Wheaton another year."

October 11 Je - "I need to spend more time with a small group of leaders including Harry Jones, Will Ogden, Bill Oberg, Gary Henley, Ed Schumacher, Bill Nolen, Fred Herzog, Virgil Vogt, Bill Horner, Willie Douglas, and Gary Shallcross."

October 23 Je - "I had become aware of areas in my life where I did not have victory. I concluded through reading several books on demonic strongholds that I needed to be prayed for, for deliverance. This afternoon Derek Prince cast a number of demons from me. Praise the Lord! I had heard of him and phoned the church on the north side of Chicago where he was on staff. He said he was to be in Wheaton later that day and would stop by our home. When he arrived we went to my basement study and he simply commanded the spirits to leave in Jesus' Name."

1968

January 17-18 - Two days of fasting and prayer for direction for 1968.

February 8 Je - "Secret to effective growth:
1   Start small.
2   Go deep.
3   Let God do the expanding.

Feb. 17-22 - Went to St. Paul, Minnesota, to be at Bro. Howe's annual gathering, and at Day Star and Bethany Fellowship. Also met John Lindell at his buffet restaurant. Bro. Howe was an apostle who evangelized and planted churches among Canadian Indian tribes. He also traveled throughout the U.S. and Canada meeting with New Testament church groups. His annual gathering was an opportunity for his many contacts to come together for a week of fellowship, worship, and teaching. His fellow-elder at the church in St. Paul was Lawrence Lee. We were encouraged and learned much from these two men. One time Brother Lee traveled through and tuned our piano at our home in Wheaton. He was a wonderful, humble servant of GOD.

February 21 Je - "Secret of success in Christian life and work:
1   Surrender fully to God - complete dedication of everything.
2   Be filled and led by the Spirit.

3   Spend much time in the Word and prayer.

4   Walk in the light that you have - instant and complete obedience.

5   Be part of a group of believers who let Jesus be the Head of the gatherings.

6   Submit to other Christians - open your life - let others edify, admonish, exhort, rebuke, correct, examine, minister to you, love you, and help you."

Feb. 27 Je - "Persecution is the only way that the Lord can:

1   Bring judgment upon the nation.

2   Purify the Church.

3   Bring sinners to repentance.

4   Bring an end to reliance upon the flesh in Christian work.

5   Destroy the man-made systems of theology and organization."

March 24 - Haroldsens offered $29,500 for 312 E. Lincoln including some furniture - we accepted.

April 2 Je - "Scriptures indicating a move to 528 N. Lockwood in the Austin area of Chicago - Ezekiel 35:4, 9, 15; 36:11, 2; 1 Samuel 10:7. Jo and I are in agreement. We signed a contract this p.m. for $15,000." June - We moved to N. Lockwood. July - Another printing of You Can be a Soul Winner - 30,000 copies are now in print.

Some co-laborers - Frank Foltz, Don Tomkinson, Willie Douglas, Gary Shallcross, Earl McClure, Willard Cummings, James Davis, Gary Henley, Len Harris.

The 1968 Democratic Convention in August was marred by the clashes that took place between the Chicago police and the thousands of anti-Vietnam war youth activists who were camped in Lincoln Park. This had been preceded by the deaths of Dr. Martin Luther King in April and Robert Kennedy in June. I spent one day passing out Christian literature and witnessing to many at Lincoln Park.

November 6 Je - "Most important New Testament truths:

1   The Lordship of Jesus Christ over every believer and every group.

2   Every believer has a ministry.

3   Full salvation - body, soul, and spirit.

4   Open meetings - all can minister."

December - We discontinued meeting with the Legion Hall group - we are needing something home-centered and in the Austin area.

This Christmas was the first time that Jo and I exchanged presents. We had always given something to our children, Gerry and Beth, but didn't feel that we had the funds to give to each other. But this year, for some reason, we felt we had the funds to give a simple gift to each other.

1969

May - A few, including Frank and Lois Foltz and Sterling Borbe, begin to meet on Sundays at our home at 528 N. Lockwood. Not long after that the Lord led us to merge with Gary Henley and the Oak Park brethren. There were eight adults and 13 children in that group.

June - I began working at Local Vending doing office work one day a week. Local Vending was a small company, founded and run by Christians, that put sandwiches in machines at various locations. I worked on an accounting machine that kept track of all of the deliveries. This was a door that GOD opened to us through Walter Simmons, who I had met back when I did some ministry at Pacific Garden Mission. Joanne did substitute teaching some and shipped LEI orders.

August - I am now evangelizing in Cicero-Laramie area, Wheaton, Chicago West side projects, North side (Jewish area), and South side with Len Harris.

In the Jewish area I gave the *Gospel of Matthew* to them at the door and told them that the little booklet was about a famous Jew. An older man, Bill Horner, often went with me to the Cicero-Laramie area. I would spend all day Monday fasting and praying about the work and evangelize Tuesday through Saturday.

This door-to-door work in various areas of Chicago was an exciting time, with a number of converts. Bob Thiele was converted through the work at Grant Park. Gary Shallcross came to the Lord in our home in Wheaton. Verdell Smith, Ernestine Douglas, Milsa Sepulveda, and Jean Campanero were contacts in the Cicero-Laramie area. Suzy Wall and Diana Williams were living in the projects on the West Side. We baptized Ernestine Douglas and Suzy Wall in a small lake on the West Side. We also had contact with a small girl that we called "little Evelyn" and with Virgie Taylor and James Davis.

Ernestine is an interesting story. Her father was a pastor in the Church of God in Christ but she was not walking with the Lord. She came to the weekly Bible study that we had at Dora Allen's apartment in the Cicero-Laramie area to cause trouble! But as she continued to come, the Holy Spirit got a hold of her heart and she yielded her life to the Lord. She later moved to Detroit and we are still in touch. She is very zealous for the Lord.

One of the outstanding converts was Suzy Wall. A brother had come from Denver, CO, to learn more about door-to-door work. We were working in the projects on the West side. These were federally funded apartments about sixteen stories tall. When we knocked on this one door the lady told us that she had lived a life of adultery, had four children from three different men, and "wanted to get saved." (What an open door!) We had the privilege of leading her to the Lord and baptizing her a few days later in the small lake previously mentioned.

105

Suzy had grown up in the hills of Mississippi and moved to Chicago as a teen. She had no schooling in Mississippi, tried to go in Chicago, but soon dropped out. She could not read or write and began to pray that GOD would give her the ability to read the Bible - and He did! She could read the King James Bible, but nothing else.

GOD also gave her the gift of healing - people started coming to her apartment from throughout the projects, she would pray for them, and GOD would heal them.

Je at end of 1969: "1965-69 - a ministry of investing in the lives of a few men - Glenn Wilcox, Stan Hahn, George Bolduc, Frank Foltz, Gary Shallcross, Gary Henley, and Len Harris."

"Summary of the decade of 1960-69: The Lord has given me a good understanding of many areas of His Word, a wonderful family, a growing ministry on every continent through our writings relative to New Testament evangelism and church life, and has more than provided our needs. I praise Him! Truly it pays to serve the GOD of Abraham, Isaac and Jacob."

1970

I went on an extended fast for ten days, March 3-13 - praying about our Chicago work, my relationship with Gary Henley, and a possible ministry to the Wesleyan Church again. This included my dealing with the disillusionment and bitterness that I had toward the organized church.

As we gathered with others at our home on Lockwood on Sunday at the end of my ten-day fast there was a mighty outpouring of the Spirit upon me. I went to my study in the basement and spoke in tongues for over an hour. In the evening I was led to go to three different churches on Laramie Avenue to testify about this outpouring - and they allowed me to share!

April 21 Je: "Since moving to Chicago (close to two years ago) we have had brethren visiting in our home from Missouri, Minnesota, South Dakota, New Jersey, New York, Michigan, Wisconsin, and California. We thank the Lord for the privilege."

Sterling Borbe, Gary Henley, Frank Foltz, and I meet regularly for prayer and to function as elders with the group that meets each Sunday morning at our home, or Henley's, or Foltz's.

I am spending Saturdays going door-to-door in the projects on the West Side and having a Saturday meeting at 6 p.m. at Mrs. Wall's apartment. I was often in the elevator with a guy with a switchblade and we often heard gunfire during the evening meeting.

June 15 Je: "A word from Frank Foltz: 'Our lives should be in subjection to a group of believers. Our ministry should be in subjection to the Lord.'"

July 2 - "I am beginning to feel that maybe I am to be back with the Wesleyans again - to teach personal evangelism - and put a word in for other radical things, as the Lord would open the door, including the gifts of the Spirit, the oneness of the Body, the church of the future, home Bible study groups, reaching the cities, healing, deliverance, and body-type gatherings."

In July Kathryn Kuhlman came to Chicago to have an afternoon healing service at the annual Full Gospel Businessmen's International Convention. Walter Simmons asked us to take a lady in a wheel chair to the meeting. So Joanne and I picked her up and took her to the meeting. We placed her on one side of the auditorium where all of the wheel chair folks were and we found seats in the general seating section.

Kathryn Kuhlman came out on the stage and began to tell stories of how GOD heals. The Spirit of GOD began to move. At one point people were being healed of back problems and I felt the power of GOD move down my back. After a bit of hesitation I turned to Joanne and said, "I think GOD just healed my back!" I'd been having back problems for some time.

After some more hesitation I finally felt I was to go down to the front to testify to my healing, as all were encouraged to do. I got in a line with others who had been healed. When my turn came to go in front of Kathryn Kuhlman, she looked at me with her piercing eyes and said, "Where have you been? GOD healed you forty-five minutes ago!" I looked at my watch - and it had been forty-five minutes! What an awesome experience and day that was! (The woman we brought in a wheel chair to the meeting was not healed.)

During the summer of 1970 my folks let us use their truck camper for a month to take an extended vacation trip. My Dad also gave us a credit card for our gas. (What a blessing!) We drove the southern route to Southern California and returned on the northern route. We visited Father and Mother Brannon in Oklahoma, Glenn and Darlene Wilcox in Arizona, Joanne's uncles in Southern California, and Bob and Arlene Hughes in Sacramento.

Our sightseeing included the Grand Canyon, Yosemite, Mt. Rushmore, and a dinosaur museum in Colorado. At Yosemite we were running short of cash and were a few cents short to get in until Beth found just the amount needed in her clothes box! When we arrived at Joanne's sister's in Sacramento we were out of money, but there was mail waiting for us, including the money we needed.

August and September: The Lord continues to lead us back to Marion, Indiana, and the Wesleyans. We went back to Marion a time or two to scout out the land. I visited with the various leaders at the Wesleyan Headquarters. They all assured me that there was still a place in the Wesleyan Church for my ministry. I shared with them that I now "spoke in tongues." They assured me that this would not be a problem if I did not make it an issue, which I never did. It was a very wonderful, but private, thing with me - a prayer language that GOD had given me by which I could edify myself (1 Corinthians 14:4).

On a visit back to Marion we heard of a property at 4001 S. Boots that was going to go on the market. We drove by and liked what we saw. We felt it was the house GOD had for us so I got out of the car, walked up on the front yard, and claimed it for the Lord. Later that week the folks who owned it allowed us to see it, we made an offer, and they accepted. It never went on the market! It was several months before we could sell our home in Chicago, but the owners of the Marion home miraculously held it for us.

Willie and Millie Douglas had offered to buy our Chicago home. Then they backed out of the deal, but we really felt they were to get it. The Chicago home was in a rapidly changing neighborhood, from White to Black. For Willie and Millie, who were Black, it would be an upgrade from the inner-city apartment where they lived. We kept encouraging them to take a step of faith and get it, and eventually they did - and we got the Boots home.

In December I was having problems with my eyes. I knew I either had to get my glasses changed or see GOD heal my eyes. As I waited upon the Lord about this, He told me to take my glasses off - and as I did, the Lord healed my eyes and I no longer wore glasses. (Years later, as I grew older, I did need to get glasses again.)

109

CHAPTER 9 - BACK TO MARION, IN, AND THE WESLEYAN CHURCH

1971 - 1973

1971

Having become convinced that we were to once again live in Marion, Indiana, and once again relate to the organized church, especially the Wesleyan Church, with our ministry of personal evangelism training, we moved back to Marion in early January 1971, to 4001 S. Boots. Frank Foltz helped us make the move.

One of our tasks of getting settled was to wash the windows. We did it on one of the coldest days of the year. I was all bundled up and washing the windows on the outside, while Joanne was working on the same window on the inside. It was so cold that my cleaning liquid would freeze and Joanne and I would have to trade spray bottles. The mailman came along and asked what in the world we were doing. We said, "Well, the windows were really dirty and we had to wash them." He sort of just shook his head and said, "Well, I believe I'd wait for a warmer day." No doubt he and the neighbors thought we were nuts!

The summer of 1971 was a busy one. We were revitalizing LEI, including opening an office in South Marion. And we put an addition on our home, which included a laundry room, a study for me, which would double as a guest room, a bathroom, and a garage. Frank Foltz and Mrs. Wall's son, Larry, came down from Chicago to help with the roof joists. By now my folks had traded their truck camper for a trailer, and they and Dave came over to help. Joanne's father helped. And in October Joanne's Uncle Vernon even came through from California and helped frame the interior walls. They sure went up fast with his help! A man from College Church did all of the electrical work without charge.

111

Also, as part of the addition, we put a fireplace in the living room wall that was adjacent to the garage. We painted every room and did other redecorating. Some of the upgrading in the house had to wait until there were adequate funds so the whole project was an ongoing one.

The carpet in the living room and dining room had been in the house for many years and, therefore, had gotten very worn down and really did need replacing. Joanne was very eager to get new carpeting. One day while she was vacuuming she was actually wondering why in the world she was bothering to vacuum. The carpet wasn't going to look one bit better after she had vacuumed than it did before. Immediately, the Lord reminded her of Luke 16:10, *"He who is faithful in a very little thing is faithful also in much . . ."* She felt like the Lord said, "If you can't prove yourself to be faithful in taking care of this old carpet, why do you think I'll entrust you with a new one." She immediately began vacuuming with fervor. And some months later the Lord did provide us with new carpet.

It was during the early years back in Marion, that Joanne's public ministry began. She was invited to become part of the leadership of an organization called Women Alive. This was an organization that could be described as somewhere between Christian Women's Club and Women Aglow in its purpose and emphasis. Women came from all over Grant County to be challenged to press toward a more intimate walk with the Lord. As a result of her public exposure through Women Alive she began getting invitations to speak to women's groups throughout the county. This was a challenge she readily accepted and found tremendously fulfilling.

At about the same time, the Lord led her to start a ladies Bible study in our home. This was an immensely exciting experience for her. She had hoped that it would be a way to reach the unsaved. But it was mostly Christian women so she had to give it afresh to the Lord.

It grew in numbers and Joanne watched as GOD drew woman after woman into a more intimate walk with the Him than they had previously experienced. She also had the privilege of leading her Avon lady, who had started attending the Bible study, to the Lord and she became a very sincere follower of Jesus.

For several years Joanne and the kids were involved in the Easter Pageant. It was a huge, very professional production presented in the large coliseum downtown. The pageant depicted a street of Jerusalem using the entire floor area. The stage was designed as the temple. It was presented on Easter Sunday at 6:00 a.m. and portrayed Jesus' triumphal entry into Jerusalem, His arrest, trial, crucifixion, and His resurrection. People would come from great distances to see it. Hundreds of people made up the cast, choirs, and dancers. Joanne was a Jerusalem woman, Beth was her daughter, and Gerry portrayed one of the beggars. One year I was considered for playing the part of Christ, but when they learned that I was not an ordained minister, which was the criterion for filling that role, I was passed over.

1972

In February I had an LEI Crusade with a Wesleyan church in St. Louis. Before I left there the Lord provided a new suit through the pastor, John Hedlund, who was quite interested in end-times preparedness.

May 16 Je: "This has been the most fruitful year (9 months - September, 1971, through May, 1972) that the Lord has ever given us. We have seen the Holy Spirit work everywhere - Indiana, Ohio, Oklahoma, Colorado, West Virginia, Illinois, Missouri, Arkansas, Delaware, Maryland, District of Columbia, Southern California, and Pennsylvania - 12 states and D.C. - and 35 beds!" This was because I had learned to rely more fully on the Holy Spirit.

After the crusade in D.C. we spent a couple of days of rest with a lady in Virginia. She told me that I was "an apostle to/of the laity." I took this to mean that I had a deep conviction that GOD has gifts, ministry, and a destiny for all of GOD's people, not just those in full-time ministry. This emphasis has been a big part of my work all of these years: Releasing everyone into all that GOD has for them.

There were three songs that we used as part of our crusades - *Calling the Continents to Christ* by Marvin Baker, *Win the Lost at Any Cost* by L. H. Ellis, and *Oh, Send us Revival!* by Merla Watson.

May 20 Je: "Men who have influenced my life - my Dad, G. Ousley Brown, Rev. Ogden, Abe David, Nate Scharff, Paul Jackson, Jim Knutz, Bob Clements, Hal Ward, Howard Noggle, Dad Sheets, Bill Bright, Dawson Trotman (even thought he was deceased), Hubert Mitchell, Billy Graham (even though I never met him), Brothers Lee and Howe, and Gary Henley." (See Appendix 3 for further information and an expanded list.)

During this year Marvin Baker and I wrote *The Way to God* booklet. He also helped me with a series of three Bible study books for new Christians. All were printed that summer. The Bible study books have been used around the world, being translated into several languages. (My son, Gerry, revised *The Way to God* booklet in 2012 with graphics by his son, Alex, who is an art major at Indiana Wesleyan University.) Glenn Wilcox and Tom Johnston were now full-time with us in lay evangelism training work.

In September I had several sessions with James Dean of Marion College. He helped me to see that I had basic problems with insecurity and a feeling of inferiority. These were due to overprotection/domination by my mother when I was a boy.

114

We also discovered that I had a problem with rigidity and tunnel vision, although I considered the tunnel vision an asset as it helped me to zero in on a project and not get distracted.

September: I am having many thoughts about a personal evangelism teaching ministry with Marion College. Also growing weary of traveling.

1973

March: GOD provided for me to make a trip to Israel in connection with a Key '73 Conference.   Key '73 was a movement of cooperation among evangelicals in 1973 toward the evangelization of North America. LEI was a part of this. I had wonderful fellowship with many North American Christian leaders during this trip and was asked to speak at one evening session.

March 14 Je: Our Israel tour concluded with a two-day stop in Greece. On the flight from Israel to Greece I sat with Robert Schuller and his wife. He did not yet have the Crystal Cathedral, but was known for his drive-in movie theater parking lot church. I spent one day in Greece resting in my hotel room, when GOD gave me the following revelation: "Athens, Greece: The whole world system is a system of power based on fear. Christ's Kingdom is a system of serving based on love." The second day I was able to see the Parthenon and have Greek food for lunch at a sidewalk cafe.

July 3 Je: in New Jersey - "Lifetime Goals:
1   Know, and live by, the Word of God.
2   Be a man of prayer.
3   Be constantly led by the Holy Spirit.
4   Become conformed to the image of Jesus Christ.
5   Have a marriage, home and children that will glorify the Lord.
6   Contribute to the evangelization of my community and the entire earth.

7   Be a part of a local fellowship of believers and also contribute to the Body of Christ-at-large in my community.
8   Be the Lord's - for whatever He has for me to do at anytime."

July 10 Je - "There is a definite pattern in my life -
1   The Lord lays something on my heart.
2   I find myself spending much time in prayer about it.
3   In answer to prayer, the Lord brings it to pass."

September 8 Je - "This past month has been wonderful. The Lord has given us a family vacation, two excellent ministry situations, and a trip to the East Coast. We praise Him!"

September 12 Je - "What is the Lord doing today?
1   Pouring out His Spirit upon all flesh at the end of the Age as He promised He would do.
2   Restoring New Testament power, purpose, patterns, and fruitfulness to His people in preparation for a last, great, worldwide harvest and the completion of His Church. Complete in number, oneness, purity, pattern, and power - as a testimony before the world and before the hosts of Satan.
3   Current evidences and parts of this include:
-    personal evangelism
-    small groups
-    the Jesus movement
-    the Charismatic renewal
-    Key 73 and Evangelism-in-Depth types of projects."

October 13 Je - "Whether I like it or not, God has chosen me to be a prophet - sounding the trumpet to God's people - evangelism and New Testament Christianity."

November - One Sunday Jo and I visited the Glory Barn, a church in Northern Indiana where GOD was moving, but which later got into error.

November 6 Je: "Ways the devil trips up people:
1   disillusionment
2   bitterness
3   immorality
4   materialism
5   slothfulness
6   the desk (spending too much time with paperwork)
7   a negative attitude."

"The person GOD uses:
1   Full of and led by the Spirit.
2   Person of the Word - study it, live by it, teach and proclaim it.
3   Person of prayer.
4   Person of simplicity - in life and ministry.
5   Clean life.
6   Fully yielded and obedient to GOD."

Nov. 20 Je: "The Wesleyans officially took a stand against the Charismatic renewal and 'speaking in tongues' last week. And I am weary of travel." This was a major turning point in our lives. The open door with the Wesleyans would soon close. What did GOD have for us next?

We got acquainted with John and Elaine Rea when we were both in Chicago. They had recently purchased a center in Wisconsin and invited us to be with them there. We visited it but did not feel we were to be part of it. They later offered it to Youth With A Mission but YWAM did not take it.

I spent much time in prayer in December regarding our future.

CHAPTER 10 - GOING THROUGH A TIME OF MAJOR TRANSITION

(Charismatics, leaving Wesleyan Church, Leffler Construction Co., Christian bookstore, YWAM training)

Marion, IN, and Kailua-Kona, HI: 1974 - 1976

1974

January 21 Je: "Things to emphasize in upcoming crusades:
1   Four things GOD is doing - Restoration of New Testament Christianity:
    a   New Testament evangelism.
    b   New Testament patterns of church life.
    c   the supernatural.
    d   the oneness of the Body.
2   The Church -
    a   We are the Church.
    b   The Church gathered -
    c   The Church scattered - transforming the world - preaching the Gospel, healing the sick, casting out demons, teaching about the Kingdom of GOD.
3   Training in person-to-person and small-group work.
4   Lateness of time.
5   Sell-out for Jesus and souls."

Jan. 29 Je: "I feel that things will come to a head regarding our relationship with the Wesleyan Church and the Holiness movement by spring."

February 1 Je: "Good time with Ron Howland." He was a Church of God (Anderson) pastor in Texas who had a heart for personal evangelism.

Feb. 4 Je: "Lord, I love You. May I glorify Your great Name. May I ever do Your will."

February 16 Je: Prophetic word from Henry, a speaker at a FGBM meeting in Marion, "You will travel again someday with a different emphasis." (This was fulfilled three ways - teaching at YWAM schools around the world, 1977-1982; being a voice for extraordinary prayer, 1981-1990; and being a voice for house churches, 1987-1999.)

Feb. 21-22 Je: "In Maine - another parsonage, bed, people . . . I have had it with travel!" But we did have a good crusade there, in the dead of winter with a lot of snow on the ground.

March 17 Je: "Am committed to a Church pattern that consists of:
1   Plurality of leadership.
2   Unstructured meetings - allowing the Spirit to lead - 1 Cor. 14:26.
3   Meeting basically in homes - savings of money for workers and the poor, future world conditions, future tax structure.
4   Nondenominational.
5   Submission to other city-church leaders."

April 17-19 Je: "I am at the Christian Holiness Association Convention. I feel really out of place. . . . Believe this convention will be my last official contact with the Holiness movement, Wesleyan Church, and institutional church. I must primarily relate to the Charismatic movement and New Testament church movement. . . . The CHA leadership is certainly opposed to the Charismatic movement, as they have been emphasizing that throughout the convention."

At some point in 1974 I learned about, and began meeting with, a group of Charismatic leaders who met on Saturday mornings at Jim McClure's home in Marion, Indiana. These were wonderful times of sharing and praying for one another.

About this time General Superintendent Dr. Melvin Snyder called me into his office to discuss the Charismatic renewal. He said there would still be a place for my ministry if I would renounce my "speaking in tongues." I explained to him that I did not speak about this publicly or make it an issue, but that I could not renounce what I believed was from GOD. He gave me a couple anti-Charismatic books to read, which I did. This did not change my views and I no longer had a ministry with the Wesleyan Church. In fact, the Department of Evangelism sent out a letter to every Wesleyan church advising them not to welcome my ministry. Several pastors, who had me scheduled for the fall, had to call and apologetically tell me that they could not have me come.

This was a very difficult time in our lives. We had had several annual meetings of the LEI associates at Marion College. The college president called me into his office and said that we could not meet at the college any further. So we met that summer at Taylor University.

And the College Church pastor came to our home one day and told us that we could continue to attend the church, but that we could not have any active involvement, i.e., teach a Sunday school class or be called on to pray at any meeting.

With the doors closing on our ministry with the Wesleyans we had to find some way to pay our bills. Jim Cunningham and Jim Leffler approached me about taking a job working with Leffler Construction Company in connection with their expanding to build Varco Pruden steel buildings. On May 4 my Journal entry was - "Have decided to take the Leffler job. I have peace about it and everyone (Joanne, Ralph Breede, Rob Oatis, Fred Milspaugh, Milford Adams, Marvin Baker, and Jim McClure) that I've counseled with have said 'yes'."

May 17 Je: "Have been on the job two weeks and love it." We put up Varco Pruden steel buildings.

Jim Cunningham sold the jobs. I took over from the signing of the contract to the completion of the job, overseeing the onsite inspectors, and coordinating with the office staff (draftsman and secretary), the customers, and the owner, Jim Leffler. I prepared a progress report on all the jobs for Mr. Leffler each Friday, which he seemed to really, appreciate. We built a new building for a motorcycle shop, for a new Radio Shack, several warehouses for Tony Maidenberg, and our largest job was a new gymnasium for Taylor University.

GOD surely helped me with this job. There were times that a problem would develop on a job site. I would get all of the key people together and together we would solve the problem. It was the first real paycheck we had ever received and we were able to finish the addition on our home at 4001 S. Boots in Marion. I worked this job until sometime in October.

May 20: GOD began to speak to me about the need for a Charismatic bookstore in Marion. Also, June 23. Again in September and October.

In September we tied in to Westside Assembly of God Church. Most of the other charismatic Wesleyans were also there - Ben Grays, Milford Adams, etc. In time we taught a Sunday school class for new converts. The pastor, A.W. Thomason, was actually an evangelist, and people got saved almost every week, so the convert's class was always full. We were also on staff for a short while, doing personal evangelism.

Also that fall, in concert with Marvin Baker and Wayne and Estella Pence, we opened a Charismatic bookstore in Marion. There were five other Christian bookstores in the area - one at Marion College, one at the Wesleyan Headquarters, one in downtown Marion, one in Upland, and one in Gas City, but none of them would carry books telling about what GOD was doing at that time - the Charismatic renewal. We each put in some money and started with $500 of paperbacks.

We initially opened on December 6 in a single room at Custer Lumber Company on the bypass. I managed the store without compensation for a few months. Larry Hartman and Boyce Nichols were temporarily out of work from Fisher Body and helped in the store. In time a paid manager, Jean Horner, took over, the store grew, moved to a better location, and mothered another store in Kokomo. They were two of the finest Christian bookstores in Indiana - all because three couples obeyed GOD!

1975

This was a year of major transition. What is to be our local church? What is to be our ministry? What is to be our livelihood? What are we to do with LEI? How are we to relate to Westside Assembly, Truth Temple, Milford Adams, the Saturday group, the Dave Watkins' kids group? Who are we to be submitted to? How and where are we to prepare for coming, end-time tribulation?

We began to look at property in Eastern Ohio in the fall of 1975. In November those with an interest in moving with us began meeting at our home on Sunday evenings. Some of the Charismatic leaders in Marion became offended that we would meet on Sundays and called us on the carpet on December 12. We were told to cancel the Sunday evening meetings and submit everything to a local church, which, before GOD, we could not do. Later, each of these brethren came to us and asked our forgiveness.

1976

1976 was a year of continuing to seek the Lord about our future - where to live, what to do, etc?

February 22-25 I was at the National Association of Evangelicals Convention in Washington, D.C. I was sick and asked Ray Smith, General Superintendent of the Open Bible Standard churches, to pray for me - and GOD healed me!

123

Evie Tornquist sang at the convention and I ran into her one noon at a lunch area, met her, and talked with her briefly. I bought her music tape, and she became an inspiration for our daughter, Beth.

March 25 Je: "Only requests in life to the Lord:
1   That my life and that of my wife and children and associates will glorify the Lord.
2   Be in the center of His will.
3   Be used of Him.
4   That He will supply our needs."

March 29 Je: "I need to be more relaxed around Jo and the kids."

April 19 Je: "Am still believing GOD for the training center in Eastern Ohio."

During these months of transition from the Wesleyan Church we began working some with Action Crusades, the personal evangelism training ministry of the Assemblies of God denomination. We participated with them at a conference in Detroit and a crusade in Atlanta, Georgia.

At the conference in Detroit we met Hugh Hedges and Jay Ferris, who were there from Connecticut. At one point in the conference we were divided into small groups. I went to the Sunday School room for the group that I had been assigned to. When I walked into the room of about eight men I was immediately, divinely bonded with Hugh and Jay. This was the beginning of a long and wonderful relationship with these two men as seen in later chapters in this book.

May 25: I am at the Pittsburgh Charismatic Conference. Before the conference I was looking at a brochure about it, and Loren Cunningham's picture leaped out at me, and the Lord said that it was very important that I look him up at the conference.

I heard several people associated with Youth With A Mission speak - Joy Dawson, Campbell McAlpine, Loren and Darlene Cunningham. I did meet with Loren and Darlene for lunch and Loren suggested that we pray about coming to Montreal in August to see YWAM in action at the Olympics. And then come to Hawaii in September to go through a YWAM School of Evangelism in preparation for teaching personal evangelism in YWAM schools around the world.

May 31 Je: "I believe that GOD is calling us to go with YWAM. In conjunction with this we should (1) go to Montreal for a week as a family, and (2) get involved in being trained in September."

GOD had some work to do with Joanne before we could take this next step. When I returned from the Pittsburgh conference and presented to Joanne the proposal regarding YWAM, the Montreal Olympics, and the training with YWAM in Hawaii, Joanne thought I'd lost my mind. She had had to deal with all of my vision through the years, some of which I saw come to pass and some of which I hadn't, so she thought this was the last straw - surely not more vision. We didn't have the money even to go to Montreal, let alone pick up the family and go out to those tiny islands in the Pacific that we knew very little about.

I had brought home a tape of Loren Cunningham's teaching at the conference. I asked her if she would just please listen to the tape. She rather grudgingly agreed to do so. Loren's teaching was about an hour long. While she was listening to his sharing of all GOD was doing through the young people who were going all over the world, GOD gave her a vision. She is not one given to getting "pictures" or visions, but this one was very clear to her. She was walking barefoot along the ocean and the waves were just lapping over her feet.

While this was happening, GOD spoke to her and said, "Joanne, up to this time in your life, with the ministry you have had, you have just barely gotten your feet wet. I have a whole ocean of experiences ahead for you." In that brief hour, GOD had so changed her heart that she was willing to go to Montreal and see what GOD had from there.

So in the summer of 1976 we went to be part of the YWAM outreach at the Olympics in Montreal. Gerry and Beth were entertained during our long drive from Indiana to Montreal with a tape of all of the music from *The Sound of Music*. I think they had every song memorized by the time we arrived back home.

We were very impressed with what we observed and experienced during our time in Montreal: The quality of the leadership, the depth of the speakers, and the zeal of the young people. So, as we returned home, the sense that we were to go to Hawaii continued to grow in our hearts until a moment when Joanne and I looked at each other and said, "Who are we trying to kid. We know that we know that we know that God is saying we are to go to Hawaii." We were in total unity.

On our way home from Montreal we stopped in Connecticut to see our friends, Jay and Carleen Ferris, their daughter, Missy, and their newborn son, Tim. We have enjoyed our friendship with the Ferrises for many years.

August 17 Je: "It seems strange - we don't know why - but the Lord is clearly leading us to Hawaii for training with YWAM. We trust Him to work out every detail. And we leave the next step in His hands."

One day I was in my office in South Marion. As I looked at the world map that was on the wall I felt increasingly called to a worldwide ministry. GOD was beginning to renew my vision for the world that He had first given me when I was with the Navigators. This vision began to come to pass through our years with Youth With A Mission and continued through our writings, which have gone around the world.

We began making preparations to go to Hawaii. At first we thought we were to sell our home, but the Lord spoke very clearly that we were not to do that. Five girls lived in it while we were gone for YWAM training. Then we came back and lived in it for another year and a half before selling it and going full-time with YWAM.

We had to sell our car for funds for our tickets to Hawaii. The night before we had to have the money, Len Fiene, a Lutheran pastor who had been added to the LEI Board, and was at our home for a LEI board meeting, prayed with us that the car would sell the next day. Sure enough, the next morning, while Joanne was fixing breakfast, a man came by and bought the car for exactly what we were asking - and he never even drove it! Oh, the faithfulness of GOD!! So now we could purchase our tickets and head for training with YWAM in Hawaii.

We arrived in Kailua-Kona, Hawaii, on September 7th, my 41st birthday. September 10 Je: "We are now in Hawaii! The Lord had wondrously put it all together."

Joanne and I were attending a YWAM School of Evangelism (SOE). There were about 40 students in the school, being led by Loren and Darlene Cunningham, the founders of Youth With A Mission. Most of the students lived in tents on a Hawaiian farm. We were one of the fortunate few that were housed at Casa De Emdeko condominium on the Pacific Ocean for the first six weeks.

Then we got word that we were to move to Amber Silva's house. She had her son, Delta, and two other hippie girls, one with a son, living with her. Gerry slept in a bedroom with Delta and the other boy. Jo and I and Beth slept on Amber's living room floor. Not much privacy! It was a trying time.

Gerry was taking two of his high school senior classes by correspondence, but was having to travel up the mountain to the local high school for another class. He was having difficulty getting the rides he needed to get up to the school so had been praying about getting a motorcycle. He had sold his car when we came to Hawaii so had a little money, but not much. Going to a retail store to buy something was out of the question. When we first arrived at Amber's home there was a motorcycle for sale in her front yard - a Kawasaki 250 - exactly what Gerry had been praying about. This was a huge boost to his faith and proved to him that GOD cared about his personal needs just as much as He did about the needs of his Dad and Mom.

Joanne was concerned for his safety as he rode up and down the mountain and happened to be talking about that in the women's restroom shortly after he had made the purchase. Darlene Cunningham happened to be there and overheard Joanne's comments. She piped up and said, "Joanne, GOD's not going to give him something that he's going to kill himself on." That made total sense to her and she ceased her worrying. And, of course, GOD did protect him.

Our SOE classes were held in a room in a warehouse section of Kailua-Kona, Hawaii. Each week a different spiritual leader would come from around the world and teach. Some of these included Gordon Olson, Joy Dawson, Corrie ten Boom, Ramona Peterson, Don Stephens, Loren and Darlene, and others. Much of the teaching centered on world vision, trusting GOD, and hearing His voice. And I was asked to teach a couple of days on different aspects of personal evangelism.

One evening we were given an opportunity in class to give to those in the class who yet owed on their school tuition. We had only five pennies so we gave one cent to each of five fellow students. The next week we received an unexpected check in the mail for $100 - we believed that GOD was honoring our obedient giving.

Each day was begun with our dividing into small groups and having an hour of intercession. This was one of the most exciting aspects of our training. GOD would show us what to pray as a group as we all listened to His voice and shared with the group what He had spoken to each of us.

Beth was in the ninth grade and was attending YWAM's new International Christian School (ICS) under the leadership of Paul Hawkins. The dining hall where we ate our meals was right next to our classroom. The kids spent their evenings, while we were in evening classes, in the dining hall doing their homework. Since we were in Hawaii for only five months, both the kids were able to return to their schools in Marion to finish out the year - Gerry was able to graduate from high school with his class and Beth finished her ninth grade.

October 17 Je: "I am very grateful to the Lord for the time here in Hawaii:
1   The vacation at the condominiums.
2   The inner-healing at the hands of Alan Williams.
3   The being built-up by the teaching, fellowship, and corporate worship.
4   The renewed vision for world evangelism.
5   The practical lessons of putting others before self.
But I am getting anxious to push on with what GOD has - whatever that is."

Oct. 21 Je: "Things shared by the group about me: mature, wise, compassionate, a weeping prophet, have the fear of GOD, able to flow with younger generation, relationship with Jo impresses younger generation."

During our SOE one of our teachers for a week was Corrie ten Boom. She had lived in Holland when it was occupied by the Germans during World War 2 and was sent to a prison camp, but miraculously released. I had hoped that she might write the foreword for my book, *The Omega Generation*. She spoke at a Friday evening meeting at the local high school in Kealakekua, open to the Kona community. Loren Cunningham arranged for Jo and me to take her back to her hotel after the meeting so that I could approach her about this.

While we were driving down the mountain, Corrie asked us to come to her room at the Kona Inn and have tea with her. We, of course, graciously accepted her invitation. While her nurse left to get the tea, we were left alone with her, felt that we were in the presence of royalty, and were quite intimidated. Joanne was standing with her tongue totally tied. Shortly, Corrie looked at her and with a quick wave of her hand said in a commanding tone, "Sit down!" As Joanne tells the story, upon that command, "I sat down!" The tea was served and we had a delightful visit with her. She, however, informed us that her board had decided that she was not to write the foreword for books.

However, at some point when Loren was talking with Corrie about Nate's book, she made the statement, "The message of this book needs to get out now, very quickly. A few months from now may be too late," at which time Loren quickly said to her, "Can he quote you on that?" She said, "Yes." Thus the quote made it on the front jacket of Nate's book. What a memorable time it was to spend time with Corrie ten Boom.

For the two-month outreach phase of the SOE our entire team of about twenty-five lived together at a rented property, later purchased, which YWAM named the House of Barnabas. We all were involved in different types of outreach in the community. I, however, was gone for several of those weeks, being involved in a Bibles for Mexico outreach. (More on this in Chapter 11.)

Our Christmas time that year was very unique and special. The children's singing group called The King's Kids was just getting started under the leadership of Dale Kauffman. This group was made up of the children of parents who were either going through a school on the base in Hawaii or on staff. And a few local kids got involved as time progressed. Dale's vision was to see groups like this raised up all over the world at the different YWAM training centers and for those groups to go out on mission trips to spread the Gospel. As soon as we arrived on the base in Hawaii, Beth got involved and actually ended up doing quite a bit of solo work with them. She ended up working with King's Kids for several years either as just part of the singing group or also part performer/part staff.

So, this Christmas, during our outreach time, Dale had made arrangements for the King's Kids to sing in a different hotel each night of the week leading up to Christmas. There was one vacant lot in downtown Kailua and permission was granted from the owner for the Kids to use that lot for a Christmas pageant. Each night, after singing at the scheduled hotel, they would parade from that hotel down the main street of town to that vacant lot. As the Kids walked down Alii Drive, they were followed by Mary and Joseph with Mary riding on a donkey. On the lot a stable had been erected so that the true story of Christmas could be enacted culminating with Rod Wilson, who was a part of our outreach team, coming out from the shadows with a crown of thorns on his head and "blood" dripping down his body enacting the real reason for Jesus' birth - His death for our sins. It was quite powerful. Beth, of course, was part of the singing group and Gerry was in charge of the lighting for the pageant part. Both of them thoroughly enjoyed these activities.

It was a Christmas that Joanne, in particular, was not looking forward to because we were so far from family. But, with a donkey tied up outside our bedroom door at the House of Barnabas, who loudly let his presence be known, and another animal or two also being used for part of the performance, she has said that she felt like she was "living" in Bethlehem. Then with the performance/ministry the King's Kids had every night plus the outreach "family's" activities at the house each night after each performance, the birthday presents for Jesus on Christmas morning, and the huge Christmas dinner with the whole base, it turned out to be one of her most memorable Christmases.

CHAPTER 11
TRAVELING THE WORLD

Youth With A Mission - Kona, Hawaii: 1977 - 1980

1977

This year began several years of traveling around the world in connection with Youth With A Mission - teaching in their training schools, working with their outreach teams, and working with local churches.

After completing our School of Evangelism training, I was invited by Loren to be part of the Bibles for Mexico outreach. I spent early 1977 working with YWAM teams going to Mexico to place a Bible in every home. I was their in-transit teacher, sharing principles of evangelism at our various stops on the way to LaPaz, and after we got to our base there. I was also very sick at the base due to all of the travel.

After the time in Mexico I also had some ministry with a church in San Diego and wonderful fellowship with Hal Ward, who had mentored me when I was a young Christian.

In February we attended a three-week YWAM Leadership Training seminar. In March we moved back to our home in Marion, IN, to wait on GOD regarding our future. I spent a week teaching at the YWAM Base in Tyler, Texas, en route from Hawaii back to Indiana. I also stopped at the Arkansas base and stopped at Cassandra Ward's parents' place. Cassandra had been heading up the hospitality department on the YWAM Base while we were in Hawaii. Shortly after we returned home, she was killed in a private plane crash on Hawaii. We spent the summer praying about our future.

The first week of September we attended the YWAM North American Conference at the base in Arkansas. We all brought tents and slept on the ground. The meetings were held in a big tent. During the week I received word that *The Omega Generation* book was in at the publishers a few miles away. I borrowed a car and went over and got a case - on my birthday! - to make available at the conference. Also, during the conference, Loren made a phone call to Floyd McClung in Europe to arrange for me to teach at YWAM schools throughout Europe in the coming months.

September 19 Je: "I leave today for Europe via Ohio, Michigan, and New England."

September 26 Je: "What a privilege! - to sit here at Carleen Ferris's folks' cottage on Long Island Sound, to look across the water, and spend the day with the Lord." I spent much of the day praying about the training center we still hoped to develop in Eastern Ohio.

September 28 Je: "I leave in a few hours for London - beginning a new chapter in Jo and my lives." I was directed by the Lord to go to our friends, Jay and Carleen Ferris in Connecticut, to get the Lord's further direction on the trip to England since I was flying standby. When I got up on the 28th, the Lord said, "Take the 9 p.m. TWA flight tonight." I started toward the phone to call TWA, and the Lord said I was not to phone, but just go to the JFK airport. Later in the day I started to phone again - and again the Lord said, "No!"

My friend Hugh Hedges dropped me off around 4 p.m. I got in the standby line, as I had only enough money to fly standby. When I got up to the front of the line, the ticket person said the 7:30 flight was all sold out. (I didn't know anything about a 7:30 flight, only about the 9 p.m. flight that the Lord had spoken to me.) Then he looked again at his computer screen and exclaimed, "What is this? They are putting on a 9:00 flight tonight! You can go on that one." (I could have told him that!)

When boarding the plane I had a window seat with two gentlemen beside me. I went to the back of the plane to get a news magazine. When I came back the two men were gone and a young couple was seated there. I learned that the young couple had known each other a year earlier when they were college seniors - he at Harvard and she across the street at Vassar. They were now both on their way to England as Rhodes Scholars at Cambridge University. They just ran into one another on the plane, and the two men gave up their seats to let them sit together.

After we took off I overheard this couple talking about Charles Colson's born-again conversion to Christ. The gal mentioned that she had done her undergraduate thesis on Jonathan Edward's preaching. I asked them if they were born again. They said, "No." I told them that I was. They wanted to hear more, and for the next hour I shared my testimony and we talked about knowing Jesus. What a joy! I would have missed this wonderful opportunity if I had not obeyed the Lord and taken the 9 p.m. TWA flight. How it pays to obey the leading of the Holy Spirit!

I stayed overnight at the England YWAM Base. The next day on the way to the airport for a flight to Belfast, Northern Ireland, the fellow taking me handed me some money he had just received in the mail. It was the rest of what I needed for the flight to Ireland!

When traveling by auto from the Belfast airport I noticed military personnel everywhere due to the prolonged struggle between the Catholics and the Protestants in Northern Ireland. I taught for a week at the YWAM Base in Bangor, Northern Ireland. My teaching at YWAM bases was usually on (1) how to study the Bible, (2) principles of personal evangelism, and (3) the end-time Church.

The base overlooked a beautiful harbor. I would walk down there each day. A couple of times I bought fish and chips - great big chunks of fish fresh off of the fishing boats and big chunks of french-fried potatoes - what a treat.

While at the base on October 6, a young student by the name of Paul prophesied to me, "My son, know that I love you. I will repair all the hurts and cuts of the past. I will build you up again. I have a deep concern for you, My son. Know that I am with you. For I, Omega El Shaddai, have called thee to serve Me and you have answered. Care not about the areas which aren't mine; for you have laid them on the altar and they shall be mine. This is the Lord Almighty that saith."

I then taught for a week at the YWAM Base in Hawick, in Southern Scotland. It was in a little town surrounded by hills with many sheep on them. What a beautiful place!

Then I spent a few days in Northern Scotland living with a retired oil executive, his wife, and her sister in an old castle they had purchased. I ministered at various home groups in the area. On Sunday morning I attended a Church of Scotland with the couple where they sang the Psalms. On Sunday evening I had the Lord's Supper with the couple, who were Plymouth Brethren in background. Following that I took the train back to London for a week of teaching at the England YWAM Base south of London.

On Friday, October 28, the base in England had words of prophecy and knowledge for me - "GOD is going to release the property in Ohio, but mine is to be an itinerate ministry of great scale. I will affect nations. The end-time emphasis is to be part of it. There is now the release of much greater authority against the enemy. There will be a much greater supernatural, signs-following aspect. Whole groups of people will come into deliverance, inner healing. 1 Samuel 17:46."

Additionally they said, "Finances on this trip have been only what you've needed - GOD has been proving you - this will not be the case in the future - there will be an abundance. GOD has invested a great deal in you. Your family will be with you in future moves. You must be careful not to get ahead of them. There will be 'a word of the Lord' aspect to it. The center will be a place for you to rest and be renewed. Humility mentioned. There will be much opposition, but GOD will clearly and mightily vindicate. GOD will give wisdom." (Added in 2013: I don't have much understanding about these words. The center never came to fruition, nor the worldwide traveling ministry. But GOD has given us a worldwide ministry through writing, publishing, and mentoring others. Regardless of the past, we are very content being and doing what we are now doing. GOD is faithful!)

In November the Lord made it clear that we should turn the LEI materials over to Marion Noll, who had been part of LEI for several years.

Nov. 20 Je: "I believe the 'moment of truth' has come:
1   My ministry is that of an evangelist-teacher-prophet. It is not a ministry of people being built around me. I'm a loner like Joy Dawson.
2   I have no desire to be a YWAM leader. I do desire to travel, speak and teach, give prophetic leadership on principles of evangelism, the Church, end-time persecution, the person GOD uses, etc. I want to be free to study, pray, write, and teach.
3   I am a second-tier leader. I need others beside me and over me. I need to submit to Loren Cunningham and the YWAM-Hawaii elders.
4   I have no desire to head up a base, or a team, or a division.
5   Move to Hawaii.
6   Forget the Eastern Ohio center."

December 18 Je: "If we move to Hawaii for three or four years, my areas of interest are:

1   LEI/local church emphasis worldwide.
2   Help develop the university, which YWAM was starting.
3   Develop a Church Ministries department - at the university and worldwide.
4   Teach at YWAM schools.
5   Work with outreach teams.
6   Put out an end-times news bulletin.
7   Be a voice - Church, cities, Blacks, evangelism, person-to-person evangelism, end-times, Bible intake, Scripture memory. (Much of this came to pass during our two years in Kona, 1978-80.)

1978

My next overseas trip with YWAM was to Europe. I taught in YWAM schools in Iceland, Norway, Finland, Germany, Denmark, and Holland. Jo joined me from Germany on and we also made a stop at the base in Switzerland.

January 19 Je: "Am in Norway, teaching at the YWAM school. Went skiing for the first time in my life and spent most of it lying on the ground!" (The skiing instruction was given to me by one of Norway's top skiers who was part of the YWAM staff.)

It was winter and in Iceland the sun rose at 10 a.m. and set at 4 p.m. In Norway the YWAM Base overlooked a beautiful fjord. In Germany, since Jo was with me, we spent a day in Munich, where the waiter at a restaurant was impressed with my name being Krupp.

We were scheduled to fly from Switzerland to Denmark. There was a problem with ice so we were taken to the Geneva Airport, larger than the one at Lausanne. At the Geneva Airport I gave Christian leaflets to a number of people.

The airport was finally closed so we took a train and missed our connecting flight from Copenhagen to Vejen. We stayed overnight in a Copenhagen hotel and the next morning Joanne came across Psalm 67:1-2 in her quiet time and we realized that I had given literature to someone from every continent at the Geneva Airport. We took a walk in historic downtown Copenhagen before catching our flight to Vejen.

After the week in Holland Joanne flew back to the States and I went to Belgium for a few days to do research on "the beast," a large computer that I was told would someday rule the world.

"I don't fully understand it, but I can't get away from the burden to work with churches - and in the U.S. . . . there is an anointing I have when I work with churches that I don't have any other time."

February 22 Je: "I'm ready to sell the house, give the money away, and move to Hawaii and get on with the next chapter that GOD has for us."

Feb. 25 Je: "Have just seen the masses and filth of Amsterdam. 'GOD, please multiply me - raise up laborers for the harvest.' "

I was invited by Loren to come to Hawaii and teach and spent time with him regarding our moving there. I found out from Jeff Littleton that they were about to lose the base property. After I got home the Lord began to speak to us about selling our home and giving the money to YWAM.

April 20 Je: "Verses about giving money to YWAM:
Sell all you have and give to the poor - Matthew 19:21, Luke 18:22.
She did what she could - Mark 14:8.
Give to apostles - Acts 4:34-37.
See your brother in need - 1 John 3:17-18."

139

In May I went to Argentina to work with YWAM, preparing for the upcoming, worldwide Mundial Soccer matches. I had a young couple assigned to be my interpreters. We traveled by car to Northern Argentina. I had a wonderful time teaching evangelism principles and methods in churches in two cities. But I got deathly sick. I got up for an hour in the morning to have a quiet time and meet with my team, then spent the rest of the day in bed until I had to get up to teach in the evening.

May 13: During my morning Bible reading the Lord spoke to me to return to Buenos Aires and home to Indiana to get well and help prepare for the move to Hawaii - 1 Timothy 5:8, 3:4, 3:7. This was confirmed by Wedge Alman, the YWAM South American Director - Acts 9:15; Shirley, his wife - Luke 7:10, Jeremiah 38:26; and Wally Wenge, the YWAM Business Manager - Deuteronomy 10:11a.

I flew from Northern Argentina to Buenos Aires. As we were approaching BA, I asked the stewardess if the houses I was seeing out the window were the outskirts of BA. She went to the cockpit, I guess to confer with the pilot, and returned to invite me to come to the cockpit. The pilot invited me to sit in the single seat just behind the pilot and co-pilot. The pilot pointed out various buildings as we flew across BA to land at the downtown airport. I explained that I was not well and needed to return to the states. He radioed the international airport and got my reservations for a flight later that day.

When we landed he said that the limousine that was waiting at the plane was for me and that the co-pilot would take me to get my tickets changed. The co-pilot accompanied me to a private lounge where I rested while he got my tickets all ready for the flight home. They must have thought I was a dignitary or something - GOD was taking care of me! I then stopped at the YWAM office, then was taken to the international airport, and flew home to Indianapolis via Miami.

Shortly after getting back home I learned why the Lord had brought me home - Jo found she had to have major surgery. So I was needed at home to care for her and to get things packed for our move to Hawaii. GOD is so faithful!

One day we were doing some shopping for our move to Hawaii. The clerk wheeled around and said, "Do you practice that? - talking like Jimmy Stewart." I never realized that I sounded like the actor Jimmy Stewart when I talk!

In July we turned publishing of the LEI materials over to New Leaf Press in Arkansas. I drove our Volkswagen Rabbit to the West Coast to be shipped to Hawaii. While in Los Angeles I saw Vic Munyer who had been part of LEI.

We moved to Hawaii in August. We were given a room on the second floor of Building No. 1. What a view of the Pacific Ocean and town of Kona we had! We spent much of the first month remodeling our apartment, putting in a stairway and loft and mini-kitchen with sink. George Wilde, who was attending a Crossroads DTS, did the plumbing for the sink. We became friends with him and his dear wife, Joyce, there and later in Washington State.

One of the unpleasant aspects of moving back to Hawaii was leaving Gerry behind. He was to enter his sophomore year at Marion College (now Indiana Wesleyan University) and didn't have any leading to go with us. A year and a half later, however, he took a semester off and came to Kona to do a DTS (Discipleship Training School). He loved it and it was while he was there that he felt called to Christian ministry. We are so grateful to the Lord for the spiritual impact YWAM had on our children.

In October Joanne and her sisters were called back to Indiana due to Joanne's father's failing health. They arrived a few days before he went to be with the Lord. Beth and I joined Joanne and the family for his funeral.

Then exactly four weeks to the day after Dad Sheets passed away, Joanne's mother joined him in heaven. She passed away following a heart attack. Joanne was the only one from our family who joined her sisters to bury her mother. This was a difficult time for her, but she felt that the family atmosphere on the YWAM base helped to comfort her in her loss.

As soon as we moved to the base in Kona, Joanne was asked to work with the Hospitality Department and ultimately became the tour guide for the base. She drove visitors in a van around to the different YWAM locations. As she drove she told the story of how the base came to be established in Kailua-Kona and how YWAM acquired the hotel. She loved her tour guide work!

An interesting development that was such a miracle from the Lord was how faithful He was to Beth. Her experience in Kona when we were there in 1976-77 was less than pleasant, for a number of reasons. So when we had to tell her that we were going to move there permanently she was in tears. However, GOD orchestrated circumstances in such a way that by the time we went back to Marion for Joanne's father's funeral, you could not have paid Beth to move back to Marion. Oh, the faithfulness of GOD!

Almost immediately upon our move to Hawaii, Beth again became involved with King's Kids, the children's and youth singing group developed by Dale Kauffman. She had begun this involvement when we were there in 1976-77, and became one of their main soloists, traveling with the group to Japan, Europe, Spain, and the mainland USA.

December 26 - We were prayed over by the Kona YWAM elders - Paul Hawkins mentioned "revival, prophet, and 1 Corinthians 14:1." Gary Stevens mentioned "new things." Loren Cunningham mentioned "worldwide."

1979

January 17: Paul Hawkins - "You are to be a Christian statesman that will affect nations - you have an unusual combination of prophet and gentle spirit."

February 1: Loren Cunningham - "Keep free for an international ministry - prophet to the nations - LEI - teacher-evangelist. Don't get bogged down locally or with administration, work, a department, etc. Exceptions - small team, School of the Bible, School of Church Ministries. It takes time to build an international ministry."

I had a tremendous respect for Loren - too much! When we lived in Bldg. No. 1 and he and Darlene in Bldg. No. 3, and he would be on their lanai, I would watch him through my binoculars! GOD has since taken that unhealthy respect away and my total respect, worship, and submission are to Jesus alone.

February 12: With Kona elders - the vision for both schools (School of the Bible and School of Church Ministries) is right. I am to head them both up. The Bible is to come first.

Lesson from Robert Coleman's book, *The Master Plan of Evangelism* - I need to invest my life in a few.

In June and July I spent six weeks in Japan preparing the churches of Japan for an upcoming YWAM outreach to the Olympics. I traveled to Tokyo, Yokohama, Nagoya, Osaka, Kobe, Kyoto, Hiroshima, and Kyushu - preaching and teaching in churches on principles and methods of personal evangelism. It was a wonderful time and GOD has given me a lasting love for the Japanese people.

August 13 Je: "Things I am thankful for:
1   That I grew up in a small, Midwestern town in the U.S.
2   That my citizenship is in the U.S.

143

3   That English is my language.

4   That I'm tall and slim.

5   For what I learned from my Dad: thriftiness, cleanliness, respect for GOD and country, high morals, honesty, humility.

6   For what I learned from the Boy Scouts: crafts, diligence, love for the outdoors, leadership.

7   For what I learned from the Presbyterian Church: respect for GOD, right and wrong, character traits.

8   For my mother: that she took care of us children.

9   For the fun I had with my little sister.

10   For the oversight responsibility I had for my brother.

11   For my keen mind.

12   For the stretching experience of student government at Purdue.

13   For Abraham David and Nate Scharff who led me to Jesus.

14   For Jesus, my Lord and Savior, who saved me from a life of sin on March 17, 1957.

15   For His faithfully leading me to Kingsville, Texas, and all that took place there - Chaplain Day, Commander Robert E. Sparks, Lydia Beltran, Bob Clement, Calvary Baptist Church, Paul and Doris Jackson, Rusty Reynolds and his wife, Brother Chism, Jim Knutz, jail preaching, preaching in churches, men's prayer meetings, witnessing and soul-winning opportunities.

16   For His faithfully leading me to the Navigators - Mert Martin in California, Hal Ward, Glen Eyrie - and all that I learned from them - the Word, the world, discipling, personal evangelism, GOD's greatness, 2 Timothy 2:2.

17   For my relatives - Uncle Taylor and Aunt Lula, Aunt Emma and Helen, Dillons, Foxes, Hoffmans, Apgers, etc.

18   For my dear, lovely, wonderful, dedicated, faithful wife - the most beautiful and finest woman in the world.

19   For Gerry - a neat, wonderful, maturing, young man - who loves the Lord - and has tremendous potential as a pastor-teacher.

20   For Beth - a neat, wonderful, maturing young lady - who loves the Lord - and has tremendous potential with people, singing, dramatics.

21   For the love for GOD's Word that He has given me.

22   For my calling to be a prophet-teacher-evangelist as it relates to prayer, the Word, personal evangelism, the Church, end-times, discipling new converts.

23   For our association with Campus Crusade for Christ, the National Holiness Association, the National Association of Evangelicals, Key '73 - and all of the wonderful men and women of GOD I have known and worked with.

24   For the privilege of being a blessing to so many through the books the Lord has led me to write.

25   For the many years of experience the Lord has given me in evangelism and in working with churches.

26   For all that I learned from Joanne's parents - and from the Wesleyans.

27   For all of our friends in Marion, Indiana, and throughout the U.S.

28   For our expanding worldwide contacts and ministry.

29   For the blessing that YWAM has been to us.

30   For our lovely view of the ocean.

31   For the lovely homes we have always had. (He has always given us His best!)

32   That GOD is in charge of the universe - and He will win the final battle. And He is in charge of our lives.

33   What a privilege - to know Him - and that He is all-wise, loving, all-knowing, holy, merciful, just, righteous, and tender.

34   For all of our needs provided - and far beyond!

35   For the many books GOD has allowed me to read.

36   For the beauty of GOD's creation.

37   For the traveling the Lord has allowed me to do.

38   For all that I have learned from my wife."

August 18 Je: "I am a teacher-prophet-evangelist like Joy Dawson - not a leader like Loren. "Don't give me a big operation to manage - just give me time to be with Jesus - and freedom to study, write, travel, teach, preach, witness - and a place on the base to teach about evangelism, the Church, the Word, end-time preparedness."

August 29: I am at a YWAM Outreach in Fiji. Word to me from other leaders - "You have died to a national vision in order to be released into an international ministry."

During the fall the Lord began opening doors for Joanne to lead ladies' Bible studies in the Kona community. At one time she was leading three different groups. This was something she had developed a real love for in Marion and she was thrilled to be able to again be involved with women apart from the base, out in the community. This ministry continued for her until we moved to Oregon in the fall of 1980.

South Pacific trip: October 19 - November 19 -
American Samoa highlights - speaking at the Samoan Assembly of God Church, teaching at the YWAM Base, eating at Rainmaker Hotel.

Tonga highlights: The prime minister, a deeply dedicated Christian, spoke to 300 top leaders of the nation - "The greatest sin is to not accept Jesus Christ as your personal Savior." I was the guest of honor at a love feast given by the prime minister for about 20 spiritual leaders. We sat on the ground and ate fruit, vegetables, chicken, and lobster - they were the largest lobsters I have ever seen - and all that you could eat! I was also part of a national love feast on the Capitol grounds. I spoke at a charismatic meeting on Sunday at 4 p.m. at an Episcopal Church - the prime minister's wife and daughter participated. Isi, the YWAM leader, is very highly respected in Tonga.

146

New Zealand highlights: I taught at the YWAM school in Auckland. Had an all-day seminar with a Roman Catholic priest in Auckland. Spoke in a church on Sunday. Then several days in the Wellington area - spoke at a church where Tom Marshall is an elder. Stayed with local people, Ray and Linda Howe - had lamb every day! - very good. Spoke at various churches, home groups, and luncheon meetings. "New Zealand is on the verge of a spiritual awakening."

Australia highlights: Taught at Wesleyan Bible College in Melbourne, spoke at Full Gospel Business Men's meeting in Sydney, met with YWAM leader Tom Hallas.

During the fall of 1979 we pioneered the School of the Bible. Lee Thompson and Joanne were on the staff with me. I was gone to the South Pacific during part of the school. We had only four students, but it was a very effective time of Bible study in their lives. Lee and I also started the Base library by getting boxes of free books from major Christian publishers.

Much of the rest of the fall was spent praying through the School of Church Ministries, which took place in the winter of 1980. Two well-known teachers in the School of Church Ministries were Dr. Howard Snyder, an author and seminary professor, and Paul Billheimer, author of the book *Destined for the Throne*.

During our time with YWAM-Kona we also had the privilege of meeting monthly for prayer with the Kona pastors. And we had ministry on Oahu with Roy Sasaki's two Methodist churches and with Bayview Chapel, an Assembly of God church, pastored by Leon Hiebert. During one of my visits to Oahu I went to a large outdoor concert and heard Debby Boone sing *You Light Up My Life* - what a voice!

We had the joy of getting off the base twice and house sitting: at Floyd and Ida Watson's at Christmastime, 1978; and at Francis and Mimi McMahon's at Christmastime in 1979. Being at McMahon's that year was such a blessing because Gerry had just come over to Kona to do his DTS starting in January. This allowed all four of us to be together as a family. There would not have been room for all of us in our little room/apartment on the base.

1980

January 25 Je: Time with Loren Cunningham and Ezekiel 33 - "My primary calling is a prophet-teacher-evangelist - not to run schools."

February 6: Spent the day with Leonard Ravenhill, an internationally known revivalist, at his home in Texas - what an awesome privilege.

February 10: At John 17:21 Convocation in Dallas, Texas. Je: "What a tremendous time - seeing many old friends - Gary Henley, Rich Raad, Brian Banaschak, Glenn Wilcox, Leonard Ravenhill, Jim Rogers, Robert Ewing, Jay Ferris, Marion and Naomi Noll, Chuck Farah, Fred Herzog - and meeting and/or hearing Dennis Bennett, Larry Christianson, Derek Prince, Bob Mumford, Charles Simpson, David DuPlessis, Ralph Martin, Juan Ortiz, Action Crusade people, and Kevin Ranahan. It was an historic event in recent Church history. It was wonderful to see GOD bringing His Church together; to meet people who had read *The Omega Generation*; to have the Lord give me an even greater desire to meet, fellowship with, serve, labor with my brothers and sisters worldwide."

February 18 Je: "Issues I am struggling with:
1   Where is our home to be - YWAM or some local church like Calvary Community Church in San Jose, CA?
2   How much ministry is to be local versus out traveling internationally?

148

3   How much of my ministry is to be to YWAM versus to local churches?
4   Can I remain here in Kona when my burden is the Church, not a ship, refugees, or a University?"

March 21 Je: "GOD is beginning to make real to me that people are more important than programs, projects, vision, etc. Our goal in life must be to love people and minister to their needs."

In the spring I had to die to everything and become a participant in a Disciple Training School at King's Mansion, at Loren's direction.

April 13 Je: "I have been slow in the past to build relationships because of the fear of man, inferiority, insecurity, hurts from people, improper relationship with females, and my parents, particularly my mother. Also, because my contact with people was to use them, to lead them to Christ, to teach and preach to them. Also, because of the traveling ministry, only being in one place for a week or so. I need to accept, love, get to know, give myself to people - for no reason other than that!"

April 25 Je: "Things I 'know' for this next year:
1   The Lord has given me a message to deliver - the Church in the 80s: revival, restoration, unity, world evangelization, and persecution.
2   I've got to find a quiet place and time to seek the Lord and a home where there is security and quietness.
3   I've got to multiply myself throughout the younger generation.
4   I need to get some time with Loren - in May."

April 30 Je: "Things that have happened in the past four years - since our YWAM link-up:
1   Learned about intercession.
2   World vision renewed.
3   Ministry on every continent except Africa.

4   Clarification of calling - prophet-teacher - not people following me.
5   Gerry's DTS.
6   Beth's music and spiritual growth
7   LEI materials into several languages.
8   What GOD is doing in my life - team, servant, submissive, have fun, etc.
9   Experience running two schools.
10   Fresh release into ministry.
11   Jo's further experience with ladies' groups.
12   Getting us out of the Marion, Indiana, anti-charismatic situation."

May 3 Je: "Ezekiel 37:14 - *'And I will put My Spirit within you, and you will come to life, and I will place you on your own land. Then you will know that I, the Lord, have spoken and done it,' declares the Lord.'* GOD to give us a place of our own to live - Oregon?"

May 17 Je: ". . . I need a quiet place."

Around this time I began to have a growing unrest in our remaining on the base in Kona. Gerry Fry, the pastor of a large church in San Jose, California, told me that he felt that "the Lord was stirring my nest." As I continued to pray about it, the Lord clearly began speaking to me about moving to Salem, Oregon, to be part of the YWAM Base there.

We also had an invitation from Roy Sapp, the senior pastor at Honolulu First Assembly of God, to join the staff and develop evangelistic small groups to reach the many who lived in high-rise apartments. We really wanted to do this, but GOD said, "No."

During our time with YWAM in Kona we spent a few days on Oahu and went to the beach of the Kahala Hilton Hotel one day. There a few yards from us was Michael Landon and his family! Life is sure interesting!

150

May 19 - 23: I was released from the YWAM Base to stay at Graham and Treena Kerr's home to fast and pray and seek the Lord about our future.

May 19 Je: "I believe that, as a prophet, I am:
1   Not to be officially connected with any religious organization in a staff status.
2   To be free to be a voice.
3   But be close to, related to, in fellowship with, others."

May 20 Je:
"Jeremiah 6:1 - Move from Kona.
Jeremiah 6:3 - Have our own place.
Jeremiah 6:4 - It's getting late.
Jeremiah 6:16 - Have our own place again.
Jeremiah 7:18 - Walk in light we have - not others' visions. Prepare for end-times.
Jeremiah 7:23 - Move to Oregon.
Zechariah 8:12 - A place in Oregon.
Zechariah 10:7 - Our kids will rejoice in our move to Oregon.
Joshua 24:13 - GOD to give land to build on in Oregon.
Zechariah 3:10 - Have own home.
Jeremiah 30:1 - Write new book - *Church in the 80s*. (When it was published it was actually titled *The Church Triumphant at the End of the Age*.)
Jeremiah 30:7 - Get ready for hard times.
Jeremiah 30:10 - A place for us.
Isaiah 49:1-9 - Worldwide ministry.
Numbers 10:29 - Someone to ask us to come with them to Oregon and they will do us good - Kerrs?
Luke 9:62 - Push ahead - Oregon, new book, and world travel.
Genesis 12:5 - Take most of our possessions to Oregon - whatever Jo wants.
Jeremiah 29:11 - GOD is concerned about our welfare - a quiet place.
Exodus 23:20-22 - Obey GOD in every detail.
Hosea 4:6 - Need to study more relative to my teaching ministry.

151

Jeremiah 29:5 - Build a home, plant a garden.
Jeremiah 29:8 - Do not be discouraged by what leaders say to persuade us to stay.
Isaiah 46:4, 10-11 - GOD will provide.
Isaiah 54:11,17 - GOD to give us a quiet place."

May 21-22: Further Scriptures about having our own place in Oregon.

May 23 Je: "Conclusions - Week of Prayer, May 19-23:
1   My calling is to be a voice to the Body of Christ.
2   I do not have a burden for a Christian University.
5   To Oregon - a place to rest, study, pray, write."

May 29 Je: "I have got to find a quiet place and time to be with GOD - study and prayer. Future ministry - teaching, writing, speaking, etc., will flow out of that."

June 5: Words given to me by the DTS staff:
"a man of much knowledge, which the Lord is turning into wisdom to be imparted in increasing ways . . . teacher and leader of leaders.
"analytical, truth-seeking attitude.
"desire and ability to wait on the Lord.
"a man after GOD's own heart.
"gentle.
"a man of the Word . . . gentleness, compassion and humility . . . a heart for the lost . . . one who desires to raise up and empower workers for the harvest."

Throughout June and July GOD continued to confirm the move to Oregon.

June 29 - July 4:   At YWAM International Conference in Chiang Mai , Thailand.

July 3: Time with Joy Dawson there:

"1   You are a prophet - not with leadership responsibilities.

2   Main method of communication to be in writing, but not limited to that.

3   A teaching gift including research.

4   Because of your character level, I would recommend you to an eldership role.

5   The prophet to the nations will be through your writings.

6   Don't announce your ministry or say you're available. Concentrate on writing. Don't be frustrated if no or few invitations to travel come.

7   You are a second-level leader - do not have natural leadership or communication abilities.

8   You are a prophet-writer like Amos."

July 3 Je: "Psalm 78:54 - Oregon."

I left the International Conference early so that I could be part of the Annual LEI meeting in Indiana in July and a speaking invitation at the YWAM Base in Salem in August.

July 14 Je: "Thank you, Lord, for a terrific LEI Annual meeting." Loren and Darlene Cunningham were with us for the meeting. We were able to introduce Dr. Glen Martin to Loren, which resulted in Glen's having a worldwide teaching ministry in YWAM in slots of time that he was not teaching at Marion College.

During my time in Salem I recorded the following observations:

July 19 Je: "Psalm 81:16 - get decent furniture, etc., in Salem."

July 24 Je: "The best we are able to determine, it is GOD's will to:

1   Move to Oregon YWAM Base.

2   Purchase 14 x 60 mobile home for $7,990.

153

3   Put it on prescribed lot.
4   Get a wood-burning stove.
5   Change the carpet.
6   Get auto."

August 19 Je: "Blessings of being in Oregon:
1   Christian atmosphere.
2   Friendly people.
3   Beautiful city.
4   Good churches.
5   Beautiful scenery.
6   Change of seasons without hard winters.
7   Driving space. (Unlike the Big Island!)
8   Shopping.
9   End-time preparedness.
10 Good YWAM Base.
11 Quiet!"

September 19: Time with Loren and Darlene Cunningham - they confirm move to Oregon - now for me - Isaiah 3:10, Zechariah 3:7; Jo to wait for Beth, who was traveling with the King's Kids in Europe - Ruth 2:8.

Our time with YWAM in Kona, Hawaii, was the best and hardest years of my life. Best because of the worldwide travel and ministry that I had. Hardest because there were more people and vision than I could cope with, and there was no time to seek GOD, study, and write. Also, because of the base layout, there was no privacy - it was like living in a fish bowl, with no place to be alone.

And I never quite got acclimated to living in Hawaii. I missed the change of seasons. I felt isolated living on an island - they call it "rock fever." And the main industry is tourism - no factories, industry, etc. It just wasn't normal living to me.

CHAPTER 12 - TO THE NORTHWEST

*(Called to Oregon, pastorate, Salem prayer,
trip to Africa, Gerry and Beth both marry,
YWAM-Tacoma, became grandparents)*

Salem, OR, and Tacoma, WA: 1980 - 1984

1980

In September, we moved to the YWAM Base in Salem, Oregon. This was a very hard move for Joanne. Gerry had just finished his DTS outreach and had returned to Marion. Beth had just graduated from high school in Kona and we left her there to work with King's Kids. So, Joanne had had to say "good-by" to both of our children and head off to a new place. I was still in Thailand at the YWAM Conference so she arrived in Salem ahead of me. She had never been in the state of Oregon and, of course, it was a new base. Also, coming from sunny, warm Hawaii, the cold rainy weather that met her was not the most inviting. I don't think she had ever been so glad to see me as she was when I arrived at the Portland airport upon my return from Thailand. Shortly after my arrival, we purchased a lovely house trailer and placed it on the base and got settled and began to feel at home.

In November, we went to New England for several weeks of ministry with churches arranged by Jay and Carleen Ferris.

December 2 Je: Today I met with the YWAM-Salem elders. They explained to me that while we were in New England, the base had made some major changes in their focus. Everything that we had been invited to the base to be a part of had been canceled. We, therefore, would need to move on. This was, of course, a major shock to us. Where do we go? Where do we live? What are we to do? "Lord You are our Shepherd."

December 18:   Word from Campbell McAlpine, who was teaching at the Oregon YWAM Base for a week:
"1   Be related to the Church.
2   GOD to provide a home.
3   Many prophets and apostles are in hiding and preparation today.
4   A prophet's ministry is (a) to the whole Church and (b) itinerate."

December 30 Je: "Psalm 37:3 - 'dwell in the land' - stay in Oregon; 'feed on His faithfulness' - He will provide."
After being with YWAM for five years we now found ourselves "on the outside." Where do we go from here? On January 5 I wrote in my journal that I needed to (1) seek the Lord and (2) to meet with various spiritual leaders in Northwestern Oregon. On January 7 the Lord reminded me that I needed a "sabbatical." On January 8 GOD spoke through Psalm 47:4 that He was choosing our future.

1981
On January 8 we had lunch with Leo and Ernestine Schlegel and discussed the possibility of joining their church staff in Aloha, Oregon. We continued to pursue that possibility for several months, but their search committee finally closed the door when they found out that I didn't have a seminary degree.

February 3 Je: "Genesis 26:2 - 'stay in the land' i.e., Oregon. Genesis 26:22 - 'at last the Lord has made room for us.' "

February 21: GOD spoke about writing a book, *The Church at the End of the Age*, with emphases of revival, restoration, unity, world evangelization, and end-time persecution.

March 12:   Today, Marty Berry, the leader of the Salem YWAM Base, told us we were to be off the YWAM Base by Sunday. (Some months later, to Marty's credit, he came to us and asked our forgiveness for the way he had treated us.)

Joanne was speaking at a ladies group at the First Nazarene Church. I went to the grocery store and got boxes. When she got home I was already packing. She was devastated by the word to move. We stored our belongings and moved to Gresham, Oregon, to stay with friends, Phil and Sondra Hampe, for two weeks before I was scheduled to go to South America to teach in YWAM schools in Columbia, Chile, and Argentina. While I was gone on that trip Joanne went to Sacramento to stay with her sister Arlene

On March 21: I noted in my journal that, "I am in Bogota, Colombia, but my mind and heart are in Oregon." I taught at the YWAM Base in the mornings and evenings, but spent my afternoons walking the streets of Bogota and praying about our future. Leland Paris had invited us to come to the Texas YWAM Base when he learned of the upheaval at the Salem Base. And Loren Cunningham called and expressed his concern for the way we had been treated and invited us back to Kona. This was a very kind gesture on his part and meant a whole lot to both of us.

Our plans were for Joanne to meet me in Texas upon my return from South America to further pursue our moving there. But while I was still in South America, I believe that the Lord spoke to me that there was a spiritual awakening coming to the Northwest, which would have worldwide ramifications, and we were to stay in the Northwest and be part of it. So we never went to Texas.

During the time in Chile I received word that President Reagan had been shot. My flight from Chile to Argentina across the Andes was beautiful. On the flight I met the captain of one of Operation Mobilization's ships, docked at the Buenos Aires harbor. He invited me to come to the ship and have dinner with him, which I did.

After getting back to the states I spent time with Jim Ammerman in Dallas and also time with Leland Paris at the YWAM Base in Tyler, Texas. In discussing our future, Ammerman asked me what I would do if I had only one year to live. I noted in my journal:

"1   Spend time with my children.
2   Finalize the *Mastering the Word of God* book.
3   Enlarge *The Church at the End of the Age* book.
4   Bless my wife."

We spent the spring seeking the Lord about our future - where we were to live and what we were to do. On April 18 we decided to move to Vancouver, Washington, to be closer to Jerry and Mary Thurston, as the next step in our lives. We had gotten to know and appreciate the Thurstons through the Portland pastors' prayer meetings.

I had some ministry out East, picked up a car in Detroit that needed driven to Portland, rented a trailer in Fostoria, picked up Gerry in Marion, picked up some of our furniture in Fostoria and Marion, and Gerry and I drove to Vancouver. He spent the summer with us.

On May 5 we spent time at Christian Center's Icthus School in Salem where we were invited to join their staff as a teacher, but GOD clearly told us, "No!" on that one. (Later there was a big shakeup at Christian Center and the school was closed!) At some point we considered going to Medford, Oregon, and working with Jim McKeavor, who had an end-times preparedness emphasis.

On June 10, my Je was: "Psalm 102:13 - It is time for God to act on our behalf." On June 16, the South Salem Foursquare Church, New Life Fellowship, was offered to us - and we accepted, believing it to be the will of GOD.

We spent two years at NLF. The founding pastor began to get a vision for nondenominational house churches and left Foursquare to do this. He thought everyone would follow him - one-third did, one-third stayed, and one-third scattered to other churches.

So we started with about 25 people. The church grew to about 75 during the two years - some of the original folks returned, new folks came, and there were some new converts. We spent much of the time just getting the people healed from the split and from the controlling ways of the previous pastor. The original core of people included Hank and Shirley Arends, Dave and Corky Hooton, Ed and Lindy Medina, Doug and Karen Stair, Debi Collins, Melvena Horst, Doug and Jan Holmes, John and Cathie Leonard, and Dennis McGill. We thoroughly enjoyed our two years there and are still in touch with many of these folks.

When we were at the Salem YWAM Base we met the South Salem Friends Church pastor, Hubert Thornberg. Shortly after we took the church the Lord spoke to me that He would bring the spiritual leaders of Salem together for prayer just as He had done in Portland, and would use us to do it, but we were to do nothing about it through the summer but make it a matter of prayer. In September the Lord spoke to me to call Hubert and see if he would be interested in getting together for prayer. He said, "Yes," because the Lord had also been speaking that to him. So Hubert and I began getting together on Wednesdays from noon to 1:30 p.m. to fast and pray. Soon other leaders from South Salem were joining us - Wendell Barnett, Bob Wineberger, John Fuiten, a retired Friends missionary, Dave Leman, and Hank Arends. We had wonderful times together. As our hearts were knit together we were able to discuss various doctrinal issues that we did not agree on without it causing a break in our relationships. We became known around Salem as "the praying pastors of South Salem."

In the spring of 1983 we (five churches) had a joint eight-week Bible Institute together. The five churches included Church on the Hill (Assembly of God), Rosedale Friends, South Salem Friends, Crossroads Community Church, and New Life Fellowship. Many courses were offered and taught by various ones of us and others. Of special interest was a course on the gifts of the Spirit, team-taught by John Fuiten, the Assembly of God pastor, and Hubert Thornberg, the Friends pastor. They did not agree on every aspect of the gifts of the Spirit, but team-taught the course. Now that's unity! God's people were flowing together in a wonderful way. We did other things together jointly, too.

In time the weekly prayer time was moved to First Baptist Church downtown and became citywide. About 12 to 20 came from across the city to pray together. It was one of the most exciting things I have ever been involved in.

1982

Je: "Goals - New Life Fellowship - 1982 -
1   Let Jesus be Lord!
2   Further wholeness in people's lives.
3   Further functioning as a body.
4   Further release into ministry for each person.
5   Continue to go deeper - Word, prayer, relationship to GOD, families, relationship with each other, small groups, praise and worship, outreach, missions.
6.   Improve process of discipling converts.
7   Develop process for training leaders.
8   Vision and preparation for the future.
9   Greater flowing with the Foursquare organization and with the Salem churches.

January 18-19 - Jo and I spent two days at the ocean.
March 5 Je: "Acts 27:23-24 - I am to be involved in a broader ministry once again - in the interests of unity, revival, and world evangelization."

April 17: A word from Joanne - "Be faithful at NLF and GOD will once again someday give you a worldwide ministry."

April 21: At Foursquare Convention in Los Angeles - "We feel part of the Foursquare family."

Gerry and Wenda were married on June 12, 1982, at the Houghton College Wesleyan Church in Houghton, NY. They met at Marion College and went together for more than two years. Wenda is a precious woman of GOD and a perfect mate for Gerry. I had the honor of serving communion to them at their wedding.

Beth came home to live with us during the summer and fall of 1982. She and Greg Bachran had had a "special relationship" at the YWAM Base in Kona, Hawaii, for more than a year and were talking marriage. We felt we needed some time with Beth before that might occur.

During the summer of 1982 I had a four-week ministry trip to Southern Africa. This included teaching one week at each of the YWAM bases in South Africa, Zimbabwe, and Namibia; visiting a gold mine in South Africa; and spending several days in Transkei, a small independent state for Blacks within South Africa.

This was still during apartheid and I was appalled at the discrimination against Blacks - in housing, employment, rights, etc. The flight over involved several opportunities to witness. The week with YWAM in Southern Africa was very enjoyable.

The week in Zimbabwe was at a beautiful country setting. One evening I was made aware of an approaching grass wildfire - some of the YWAM people there and I asked GOD to send His angels - and the fire turned another direction away from us!

The YWAM Base in Namibia was on the edge of the capital, Windhoek, a modern city of 200,000. It was once a German colony and I found Krupp Street! I preached on Sunday morning at a Charismatic Methodist Church.

During my time in Windhoek, I received a phone call from Greg Bachran asking for permission to marry our daughter, Beth. I was so "shook up" over the call that all I could say was, "I'll pray about it." (Upon returning to the states though I called Greg and said, "Yes.")

Upon returning to South Africa from Zimbabwe and Namibia I visited a gold mine one day, which was very interesting! Then I took a small plane to Umtata, the capital of Transkei, a small Black nation within the country of South Africa. We landed on a dirt runway. The houses were all mud huts with thatched roofs. Lewis and Arlene Ziegler, the Foursquare missionary supervisor in Transkei, met me.

Lewis' father was a pioneer missionary to the area. He (the father) was converted as a young man at Aimee Semple McPherson's Angelus Temple in Los Angeles, California. He went in because he thought it was a movie theater!

Lewis' future wife, Arlene, came to know the Lord in a Methodist Church in Portland, Oregon. One Sunday evening she had a vision of black sheep covering the hillsides, and the Lord showed her that He was calling her to go to Africa to take the Gospel to the Blacks there.

She and her husband-to-be met at the Foursquare Bible College in Los Angeles. They were both called to Africa. Upon graduating they took a ship to England, then to Cape Town. At Cape Town they boarded a train for the interior of South Africa. One morning on the train, as the window shades were being raised, Mrs. Ziegler saw the same hills she had seen in her vision, and she told the conductor, "We'll get off at the next stop."

The Zieglers did not know it, but the Lord had spoken to a traveling pots and pans salesman in the region that a white couple was going to bring the Truth to Africa. On the morning that the Zieglers were about to get off the train, the Lord spoke to the native that this couple was coming that day and he was to go to the train station and meet them. So GOD providentially brought them together and this was the beginning of the missionary work to the "Red Blanket people" of the Transkei in South Africa.

The younger Ziegler, Lewis, grew up in South Africa, but returned to the U.S. to attend Bible College. There he met his future wife, Arlene. Upon completion of their training they headed for South Africa. Lewis' first task was to build a home for his parents who had up until then spent all of their years living in a mud hut. He also built one for him and Arlene. It was this second-generation Zieglers that met me at the Umtata airstrip. I rested on Saturday and on Sunday we headed farther into the interior where I was only the second white man they had ever seen, Lewis being the first.

The church service was in a simple tin-roofed building in the middle of nowhere. The people walked from all directions for two-to-three hours. One of the elders of the tribe heard I was coming and carved a walking stick for me that they presented to me during the service. It is one of my most prized possessions! (I have since passed it on to my son, Gerry.) They also took up an offering for me. It was about $15. These were very poor people, and I was deeply honored and humbled by this act. After the service we all walked down a hill to a river where Lewis baptized several new converts. Then we went back up the hill for a meal that some of the women had been preparing, followed by the Lord's Supper. Then they had the two-to-three-hour walk back home after the all-day meeting. It was a great privilege to be part of this all-day gathering of believers.

The Lord had spoken to me from Psalm 2:8 that I would have a ministry "to the very ends of the earth." Where I was in Transkei was almost exactly halfway around the world from Oregon - "the ends of the earth!"

It was a real privilege to teach at the three YWAM bases, speak in churches in all four nations (including Transkei), meet with spiritual leaders, observe the racial discrimination, be out in "the bush," witness wherever I went, and all that was part of this four-week trip to Southern Africa. I had now been on every continent - North and South America, Europe, Australia, Asia, and now Africa. Just a nobody from a little town in Ohio, obediently trying to follow GOD's leading and do His will.

October 8 Je: "I have been going through a valley lately - the attack of a 'lying spirit' revealed to me today - trying to get me to doubt my planting/calling to Salem - because of the prayer responsibility in the city - and what GOD is doing at New Life Fellowship."

October 12-17: A time of fasting and prayer. Je: "GOD has given me a five-fold ministry:
1   NLF.
2   South Salem praying pastors.
3   Salem citywide prayer.
4   Writing.
5   Plus an occasional trip overseas.
That's enough!"

During the time at NLF, GOD spoke to me to write two books - one on GOD's attributes and one on what He desires in us. (These did come into being in 1998 and 2001, 15 years later! See Appendix 5.)

1983

Beth and Greg Bachran were married on January 1 in Kona, Hawaii, at the Keauhou Beach hotel with the reception at YWAM's King's Mansion. Joanne spent weeks sewing Beth's wedding dress and planning the wedding with Beth. I had the honor of doing the ceremony, but was a bit intimidated by all of the YWAM leaders who were at the wedding.

January 25 Je: "John 15:2b - 'Every branch that bears fruit, He prunes it, that it may bear more fruit.' There have been six major times of pruning in my life - each leading to a larger, more fruitful, different ministry:

1   The initial pruning as a new convert that led to the ministry at the Naval Auxiliary Air Station in Kingsville.

2   The pruning at Glen Eyrie that led to the ministry at Marion College, Pacific Garden Mission, the Wesleyans, and Lay Evangelism, Inc.

3   The pruning in the mid-1960s that led to the Chicago work, gifts of the Spirit operating in my life, and New Testament church concepts.

4   The pruning in the late 1960s that led to a broader, more fruitful time back in the Wesleyan Church.

5   The pruning in the mid-1970s that led to a worldwide ministry with YWAM.

6   The pruning through YWAM-Hawaii and YWAM-Oregon that led to New Life Fellowship and the ministry of prayer in Salem."

As I write this biography I would add these:

7   A time of pruning in 1983 - 1984 that led to the writing of *The Church Triumphant at the End of the Age* and the prayer ministry in the Pacific Northwest and nationwide.

8   A time of pruning in late 1980s that led to our leaving YWAM, the establishing of Preparing the Way Publishers, and the worldwide house-church ministry.

9   A time of pruning with regard to our relationship with the Salem church leaders that led to our flowing with them beginning in the fall of 2003.

165

Over the summer of 1983 GOD made it clear that our time at New Life Fellowship was over. We had laid a new foundation for the church and others were to take it from there. We were to return to YWAM. We thought it would be Salem, but various YWAM leaders (Leland Paris, Jim Dawson, Denny Gunderson, Graham Kerr, the Salem YWAM leadership) all felt it should be at Tacoma, Washington. We were to be part of the base, Joanne was to work with the staff women, and I was released to write the book, *The Church Triumphant . . .* (finally!).

Pat and Bonnie McCullough offered that we could live from September through May in their summer cottage on Hood Canal near Belfair. What a joy! It was a quiet place to write. And we gathered oysters off the beach in the front yard anytime we wanted some. We really enjoyed being under Denny Gunderson's gentle leadership. And we enjoyed touching base with Graham and Treena Kerr weekly.

As we left NLF, Kathy Mader prophesied to us that GOD was calling me to Himself. (I took that to mean there would be more time with Him, and more time writing.)

In December Greg and Beth came from Hawaii with their little baby daughter, Jamie Elizabeth. She had been born on August 31. Greg and I went into the hills and found a Christmas tree. We enjoyed the Jacuzzi that was on the back deck. Little Jamie was such a dear!

I have a photo of me holding her and all she could do was smile. So we were now grandparents!

1984

From September 1983 through May 1984 we lived in the cottage and I worked on the book. We attended the weekly staff meeting - otherwise I hid out at the house and wrote. On the weekends various YWAM staff would come out from Tacoma and stay in our guest room to get away from the city.

We also got to spend some time with my cousin, Gary McPherson, and his wife, Deb, who lived in Bremerton. And we enjoyed visiting the Navy ships anchored at Bremerton, including the battleship Missouri, on which the WW2 armistice with Japan had been signed. (The Missouri is now permanently docked in Hawaii.) Our only financial support during these months was from Bill and Pat Parker - how we thank GOD for their faithfulness!

We attended an Assembly of God church in Port Orchard. There we became close friends with Jack and Wilma Eads. Wilma was an English teacher at the local high school and helped me some with editing the book. I taught a Sunday School class on *Mastering the Word of God* and after we left the area Jack continued teaching the course.

During this time I also went through Dr. Bruce Thompson's *Plumbline* tape series. February 1 Je: "Through Dr. Bruce's tapes and since, GOD is doing some amazing work in my life, and Jo's, and our relationship."

In May it became time to leave the summer cottage. We spent the summer living in a room at the YWAM Hospitality House in Tacoma. During this time we got acquainted with LaVern and Nancy Webb who later returned to their home in Madras, Oregon, where we had further contact. We also began attending Puget Sound Christian Center where Tom Isenhart was the pastor. He became a dear friend and sometimes introduced me as "a Christian statesman," which was very humbling.

167

June 22: The Lord reminded me that He was going to provide a place for us where we could be prepared for end-times. Psalms 37 - those who will inherit the land - "the humble, the righteous, those who wait for the Lord, and those who keep His way."

June 23: GOD spoke to me that He was raising up many end-time preparedness places in British Columbia, Alberta, Saskatchewan, Canada; and Washington, Oregon, Idaho, Montana, and Wyoming, USA.

In July we traveled to Southern California to be part of the YWAM outreach at the Olympics. This was a huge outreach - 1,800 local churches; 10,000 Christians coming in from other places, including 3,300 YWAM'ers; 73 participating denominations and organizations.

In the fall the Lord led us to a new, two-bedroom apartment in Tacoma, so I was able to have a study once again. We became YWAM Base pastors and I began to serve on the Leadership Council. Some of the staff began studying my *New Testament Survey*, meeting one noon a week to discuss it. During this time we also began networking with various prayer leaders and ministries as GOD had burdened my heart with the need for extraordinary prayer for revival.

During our time at the apartment the Lord began to speak to me about Boilermakers for Christ. This was to be a network of Purdue students, faculty, administration, and alumni, who knew Jesus, for the purpose of mutual encouragement and extension of Christ's Kingdom.

CHAPTER 13 - MOBILIZING PRAYER

*(Prayer for revival, prayer retreats, AIMS,
Israel and England, Church Triumphant book,
LTS and Master's degree, leaving YWAM)*

Salem, OR; Tacoma, WA; Kona, HI: 1985 - 1987

1985

In early 1985 GOD began to speak to me about having a Retreat Center/Prayer Mountain. In cooperation with other prayer leaders in Tacoma we also began to have Nights of Prayer. We would use some church facility, often the Methodist Church in Tacoma, and folks would come, and we would pray all night, until dawn. We were beginning to work some with Hal and Carol Holmberg, Jim Vitzthum, and Rosemary Lambert in these prayer activities.

The Lord also began to speak to me about having another YWAM School of Church Ministries. Darwin and Ann Newton, whom we had gotten acquainted with in Kona, moved from their home in Eugene, Oregon, to be with us in Tacoma to help develop the SChM.

May 22 Je: Time with Jim Dawson, YWAM's international pastor:
1   GOD has called us to live in the Pacific Northwest, not Kona.
2   I am a prophet-teacher - don't get involved in daily routines and in running things - spend time with GOD and as He directs.

We had gotten to know Vic and Annette Lipsey during our time in Kona. Vic was a retired Air Force colonel and was heading up the YWAM Ship Ministry. At some point they left YWAM and moved to the Seattle area.

Vic and Howard Foltz began working on a new entity called AIMS, which was to be an association of independent charismatic mission organizations. We attended the founding meeting at Vic's invitation. At one point I mentioned that they needed a greater foundation of prayer. Before the day was over (June 13) I had been appointed their prayer chairman!

On June 14 the Tacoma YWAM Council confirmed my prayer ministry. They said I was "to be like the warhead of a missile, calling the nation to prayer."

June 20: At the North American YWAM Conference in Texas - I had a vision from the Lord - a map of North America, with everyone on their knees, praying for world evangelization, which would stay the hand of GOD's judgment. The word of the Lord, "He is now calling His Body in North America to prayer."

June 21: A note from Joanne : "I am a trail blazer:
1   LEI.
2   Chicago house churches.
3   YWAM School of the Bible, School of Church Ministries, emphasis on local church.
4   Salem - pastors' prayer movement.
5   Tacoma - Nights of Prayer, Prayer Retreats, revival emphasis."

Next: Work with the Body of Christ in the interests of revival, restoration, unity, world evangelization, and coming persecution.

June 28: I was released from all YWAM responsibilities to do whatever GOD calls us to do.

August 1 Je: "How wonderful it is to live by faith and to watch GOD provide."

August 2:   Am back at Glen Eyrie, the Navigators headquarters, for a visit - while there I got to see those we had known when we were being discipled there in 1959-60, including the Nav President, Lorne Sanny; Jim Downing, Rod Sargent, Jack Mayhall, Bob Stephens, Francis Cosgrove, Wil Hopkins, Jerry Bridges, Jerry White, Millie Hopkins, Betty Skinner, Chuck Strittmatter, Len Froisland, and Dean and Irene Meeker. What a joy!

Je: "Significant things GOD did during my time with the Navigators in 1959-60:
1   Luke 16:10 - learning to be faithful in the little things.
2   Philippians 3 - giving up all to know Him.
3   Jeremiah 33:3 - prayed for a ministry on every continent by the age of 30.
4   Beginning to be open to marriage.
5   Learning about Bible study, Scripture memory, world vision."

August 18:   Ordained and commissioned today by Tom Isenhart and Puget Sound Christian Center with Denny Gunderson, Darwin Newton, and Ron and Evelyn Rhoades also participating. Word from Rosemary - Ezekiel 39:25-29, 40:1-4, especially 40:4 - GOD is releasing us in a major way (1) to hear from Him and (2) to speak to His people. Word from Holmbergs - Joshua 1:5 - no one to be able to stand before us.

August 26: Pacific Northwest Prayer Retreat. This was the first of many prayer retreats that we would lead for the next years. It was sponsored by a band of prayer leaders in the Northwest that GOD had been drawing together for a couple of years including Al Gamble, Hal and Carol Holmberg, Bob Penton, Rick Lundsford, Phil and Sondra Hampe, Lance and Jill Miller, Dave Woodrum, Georgia Penniman, Cal Ludeman, Jim Watt, Peter Anello, etc.

We began hosting a five-day Prayer Retreat somewhere in the Northwest - Washington, Oregon, Idaho, Montana - about twice a year for several years. These were powerful times of tearing down strongholds and laying a foundation of prayer for revival in the Northwest.

This was later followed by another prayer ministry called Prayer Summits, developed by Dr. Joe Aldridge, the president of Multnomah School of the Bible. (This was not the same Prayer Summit ministry developed by Ray Bringham.)

In late August Joanne and I left in our auto for a four-month ministry trip. We had $25 in our pockets when we headed down the West Coast - then across through Colorado to the Midwest - then to New England - down the East Coast to Florida - across the southern states to Southern California again - and home to the Northwest. This was a combination of ministry connected with YWAM, AIMS, and ministry to churches and individuals all along the way. And GOD abundantly provided all along the way!

November: I am resting for three days at Carleen's Mom's cottage in Connecticut on Long Island Sound. "GOD is faithful!"

Nov. 29 Je: "I have just finished reading *From Sea to Shining Sea*. I dedicate the rest of my life to seeing revival come to America."

1986

January Je:
"I.   Life Goals -
1   Know and live by the Word of GOD.
2   Be a man of prayer.
3   Be constantly led by the Holy Spirit.
4   Be conformed to the image of Jesus Christ.
5   Have a marriage, home, children that glorify the Lord.

6   Contribute greatly to the evangelization of the world.
7   Be a part of a local fellowship of believers - also contribute to the Body of Christ at-large in my community.
8   See a glorious Church presented to Jesus.
9   Be a prophet to the nations (primarily through my writings and reproduced through others) - Jeremiah 1:7, 6:27; Ezekiel 37:10.
10   Be at the Lord's disposal - for whatever He has for me to do at anytime.

II.   My commitment - I am committed to -
1   Jesus, my Lord.
2   The Word of GOD.
3   My family.
4   All believers in the world.
5   World evangelization.
6   To what GOD is doing today -
       a.   End-time revival.
       b.   Completion of the restoration.
       c.   Unity coming to the Body of Christ.
       d.   Completion of the task of world evangelization.
       e.   Preparation for end-time persecution."

January Journal entries: GOD continues to burden us for our own, quiet place that is end-time prepared and a place of prayer.

February 7: Time with Don and Ruthie Hawkinson:
"1   Ruthie - I am a weeping prophet.
2   We had to leave Kona when we did.
3   I am very grateful for all that has been part of the past years since we left Kona - pastorate in Salem, *Church Triumphant* book, prayer ministry.
4   GOD is leading us back to Kona for six months - renew and deepen relationships, to go through YWAM's Leadership Training School, and get a master's degree."

March 18-23: We are in Israel, on Mt. Carmel, participating in the Prophets Gathering. There are 153 (see John 21:11!) prophets and intercessors from around the world that have been invited to spend a week together on Mt. Carmel. How I was included I will never know! We spent from Monday evening until Friday evening coming into unity. Then on Saturday "the word of the Lord" flowed through many. I shared the five things that would characterize the end-time Church - revival, restoration, unity, world evangelization, and persecution.

March 24-30: The week on Mt. Carmel was followed by a conference for a week in Jerusalem attended by several thousand. Many spoke at the conference - I spoke to a seminar session on Thursday, March 27, 1986, on *The Church at the End of the Age.*

On Sunday, March 30, we had the awesome privilege of being at a Sunrise Service on Easter Sunday at the Garden Tomb in Jerusalem - quite possibly the very place where Jesus was crucified, buried, and rose again.

Some words given throughout the two weeks included:
GOD's dealings are painful - to fashion a people for His glory.
GOD's love will not allow us to remain as we are!
Cancer is caused by one cell that breaks away and does its own thing.
Jesus has to be Lord of every detail.
We are in a time of awakening and harvest now - judgment is coming soon. Now is a time of preparation - warn the nations - they will soon be shaken (Hebrews 12:25-29).
Israel is at the heart of a worldwide spiritual conflict. World shaking accelerated since 1973. Nations to be judged soon - by natural disasters, economic collapse, war, and diseases.
The government of GOD is coming.
Jesus cannot come back until the world is evangelized and the Bride is prepared.

174

Love and respect the prophets.
A majority of the Church will reject "the word of the Lord" - a remnant will come through - prophets will receive persecution from the Church.

After the two weeks in Israel, we had two weeks of ministry in England. The first week was with Frank Wren and an independent, charismatic church in Watford, north of London. The second week was with John and Sheila Sutton in Stebbins, east of London, at a Charismatic Episcopal Church. The church building went back to when the Christians first came to England in the 400s.

April 10 Je: "Our ministry was once to the lost. Then to Christians. Now to leaders."

Throughout May and June the Lord continued to confirm to us that we were to go back to Kona to attend the Leadership Training School. We stored our belongings in the garage of Tony and Kathy Mader in Puyallup, near Tacoma. We had gotten to know the Maders when pastoring in Salem and had continued to keep in touch.

We went to Kona in July to be on the staff, giving us a chance to fit back into the "feel" of the base before the school started in September. Attending this school allowed me to finish a master's degree, using *The Church Triumphant* as my thesis. I was spending part of my time perfecting *The Church Triumphant* with the help of Wil Turner, Gene Hackett, and Andy Beach. My master's work was done under the supervision of Dean Sherman and Dr. Doug Feaver. I made my thesis oral presentation to them and Dr. Howard Malmstadt. During the summer I was in an office with Joe Portale, assisting Loren Cunningham in his international work. Joanne worked as a receptionist in Loren's International Office.

As part of the LTS we had to write a paper. The subject of my paper was *Presenting to Jesus a Beautiful Bride*, with a subtitle *Revival - the Missing Ingredient in Fulfilling the Great Commission and in Presenting to Jesus a Beautiful Bride*. I was attempting to outline what GOD had for me to do in the years I had left. Joanne audited some of the classes, but also went to Oahu to help Beth for three weeks when Kelly was born on October 22, 1986.

Joanne's sister, Evelyn, was going through a Crossroads Disciple Training School at the Base in Kona after the death of her husband, Ron, and she and Joanne had many precious times together.

During the LTS, we each had a personal evaluation of who we are, called SIMA. Here are the results they gave me - I need to be involved in:
1   Working with concepts and people.
2   Teaching and writing.
3   In an unstructured, quiet place.
4   Exploring new areas - geographic and concepts.
5   Working with the broad picture - and how the pieces fit in.
6   Analyzing information, people, and situations.
7   Getting things (ideas, people, projects) started - then moving on.
8   Influencing.

The application GOD spoke to me from this was:
1   Live in the continental U.S. to influence the Church.
2   Travel - preach/teach/implement the five things in *The Church Triumphant*.
3   When not traveling, have a quiet place to study and write.
4   See *The Church Triumphant* perfected and published.
5   Push ahead with pioneering Prayer Retreats and 40 Days of Prayer.

6   Perfect *Mastering the Word of GOD* and *New Testament Survey Course.*
7   Get a computer.
8   Deepen relationships in the Pacific Northwest.

November   22   Je: Time in Kona with Tom Marshall   of New Zealand:
"GOD's Structures for His people:
1   New Testament fellowships with elders and deacons.
2   The city church with elders.
3   Traveling ministries."

Throughout the LTS I continued to perfect *The Church Triumphant.* I also spent much time with YWAM leaders from around the world - often having lunch with one of them - to get better acquainted and to try to find out where we "fit" in YWAM. We increasingly could see that we were to return to the mainland, have our own home, and be a prophet-teacher to the Church regarding the things in *The Church Triumphant.*

1987

As 1987 dawned I was involved for three weeks in YWAM's School of Biblical Studies at their campus at Makapala on the north end of the Big Island. This was the last requirement to complete for my master's degree. I taught some, attended classes, and wrote assigned papers.

We were also praying much about our future and sensing that we were to return to the continental U.S., have our own place, write, travel, and be a voice to the Church. GOD was burdening us with a 40 Days of Prayer vision and renewing our house-church understanding.

January 12 Je: "Revelation 3:7 - GOD is sovereignly opening and closing doors - we need to <u>sit</u> <u>still</u> and walk through the doors that He opens."

January 28 Je: "GOD has given me the master's degree so that I will be more credible in certain settings in the future." Before leaving Kona I was conferred a Master of Arts degree from the College of Christian Ministries based upon my attendance at the LTS and SBS, my *Church Triumphant* thesis and other writings, and years of other ministry experience.

We returned to Tacoma about February 1, re-established our relationship with our church, Puget Sound Christian Center, and began our traveling ministry across the U.S. We were also working with prayer leaders in the Northwest in the interests of Prayer Retreats and 40 Days of Prayer.

We were with Jay and Carleen Ferris in Connecticut when we received a phone call from Nancy Shelton in Tacoma offering us to live in a rental home they owned. We took it, sight unseen! We were a bit disappointed when we arrived back in Tacoma and first saw it from the outside. But once inside we fell in love with our own little home, at 6813 N. Eleventh Street, near the Narrows Bridge that goes from Tacoma to Gig Harbor.

While in the East, Jay introduced me to Dale Rumble who told us about a new publishing company, Destiny Image. We met Don Nori, the publisher, on May 8 and ten days later decided to let them publish *The Church Triumphant*.

We also decided that month to give the LEI corporation to Joe Sawyer and Tom Johnston.

May 29 Je: "This date Joanne and I have concluded that we are:
1   Not to be YWAM staff.
2   To relate to PSCC.
3   Be in submission to PSCC and a network of relationships across the U.S."

Some months later I noted in my journal some of the things that happened by our being associated with Youth With A Mission:

1   Our getting out of Marion, Indiana.
2   What we learned from the emphasis on intercession.
3   All that I learned by observing Loren Cunningham.
4   The inspiration for *The Church Triumphant* book.
5   Loren's Foreword in *The Omega Generation* and *The Church Triumphant*.
6   All that I learned about networking.
7   Our input into YWAM - the emphasis of the church, revival, evangelism.
8   Our starting the YWAM schools - School of the Bible and School of Church Ministries.
9   My having a ministry on every continent and Joanne in Europe and Asia.
10   Our getting acquainted with various YWAM leaders from around the world.
11   Gerry's DTS and being called to full-time ministry.
12   Beth's involvement with King's Kids, her spiritual growth, and her meeting Greg Bachran, her future husband.
13   Living in Hawaii.
14   Our relationship with Jim and Joy Dawson.
15   The experience of selling our home in Indiana, giving the money away, and having to trust GOD for any future home we might have.
16   Our getting to the Pacific Northwest.

The summer was a relaxing time - having our own home and garden again. My folks and Dave came and visited us. My Dad was enthralled with the beauty of Washington - Puget Sound, the Pacific Coast, Mt. Rainier, etc. We were also getting *The Church Triumphant* ready to send to Destiny Image. And we were networking with various prayer leaders in the Northwest.

179

One of our prayer projects during this time was trying to procure the Big Muddy Ranch near Antelope, Oregon, as a worldwide place of prayer - not for ourselves, but for the Body of Christ. It was a huge (100 square miles) property that had been developed by Bhagwan Rajneesh from India and his followers. It had facilities for housing 5,000. In time he was deported from the U.S. and the whole thing fell apart. An insurance company who would sell it for one million dollars now owned it. We made several trips there with a team of praying people, to pray over the property, cleanse it, and claim it for the Lord. I also made a video about the property and Cal Ludeman and I did some traveling around the Northwest sharing the vision. We were not able to purchase the property but in time it was given to Young Life. The Lord showed us that our part was our prayer trips to the property and that we were never meant to have the property for ourselves. We rejoice that we had a part in seeing this wonderful property procured for GOD's work.

We had a ministry trip to the Midwest and East Coast in the fall. GOD provided us a second car, a Ford Tempo, in New Jersey where we were visiting Gerry, who was pastoring a Wesleyan Church in Glassboro. We used it for ministry trips in the Midwest and East, flying into Detroit. We stored it in my folks' garage in Fostoria, Ohio, when we were not traveling in the East.

In October the Lord began to speak to me about making Salem, Oregon, our permanent home. In November we visited Salem and talked with a number of people about a possible move there.

180

CHAPTER 14 - MOBILIZING PRAYER
(Continued)

(40 days of prayer, returning to Salem,
Beth and family move to Salem, Crossroads Church)

Tacoma, WA; Salem, OR: 1988 - 1990

1988

Destiny Image publishers had agreed to partially finance the publishing of our book, *The Church Triumphant*, and we were to raise the rest. We sent out a letter and received some funds. After awhile no more came in. Things seemed "dead in the water." On January 8 Don Nori phoned and said that the Lord had spoken to him that they were to finance the rest of the book. How we praised the Lord for this miracle!

In addition to the Prayer Retreats, we were also being called to call various areas, states, etc., to 40 Days of Prayer. The city of Tacoma had a 40 Days of Prayer January 20 - February 28, 1988. More than 100 churches participated. It was a real spiritual battle - I was sick much of the time.

Later in the year Joanne and I were guests on a Christian TV station in Pittsburgh, Pennsylvania. The host said that they were having Reinhardt Bonnke, the German evangelist being used so widely in Africa, come to speak to the city in a few months. It popped out of my mouth, "You should precede that with 40 Days of Prayer." They were struck with the fact that this was a word from the Lord and they called the city to 40 Days of Prayer.

I shared the 40 Days of Prayer concept at a gathering of national prayer leaders held in Seattle. Dr. Bill Bright was sitting right in front of me on the front row.

181

A few years later he began to promote 40 days of prayer. I have wondered if I might have planted the original seed.

On April 29 I was with Ray Bringham at a huge rally of Christians in Washington called Washington for Jesus. Ray was a national prayer leader and founder of Prayer Summits (not the same Prayer Summits that originated later in Portland, Oregon). I mentioned to him that the entire U.S. should be called to 40 Days of Prayer leading up to the National election in the fall. He concurred. We shared it with several other prayer leaders - Vonette Bright, David Bryant, Dick Eastman - and they all concurred. So the entire United States of America was called to prayer September 30 - November 8, 1988. Our home in Tacoma became the coordinating office for this project.

The Maders had a friend, Barb Bailey, who became our secretary for this project. We produced a flier and mailed it to churches, denominational headquarters, prayer leaders, and Christian organizations all across the U.S. Hundreds of thousands of Christians humbled themselves, prayed, and sought GOD's face for our nation (2 Chronicles 7:14). George H.W. Bush was running for president. He was twenty points behind in the polls in August. He was elected in November. We believe that GOD changed the course of history because GOD's people prayed!

After our return to Oregon, we were able to call the state of Oregon to 40 Days of Prayer, September 27 - November 6, 1990, leading up to state elections in Oregon. We had an oversight committee of eleven. The effort was supported by about forty organizations. More on this later in this chapter.

Some of us in Tacoma met for prayer each Tuesday a.m. from 9 to 12 - Bob Penton and Al Gamble were two of the main ones in this. Sometimes Jim Watt came from Federal Way. He had been in the Latter Rain outpouring in 1948 as a Bible school student in Canada.

182

Some of us also began to meet for early morning prayer at our church, Puget Sound Christian Center. Dick Simmons from Bellingham, Washington, who traveled all over the U.S. encouraging early morning prayer for revival, sparked this. He especially spent time in Washington, D.C., praying at the Congress and Supreme Court. Jim Vitzthum and Hal Holmberg were regulars at these early morning times.

Steve Seabury and I began getting together once a week for fellowship and prayer. He became a very close brother. We both had a vision for revival and for home church. He and Cindy are now missionaries in Turkey with a vision of reaching the Muslim world by reaching and discipling Turks.

This spring we left PSCC and began meeting with Fred and Nancy Shelton and Russ and Barb (I can't remember their last name) in our homes. Steve Seabury and others also began meeting in homes on the south side of Tacoma.

I also had hernia surgery. I had been having abdominal problems for years and finally looked into it and discovered that I had a hernia that needed repairing. My doctor was Dr. Zielinksi. He was a born-again Catholic and had prayer with me at the conclusion of my initial appointment and just before we went into surgery. He was such a blessing.

In March I spent a week with John Lindell visiting various groups and people in the Bellingham area. John Lindell made an interesting statement one day, "The beginning of Babylon is membership."

March 15 Je: "Today Jamie, our granddaughter, invited the Lord into her life. She called us from Hawaii and in her little high-pitched voice said, 'I have something to tell you - I have invited Jesus into my heart and we're going to have a party.' Those were precious words for us grandparents to hear. Praise the Lord! May He mightily use her!"

183

Now she is married to Andrew Palmer and is the mother of Audra and Aaron. She and Andrew are doing a marvelous job of teaching them to love Jesus. Audra has already invited Jesus into her heart - at 3 1/2 years old.

April 16-17 a group of us had a conference in Bellingham, WA, on GOD's plan for His Church. Here are some of the things that were shared:

1   Have GOD's heart for His Body.
2   Die to self.
3   Recognize and respect our Jewish heritage.
4   Ezekiel 34 - Jesus will care for His sheep.
5   We should be Full (of the Spirit), Free (from the control of man), and Functioning.
6   The church often takes the place of GOD - if you bow down and serve the church you can be someone.
7   There is only one Body.
8   Reject the works of man.
9   Babylon - the desire to be somebody, do something, and have something.
10   Don't build Babylon - love the brethren - GOD wants to do a new thing.
11   Listen to GOD and each other.
12   What you lack in Jesus you will fill the void with a system that you invent.
13   Do not usurp the Headship of Jesus.
14   1 Timothy 1:1-5 - "Love from a pure heart and a good conscience and a sincere faith."
15   It is enough to have Jesus.
16   Prepare for battle.
17   Two deaths - die to having a king and to wanting to be a king.
18   We need to repent and be broken.

In late April I was part of another Prayer Summit with Ray Bringham in Washington, D.C. It was a wonderful time with prayer people from around the country. We also participated in the Washington For Jesus rally on April 29.

In May Beth and her two girls came to Tacoma to visit us.

June 9 Je: "Satan's traps for spiritual leaders and the antidote:

1	Immorality	purity
2	Greed	simple living
3	Authority	being a servant
4	The desk	having a fruitful ministry
5	Bitterness	forgiveness
6	Pride/prominence	humility"

In June Gerry graduated from Fuller Theological Seminary. We made a trip down the West Coast to be at his graduation. We were so proud of him! We received the first copies of *The Church Triumphant* from Destiny Image while on this trip.

In July Joanne and I attended my 35th high school class reunion in Fostoria, Ohio. It was the first time that I had seen most of my classmates since our graduation in 1953.

On July 22 Gerry and Wenda had their first child - a boy - Geoffrey Nathan. I was sure blessed to have a grandchild named after me. I call him "G. Nathan" and he calls me "Nathan G."

In August I was part of a nationwide congress on evangelism called Evangelism Congress '88, held in Chicago. I was asked to pray the closing prayer and GOD really anointed me, for which I praise Him.

Much of the summer was also spent working on procuring the Rajneesh property in Oregon.

In the fall we had a major East Coast trip.

In December I was involved with an annual gathering in Washington, D.C., called Evangelism Roundtable.

Dr. Paul Benjamin, one of America's evangelism leaders, hosted it. We had met by phone when he was an evangelism professor at a Bible college in Illinois and we had our LEI offices in Marion. The Roundtable was a time for those involved in evangelism ministries to share with each other what GOD was doing. They were always a time of real blessing.

1989

In early 1989 I noted in my journal that there are six types of relationships:
1   family.
2   friends.
3   those you co-labor with.
4   those you serve.
5   those you network with.
6   your financial and prayer support base.

I had met Carol Preston during the YWAM Outreach in Fiji in 1979. She eventually came to Oregon and in January we learned that she was going to come and work with us. Because of our vision for a prayer center, she came to be our secretary because she had a similar vision. She was such a blessing, coordinating all of the various prayer and other projects we were involved in. GOD provided a place for her to live without charge and she was simply a servant to our ministry, without pay. She just lived totally by faith and GOD provided her needs even as He provided ours. She is a true woman of GOD with a huge servant heart. We are still in touch with our dear friend and co-laborer.

In April Dave Woodrum and I went to a two-day prophets' gathering in Montana. It was a time for Dave and me to get further bonded together, a relationship that has continued for many years, resulting in much fruit worldwide. He and Jan took over our publishing ministry and use many of our writings in their Bible schools around the world.

July 10-20 I had the privilege of attending the Lausanne II Congress on Evangelism in Manila, the Philippines. I was invited to be part of a prayer team that met and prayed throughout the Congress. This was coordinated by Ben Jennings of Campus Crusade for Christ. I had been invited, but did not have the finances. At the last minute a dear couple was led to underwrite our way. GOD is so faithful! Some of the others who were part of this prayer ministry included Jim and Joy Dawson, Paul Hawkins, Ray Bringham, and a host of others - about thirty in all. Loren Cunningham and Floyd McClung of YWAM both had prominent speaking roles in the Congress.

During this year we had a growing sense that we would be moving back to Salem, Oregon, soon. In August we met with a church group in Salem called Crossroads Church that wanted to move into more of a New Testament model, with an open meeting, and elders. We found ourselves praying more and more about having a home in Salem and being part of that church. Greg and Beth were also praying about moving to the mainland. When we called and told them we were definitely moving back to Salem, they felt that was their cue to also move to Salem, which they did. We had the privilege of living either with them or close to them for the next 20 years and watching their three children (our grandchildren) grow up. (More on this later in this chapter.)

The Lord was also speaking to us about starting a publishing venture. Beth suggested that it be called Preparing the Way Publishers based on Luke 1:17.

On August 15, Beth and Greg finally got their boy, Daniel Gregory Bachran. Joanne was able to watch him be born, which was an amazing experience for her.

September 14-15 found us at a gathering of Christian workers in Helena, Montana. Someone shared the characteristics of a true prophet - "integrity, character, dead to self, a heart for the Bride (Revelation 19:7), concerned about getting the spots and wrinkles out of Her garment (Ephesians 5:27), and the cross."

Our fall ministry tour this year included stops in Washington, Montana, Iowa, Ohio, Indiana, Wisconsin, Eastern Wyoming, and Idaho.

On December 2 we found out that we needed to move from the house we had been renting in Tacoma. On December 3 the Holy Spirit said to me, "You're going home." I knew what He meant - Salem, Oregon. Through the rest of December we got many promises from the Word about our move back to Salem.

December 14-17 was an interesting gathering in Bend, Oregon, of apostles and prophets from around the Northwest that I was led to call.

In late December we drove my folks and Dave to Florida to have Christmas with my sister Janet and her girls. It was a very enjoyable time being with all of my family once again.

1990

During the Florida time I went to a prayer conference January 2-5 with about 90 people from around the U.S.

On January 4 I noted in my journal: "We need a home, Lord:
1   in South Salem.
2   near Kuebler Avenue.
3   quiet neighborhood.
4   nice, quiet backyard with garden area.
5   2-car garage.
6   1 1/2 or 2 bathrooms.

7   living room, dining room, kitchen.
8   a study for Nate.
9   a study for Jo.
10   a guest room.
11   a laundry room.
12   a patio.
13   near Greg and Beth
14   with a play room for the grandchildren.
15   for $60,000."

ALL of this was fulfilled in both our Cabin Ct. home and 2121 Barnes Avenue, later changed by the city to 5025 Barnes Ct. GOD is so awesome!!

Carol Preston, our secretary, packed our things while we were in Florida and we moved to Salem. Carol moved in with some friends on a farm north of Keizer. We stored our belongings at the Old Pringle School building used by Crossroads Community Church and were invited to live with Lance and Jill Miller.

CCC became our church for several months. They were moving toward an open meeting based on 1 Corinthians 14:26; had an eldership of Don DeBoard, Nathan Allen, Bruce Fowler, and John Sparks; and were open to home meetings. We enjoyed our time with them. I met with the elders occasionally when they asked for my input. And I was able to set up an office in the CCC space at the Old Pringle School.

Joanne also spent time at the CCC location working on her book on women. I was given Bushnell's book on women on one of my trips to DC by a sister of Joan Schnabel. Joanne began to read it and was overwhelmed with a desire to search out everything she could find on the subject. She began to teach on the subject while we were still living in Washington.

Then she was led to put it all into book form. The title: *WOMAN – God's Plan not Man's Tradition.* In it she deals with every scripture where the role of women is addressed. It clearly repudiates the traditional teaching that woman is to be under man's authority and that her area of ministry is greatly curtailed. There is no scripture to support either of those "doctrines." It has since been translated into Arabic and Urdu and has been used in many parts of the world.

January 15-19 we had a 5-Day Prayer Gathering at the Assembly of God campgrounds north of Salem.

Late January through early April we were on the East Coast for six weeks. Stops included:
Washington, D.C.
Glassboro, New Jersey, where Gerry and Wenda were pastoring.
Glen Burnie, Maryland.
Baltimore, MD.
Revival Corps in Pennsylvania.

February 17-18 Je while at Revival Corps: "GOD is ready to assume full responsibility for the life totally yielded to Him. GOD is responsible for the consequences of our obedience."

March 1 - 4: I am at a House Church Consultation at Salem, Massachusetts, where I met Hal Miller and Chris Smith, who were leading the consultation. Jon Zens and Gene Edwards were also there. It was a wonderful time of getting oriented to home church once again.

March 23 Je: "It's GOD's responsibility to open doors, provide, give fruit. It's my responsibility only to walk with GOD and obey Him."

March 26-30: A 5-Day Prayer Retreat with Leon and Arlene Franck at their Prayer Retreat property in Wisconsin.

May found us in Kona for two weeks, teaching at the School of Church Ministries. We also spent a weekend with a church in Kauai. What a beautiful island!

In June we looked at a house in Salem that Dave Dryling showed us - and signed papers - but GOD closed the door. GOD had something so much better in mind for us.

On June 24 I was discouraged and GOD sent Harold Eberlee along with a fresh word for me.

One Saturday in late June, while we were living at Miller's, I got up to have my quiet time, and the Lord said, "Today I will provide you a home." I checked the newspaper, made some phone calls, met with a realtor and saw 5255 Cabin Ct. It was a fixer-upper for $55,000, and we made an offer.

On July 2 GOD spoke to Joanne through Jeremiah 23:8 that we were to have our own place again and on July 3 through Jeremiah 23:15 that it would be near Wormwood. Cabin Ct is a short cul-de-sac just off of Wormwood!

In August we were at a large Charismatic gathering called Indianapolis '90. Greg and Beth were there, as part of the leadership of YWAM's King's Kids ministry. And Joanne was there being a nanny to their kids. They made a final decision to move from Hawaii to Salem and to help with the down payment on Cabin Ct. We finally signed the final papers in October. But we had moved in, in early August, before going to Indianapolis.

And Greg and Beth and their three moved in with us; we lived together for about a year, and got the house fixed up and ready to sell. Greg did most of the work.

August 22 Je: "Matthew 2:6 - I am not to consider myself insignificant with regard to what He is doing in the Northwest and America. Our biggest battle will be with religious leaders, controlled by religious spirits, who are unwilling to give up control of 'the work of GOD.' "

September 2 Je: "All religions have a founder, writings, creeds, morals, and belief in the hereafter. What makes Christianity different - a changed life and the power of GOD to do the supernatural."

September 23-27: We conducted another 5-Day Prayer Gathering, in Montana - about 50 prayer leaders and intercessors from MT, ID, WY, WA, OR, and CA.

In the spring GOD began to speak to me about calling Oregon to 40 Days of Prayer. I began to share this with various Oregon prayer leaders; an oversight committee was formed including Peter Carlson, Craig DeMo, David Hoover, Jenny Matteson, Cathy Ramey, Frances Rath, Ron and Karen Rohman, Kathy Tillson, John Whitman, and me; and the entire Church of Oregon was called to 40 Days of Prayer September 27 - November 6, 1990. Close to 40 ministries were supportive of this call and hundreds of churches all across the state participated.

We also began working with Dr. Jay Grimstead some, facilitating a prayer emphasis at his various gatherings of spiritual leaders around the country.

December 20 Je: "What GOD has done in 1990 - He has:
1   Moved us back to Salem, Oregon.
2   Begun to bond us into Salem - Crossroads Church, the elders there, New Life Fellowship reunion, etc.
3   Begun to bond us into Oregon - 40 Days of Prayer.
4   Brought Greg and Beth to Salem.
5   Provided a house.
6   Provided office space.

192

7   Helped Joanne write her book.
8   Fruitful ministry in OH, IN, IL, WI, IA, PA, VA, DC, NJ, MD, CT, HI, OR, MT, and FL.
9   Provided our every need!
10   Closed down the Big Muddy Ranch vision.
11   Given us an '86 Ford Tempo."

This year I also wrote three booklets, *Fulfilling the Great Commission by A.D. 2000, New Wine Skins,* and *Characteristics of the New Testament Church.* Orval Johnston printed them without charge at his printing company in Detroit, MI. He later moved to Jamaica to reach and disciple young boys there.

Joanne has gone to garage sales for years and with our move to a home on Cabin Ct. I began to enjoy going with her some. It's amazing the deals one can get - our home is filled with garage sale purchases!

December 21 Je: "GOD blessed the Jews because 'Abraham obeyed Me and kept My charge.' - Genesis 26:5." GOD will use us to bless others if we do likewise - obey Him and keep His charge.

CHAPTER 15 - BEING A VOICE FOR HOUSE CHURCHES

(House churches, Boilermakers for Christ,
Nate's book on house church,
Joanne's book on woman, U.S. travels)

(1991 - 1993)

1991

Je: "Goals - by AD 2000 (65 years old):
Personal:
1   To be more whole and more like Jesus.
2   Deeper knowledge of GOD's Word.
3   Deeper prayer life.
4   Jo fulfilled in her life and ministry.
5   Children and grandchildren living out GOD's will.
6   Be in good health.
7   A home to live in for our closing years.
8   See relatives saved.
9   Spend more time with friends.
10   Visit each continent one more time.
Ministry:
1   The Church and world experience genuine revival.
2   The Great Commission fulfilled.
3   A string of New Testament fellowships in the U.S. that we give input to.
4   PTW established and run by someone else.
5   Do more writing.
6   Oregon Property (the Big Muddy) operated by Christians.
7   Jesus Returned?"

As of 2009 I have seen progress on 1-9 under Personal, and will probably not see 10 come to pass, except through writing and publishing.

Under Ministry, we have seen 4-6 come to pass and progress on 1-3, although we don't have much input anymore to the many New Testament fellowships that GOD has raised up. GOD is surely faithful!

Late December 1990 Je: "My present ministry - Getting the Bride ready - for coming revival, harvest, persecution, His coming. - Revelation 19:7.
Specifically:
1   Be with GOD.
2   Call for, and sometimes facilitate, extraordinary prayer.
3   Call and help 'the church in transition.'
4   Reaching cities.
5   Writing."

December 31 Je: "GOD is raising up a new thing. He wants to raise up a new thing in the Willamette Valley. We need to walk very carefully before Him."

January 3 Je: "Many people are fearful of leaders because of being wounded and oppressed in the past. May I always be a serving/releasing/encouraging leader who does not dominate/control/manipulate - so that those around me are healed from the past and released into GOD's full potential and plan in the future."

January 7-11 - 5-Day Prayer Gathering in Yelm, Washington, with participants from CA, OR, WA, ID, MT, British Columbia, Egypt, and India. Gideon Chiu and Masa from Egypt had significant input. A brother from Tacoma, who had some involvement with the Big Muddy Ranch project, and I got reconciled after a break in our relationship. GOD began to release me from the Prayer Team.

January 15 - Gerry and Wenda are the proud parents of TWINS! - can you believe it?! - Allison Joanne and Alexander Jason.

196

January 20: We were prayed over at Crossroads Community Church for our traveling ministry - "You will always have a nest to come home to."

January 31: We flew to Wisconsin - stayed with Ernie and Mary Ann Holman in a lovely, old, restored farmhouse. Good prayer seminar, good time with Leon Franck, I spoke at Iowa FGBMFI, Jo spoke on "The Fear of GOD" at a West Union church.

Word from Rosemary Lambert in February:
- You will begin to see fruit.
- Small groups.
- Colossians 2:1-10 - proper order.
- End-time leaders now being set in.
- Acts 13 - apostolic/prophetic teams to be released.
- Koinonia coming soon in Salem for us.
- Something is going to happen soon.
- We are the teaching - as we walk.
- John 17:5 - the hour has come for our ministry.

To "inherit the land" in Psalm 37 (regarding our having a home again):
wait for the Lord - 9, 34
be humble - 11
be righteous - 29
keep His way - 34
be dependent upon His blessing - 22

Greg, Beth, Joanne, and I fixed up the Cabin Court property. Then they purchased a large piece of land at the northwest corner of Reed and Barnes. They discovered a .45 parcel, left over from when Kuebler was put in, that was next to their land, and suggested we try to get it. We had been getting scriptures about land and decided to make an offer to the city for these two lots. We offered $2,555.55, which was the amount the Lord had given us in prayer.

197

Ezekiel 48:35: We are to name it "YHWH Shammah - the Lord is there."

On March 15 we were in Elizabethtown, PA, and got word that we had been awarded the property. Joanne and I were the guest speakers at a missions conference at Grace Chapel and their generous offering to us helped pay for the land.

March 19 Je: "Evidences of GOD's judgment upon the U.S. :
1   North Korean War lost.
2   Viet Nam War lost.
3   Watergate.
4   Failed attempt to get U.S. hostages in Iran.
5   Challenger space explosion.
6   Space program problems.
7   AIDS.
8   Drought.
9   Savings and loan failures."

March 29 Je: "GOD has a remnant - Exodus 19:4-6:
1   Born on eagle's wings.
2   Brought to GOD by Himself.
3   Who obeys His voice.
4   Who keeps His covenant.
5   Who will be His own possession.
6   Who will be a Kingdom of priests.
7   Who will be a holy nation."

April 3: Given to me in Connecticut by a friend of Jay Ferris: I have an apostolic calling, with prophetic revelation and insight, delivered with a teacher's style.

I was in Connecticut for a few days - time with Hugh Hedges, Jay Ferris, a leaders' retreat, at Yale University, two home meetings.

April 14, Sunday: In Jersey City, NJ, with Donivan Shoemaker, a Wesleyan pastor, and the church there.

April 16: Another time with Revival Corps. Also with Don Nori, the publisher of Destiny Image.

April 18-20: 3-Day Prayer Retreat at Roxbury, PA.
Sunday, April 21: At Cumberland Valley Church.

April 22 Je: "My mentors through the years: Abraham David, Nate Scharff, Mert Martin, Bob Clement, Brother Chism, Jim Knutz, Hal Ward, Howard Noggle, Hubert Mitchell, Gene Edwards, Dad Sheets, Maynard Howe, Loren Cunningham, Armin Gesswein, Leonard Ravenhill." (See Appendix 3 for additional people and further details.)

Sunday, April 28: At Glassboro Wesleyan Church with Gerry and Wenda.

May 1: Met with National Prayer Committee. I presented the vision for national leaders' 3-4 day prayer gathering to become more bonded - I feel that it was accepted.

May 2: National Day of Prayer with prayer leaders in Washington, D.C. - saw Bill and Vonette Bright, Jim and Joy Dawson, Ed and Linda Davis, Norval Hadley, Ray Bringham, Leon Franck, Glenn Sheppard, Terri Bork, Jill Miller, and others.

May 7 Je: "Wonderful time honoring my folks' sixty years of marriage - about 40 present."

May 13 Je: "Today the Lord gave Jo and me basic house plans - a split level." I drew up plans, but we couldn't get financing. We decided to sell the lots on Barnes and stay at Cabin Court. After a year of trying to sell the lots, we realized that GOD did want us to be on Barnes. Then we began to look at manufactured homes.

Sunday, June 2: Today the Crossroads Church gathered with us to pray over our land.

June 13-15: 3-Day Prayer Gathering with Dr. Jay Grimstead and others in Northern California.

Sunday, June 16: Today GOD gave me an enlarged plan to take cities, which I gave to Jay Grimstead.

June 23: GOD began to speak to me about leaving Crossroads Community Church and being part of a home-centered fellowship in Salem.

July 16 Je: "Hosea 14:8 - 'It is I who . . . look after you.' - what a promise - GOD has assumed responsibility for us and our needs!"

In July we began meeting on Friday evenings in our homes with Ron and Sylvia Zook, but the Lord soon showed us that we were ahead of Him on this.

We spent most of August resting and seeking the Lord.

August 27: Went to the Oregon State Fair - what fun! It became an annual tradition.

September 9 Je: "Places Jo and I have lived:

Midwest - Franklin trailer that we began our marriage and ministry in; Sheet's home at 125 W. 43rd St. in Marion, IN; Sheet's apartment in Marion, IN; our home at 312 E. Lincoln St., Wheaton, IL; our home at 512 N. Lockwood, Chicago, IL; our home at 4001 S. Boots, Marion, IN.

Hawaii - Casa De Emdeko condos in Kailua-Kona, HI; Amber's home in Kailua-Kona; the House of Barnabas, a YWAM outreach house in Kailua-Kona; Gary Stephens' apartment in Building No. 3 on the YWAM Base in Kailua-Kona; our apartment in Building No. 1 on the YWAM Base in Kailua-Kona.

Northwest - a room at the YWAM Base in Salem, OR; our house trailer there; Hampe's apartment in Gresham, OR; our apartment in Vancouver, WA; the Foursquare Church apartment on S. Sunnyside, in Salem, OR; the Hood Canal summer home, at Belfair, WA; a room at the YWAM Tacoma Hospitality House; a new apartment at 6813 N. 11th in Tacoma, WA; Miller's home in Salem; our home with Greg and Beth at 5255 Cabin Ct. SE in Salem - 22 places in 30 years!" (To this can be added our current home at 5025 Barnes Ct. SE, Salem. The city changed the address from 2121 Barnes Ct.)

September 25-27:   Northern California 3-Day Prayer Gathering of leaders with Jay Grimstead.

Sunday, October 20:   Crossroads Community Church disbanded! It became increasingly clear that there were two groups of people there: Those who wanted a traditional Charismatic church with a pastor, building, etc., and those who wanted a more New Testament fellowship. Those who wanted a traditional Charismatic church scattered and began going to various churches. Those who wanted something more radical started meeting on Sundays in one of our homes.

On November 1 we learned from Wendell Barnett that he had been asked to leave the Friends Church in Silverton.

Sunday, November 3: First home gathering - at Bob Morin's apartment. It was a good time of beginning to define who we are and what we're to do.

Several house church leaders begin to get together on a semi-regular basis - Dan and Jodi Mayhew, Wendell and Donita Barnett, Don and Sue DeBoard, Robbie and Jean Moule, Lane and Marsha Witt, and Joanne and I.

I also got together occasionally with Ron Rohman and Al Schubert. Ron was a prayer leader and street preacher in Portland and Al carried the cross around the U.S.

In the fall I built a study in the corner of the Cabin Court garage since the CCC area, where I had a study, was no longer available.

Also during the fall I wrote a little booklet, *New Wine Skins - the Church in Transition*. It was soon being used around the world. We began getting phone calls from various locations wanting more copies. It was greatly used by the Lord during these early days of GOD doing a new thing in His Church.

On Friday, December 13, Don DeBoard, Wendell Barnett, Dan Mayhew, Al Schubert, Ron Rohman, and I spent a day together in prayer.

1992

My present ministry - getting the Bride ready - Revelation 19:7:
- for coming revival.
- for coming harvest.
- for coming persecution.
- for His Coming.

January 16 Je: "My ministry - hearing GOD's voice and:
- saying = prophetic.
- doing = apostolic."

January 21 Je: "Genesis 26:4 - '. . . by your descendants all the nations of the earth shall be blessed.' - Gerry and Beth."

January 25 Je: "17 house church leaders from 12 groups together to get acquainted."

February 22 Je: "GOD has a place for us out somewhere that will be paid for and self-sustaining - water, septic, large garden and orchard area."

Feb. 25 Je: "Signs of an apostle - traveling, pioneering/giving birth to new things, paving the way for others, signs and wonders, persecution/suffering, miraculous provision, fruit, networking."

Feb. 27 Je: "On Anderson Island in Washington - 'Tall evergreens are so straight, tall, unmovable, always looking upward, growing, bearing fruit, giving shade, reproducing - Lord, make me like them.' "

March 2: Extended prayer time with Rosemary Lambert, Hal and Carol Holmberg, and Jim and Julie Vitzthum.

<u>March 14: I am flying to Detroit to begin a 6 1/2-week trip in the East without Jo.</u>
March 15: With Fred Copple whom I presented the Gospel to when we were CEC officers together in Texas.
21 Je: "My traveling days are over - get settled in the Willamette Valley - people will come to us for input."
22 Je: "Good time with Gerry and Wenda and their children." I spoke to their church on "Intimacy With GOD and With One Another."
23 Je: "Travel on to Earl and Helen Martin's." Helen is Joanne's cousin.
26: With John Niesley, another cousin of Joanne's - traveled to Connecticut.
27: With Dave Wilkerson at a meeting at Yale. I offered him a copy of *The Church Triumphant,* but he said he had already read it!
28 Je: "Powerful meeting at Ferris'." I spoke on "GOD's Plan for His Church."

March 29 Je: "Powerful day at Yale." This included speaking to the new International Church there. And as Hugh Hedges and I were walking across the campus I was led to shout out "Jesus is Lord over Yale."

April 1 Je: Time with Connecticut Shoreline elders.

Met with a house church group near Elizabethtown, PA - "what a group!"

April 4 Je: With Hank and Mary Niewola in Wexford, PA (north of Pittsburgh). A word from them - "Our new ministry (not traveling), new home (in country), new lifestyle (semi-retired) is a promotion - GOD has it all arranged. Things that have been on my heart for years will now come to pass. He will 'guide us until death.' I am to write my autobiography."

About 35 leaders together for prayer in Pittsburgh.

April 8: In Fostoria for three days of rest.

10 Je: "Proverb 23:4 - Don't try to figure out financial provision - trust GOD!"

11: With Gar and Rachel Darnes, Ernestine Stewart, Fred Copple in Michigan.

12: With Don Pann in Michigan and Joyce and Cody Cull in Indiana.

13: With Glen and Betty Martin in Marion, IN.

14 Je: "Apostles are those who go first and pioneer - for others who get the credit."

14: With Evelyn Rhoades, Joanne's sister; Larry Hartman; and Glen and Betty.

15: Met with Purdue alumni regarding Boilermakers for Christ. GOD had spoken to me about BFC in 1984.

16: Met with some Purdue Christian faculty. Later at Don and Ruthie Hawkinson's place in Chicago area.

20-22: 3-day Prayer Retreat in Wisconsin with Leon and Arlene Franck at Prayer Valley.

25: Boilermakers for Christ is born by four others and me.

April 26-27 Je: "Tomorrow I fly home to Oregon - 6 1/2 weeks away from my wife - too long! - but one of the best trips ever - 'at the right place at the right time.' Gone 45 days, drove over 4,000 miles, ministered in 10 states, slept in 20 beds, and ministered in 23 meetings."

May 13-16: To Washington state.

May 17 Je: "GOD is speaking to me about a magazine."

June 10: Started new book, *God's Plan for His Church.*

June 13: Beth and Greg move to their new home.

June 24: Am spending the night in Greg's truck by a mountain stream near Laurence Lake near Mt. Hood.

June 27: Thirteen house church leaders gather for a day in Portland.

July 19 Je: "About 50 together from house churches in Salem, Stayton, and Portland. Great time!"

July 28 Je: "Finished first draft of *God's Plan* today - PTL!"

July 31: Mailed out copies of GP manuscript today for input and to publishers.

August 1: Sixteen house church leaders together. Je: "Foundation - walking deeply with the Lord and one another. Sterling - 'I need people who will make Me important.' Authority out of relationships. Don't put anything in the way of loving one another."

August 3 Je: "I sense that the Lord may be saying that I am to concentrate on the house church movement. Many others are now running with united, extraordinary prayer; bringing prayer leaders together; and reaching cities."

August 10: I visited Glen Eyrie, the Navigators headquarters, today.

August 11 Je: "I am a biblical, charismatic, historical post-tribulation, historical premillennialist, Wesleyan Arminian."

August 15: I am with house church people in Washington state - 9 people from Bellingham, Lynden, W. Seattle, S. Seattle, and Issaquah.

August 28:   In Phoenix at A.D. 2000 Taking Cities Consultation - I brought the challenge of simple church as one indispensable key to reaching cities. Also saw Cathy Hughes, Bill and Pat Parker, and Vern and Diane Nesbitt.

Late August and early September: Mom and Dave spent three weeks with us.

September 12-17: Am in Western Florida for Intercessors For America-sponsored prayer conference. I spoke to the group and had a workshop on house church.

On Sunday I saw Sister Reisdorph, widow of one of the former Wesleyan Methodist general superintendents. She remembered me from years earlier. I was reluctant to share with her about our current involvement with house churches, but did. She surprised me by saying that in 1948 GOD told her that "the church will return to the parlor (home)."

Things shared at the Prayer Conference and notes I made in my journal:
"Judgment coming to U.S., especially California, Florida, and New York City.
Life is relationships.
Importance of 'Divine linkings and appointments.'

I formally released our prayer-emphasis work to the prayer leaders and they released me to concentrate on the house church emphasis.

Live each day in forgiveness."

After the conference I drove to the other side of Florida and spent two days with my sister, Janet, and her two daughters, Aime and Lorie.

October 13: Jo and I flew to Baltimore, MD.
Oct. 14-16: We were involved in a 3-day prayer gathering with believers from Central Maryland.
17-18: With several house churches in MD.
19-22: Spent four days with Gerry and his family. One day we took Geoffrey to a Dan Quayle, running for Vice President, campaign bus stop - and got to shake his hand!
23-24: With Jay and Carleen in CT.

October 25: Jo and I were with a Yonkers, New York (north of the Bronx), house church - what a day! This was a group of about 30 people who meet in a large home that overlooks the Hudson River. A woman started the group about 35 years ago. There were musical instruments scattered throughout the group. At 9:30 the pianist's hands touched the piano and the Holy Spirit fell on the group! They spent about an hour in Spirit-led worship. Then about an hour of teaching from several. Then about an hour in prayer and ministry to one another. What a meeting! I wept through the whole meeting because of the presence of GOD!

October 29 Je: We head home today - have spent the past 2 1/2 weeks in MD, PA, NJ, NY, and CT.

November 2 Je: "I must prophesy again - Revelation 10:11.
In the past:
1   Personal evangelism to the Wesleyans and the whole Church.
2   Spiritual gifts to Wesleyans - not received.

3   Importance of local church to YWAM.
4   To Tacoma YWAM - need for more prayer and koinonia, better oversight of finances. (I don't feel that this word was taken too seriously. The base subsequently closed.)
5   United, extraordinary prayer - to North American church. Now - House church emphasis to whole Church around the world."

November 8 Je: "What GOD has done in our midst this past year:
1   We are a Body - growing in our relationship with GOD and each other; growing in our understanding of New Testament Christianity and our commitment to it; and new people having been added.
2   We have been an encouragement to Wendell, some of the people from his former church in Silverton, the Stayton group, Portland people, and people and groups across the United States."

November 10 Je: A day for prayer - "I choose to not give any thought to our financial needs - our Father will provide - Matthew 6:24-34."

November 15 Je: "I thank GOD:
1   that He has called me to Himself.
2   that He has called me to His work.
3   for my wife, children, grandchildren.
4   for bringing me into the charismatic dimension.
5   for giving me an understanding of the New Testament church.
6   for providing all of our needs.
7   for bringing us to the Willamette Valley, Oregon, Northwest.
8   for allowing me to know some of His choice servants.
9   for using our children in His service.
10   for my health.
What more could one ask for!"

December 4 Je: "I have not always flowed with others - is this due to my visionary call or an independent spirit??"

December 11 Je: "YWAM is a great movement - but we are not called to be part of it. We are grateful for the time we had and all that we learned. My calling - house church movement and writing."

December 27 Je: "Do what you can, with what you have, right where you are!"

December 28 Je: "What GOD has done this year, 1992:
1   Led us to the Cabin Ct. home - moved, settled.
2   Provided two computers and a laser printer.
3   Wrote *GOD's Simple Plan* . . .
4   Sold our two Ford Tempos - and purchased a Honda.
5   Deepened our relationship with key Oregon house church people.
6   Relinquished all of the prayer ministry (to concentrate on the house church emphasis).
7   Relinquished working with Jay Grimsted. (This was not a break in relationship - we are still in contact with a good relationship, although we do see the male-female issue differently.)
8   A whole ministry change - to house church emphasis.
9   Started part-time secular work."

1993

During 1992 I had felt the Lord releasing me to write a book about house church based on what He had shown Art Prouty and me in 1966 and taught me since then. This was a major project for 1993.

Debi Renfro had given us a used Macintosh computer, which I was learning how to operate, this being my first experience with a computer.

Our home church group learned of another group that met at Rob and Jean Moule's home out in the country southeast of Stayton. Our group began going out there occasionally and meeting with them about 10:30 on Sunday morning, followed by a potluck lunch and further fellowship through much of the afternoon. The combined group sometimes numbered forty. These were wonderful times. Once or twice a year, Jeannie would be led to suggest a weekend of prayer. Some of us would spend Saturday in prayer together at their place. The Sunday gatherings the next day were unusually powerful!

Several couples began meeting occasionally. They included Rob and Jean Moule, Lane and Marsha Witt, Wendell and Donita Barnett, Don and Sue DeBoard, and the Krupps. I saw it as the beginnings of an eldership, but found out in time that several did not believe in official elders. But we did function for a season and gave sponsorship to several things including a large gathering of about 120 on July 31, 1994, when Rob and Julia Banks came through from California.

On other occasions just Jean Moule, Dan Mayhew from Portland, Wendell, and I would get together for a few hours of sharing and prayer. These were really good times. Sometimes Jo would join us if we were meeting at our home.

January 7: I met in Portland with Gregg Harris of the home school movement who was expressing interest in the home church concept. Also Leonard Zike who taught about getting detached from all government connections.

Also saw Ron Rohman and phoned George Wilde, Lee Thompson, Sterling Borbe, Dan Mayhew, and Hans Schnabel.

January 8 Je: "We are pioneering a whole new ballgame:
- no name.
- no incorporation.
- no property.
- meeting in homes.

210

- built on relationships alone.
- releasing all to minister, including women.
- shared leadership.
- no clergy/laity division.
- humility, simplicity, mutuality.
- very natural, very reproducible.
- the Holy Spirit's full role.
- apostolic oversight.
- elders and deacons appointed.
- our personal walk with GOD.
- growth, multiplication.
- the call of GOD.

We dare not swerve, stop, change, or leave anything out. Hold to all that GOD has spoken!"

After moving back to Salem I met occasionally with the Salem pastors who were meeting for prayer. Jerry Sloan, a Wesleyan pastor in Salem, was giving leadership to this prayer movement. I did not go on a regular basis, not feeling too welcomed and not feeling led to be deeply involved.

On February 13 Joanne and I spent some time at Aldersgate, a Free Methodist Conference Center, with some Oregon Christian political activists. There were a number here in our state who were trying to see things changed toward a godly state. Through this we became close friends with Dale and Frances Rath and also came to know Frank Carpenter, the unofficial chaplain of the Senate.

During January and February, a rift began between one of the home church brothers and some of the rest of us. In each meeting he was continually pushing "the sovereignty of GOD," leaving no room for the freewill of man, and his interpretation of "freedom in Christ." Time after time he would interject these teachings, even if GOD seemed to be leading the meeting in a totally different direction. We tried to bring balance and correction, but he could never receive it.

In time some of us felt we couldn't continue in this atmosphere so on February 28 we began to meet separately. There was a very sweet presence of the Lord.

Over the past year I had gotten acquainted and had some wonderful fellowship with Emory Welch, a godly apple farmer living west of town with his wife, Clara. Emory unexpectedly was taken to the hospital and died. His funeral was March 6.

My sister, Janet, came for a visit on March 15 for a week or so. She had just gone through a horrible time - her third husband, Dan Therriault, in Florida, had tried to kill her.

Jo and I began to clean rentals one day a week for some additional income, but the work was quite taxing and we lasted only a few times. We also did some maintenance and construction work at Black Butte with Greg, our son-in-law.

On Easter Sunday, April 11, three home church groups met at Jim and Bev Carver's home - it was a wonderful time. Later in the day we had dinner with Beth and her gang.

As I finished my book on house church, which we entitled, *God's Simple Plan for His Church - and Your Place in It - A Manual for House Churches*, and Joanne finished her book on woman, *WOMAN: God's Plan, not Man's Tradition*, we were both looking for publishers. We had contact with Gene Edwards, Destiny Image, New Leaf Press, Solid Rock Books, Huntington House, and others.

I decided to let Solid Rock Books in Woodburn, Oregon, do my *God's Simple Plan*. But we also began to produce a spiral 8 1/2 x 11 edition for private distribution until the published book was available. Jo continued to look for a publisher. Destiny Image almost took it two times. And New Leaf Press and Huntington House were quite interested. In the meantime she put out a spiral-bound version.

Linda Zuck began a Christians for Biblical Equality chapter for the greater Portland area. CBE was a growing, national and international movement of men and women who believed that the Bible, when correctly interpreted, taught an equality between men and women in the home, church, and all of life. Jo and I went to a two-day CBE conference on May 7-8. The keynote speakers were Ruth A. Tucker, who co-authored *Daughters of the Church*, and Gilbert Bilezikian, author of *Beyond Sex Roles*. Both of these authors had been a huge help to Joanne in writing her book and it was a real privilege for her to meet them in person. Dr. Bilezikian later wrote an endorsement for Joanne's book. Rob and Jean Moule went with us. It was a very enjoyable time.

May 15 Je: "Life has not been easy:
- My youth - caring for my brother Dave, working, not much money, domineering Mom, couldn't be with friends and do things I wanted to do.
- College - much study, too much responsibility.
- Adult life - getting acclimated to the Christian life; finding my place in life; being a voice and pioneering; struggles with the Church - personal evangelism, gifts of the Spirit, etc.; our many moves.
Now - it's time to 'smell the roses' - have friends, write, be an encouragement to the house church movement, learn to 'rest in the Lord,' be a blessing to people."

May 19-22: GOD provided (through a contact of Wendell's) a spacious house right on the ocean for a few days. We visited Garibaldi, Tillamook, Cannon Beach, and Seaside - and had lots of time to rest, think, pray, and walk the beach.

We are still trying to sell the two lots on Barnes Avenue.

On May 25 Mary Ellen King from Indiana phoned and said she was sending $4,800 for the publishing of *God's Simple Plan*. What a miracle! We signed a contract and got the finished manuscript to Solid Rock Books the first week of June.

Sunday, June 6 Je: "Wonderful gathering - Barnetts, Yankuses, Krupps - at Krupps - real peace, openness, depth, GOD's leading and presence."

On the publishing front we were also working on putting out a new edition of our *Basic Bible Studies* booklets and the *New Testament Survey*.

June 20 Je: "I am the most fulfilled I've ever been - writing, being a voice for house church, living in the Northwest, being near one of our children (Beth), taking life a day at a time."

I had a dental appointment this week with Dr. Davis in Dallas, Oregon, but did not have any funds to pay. I phoned them to cancel the appointment and he said I should come anyway and not worry about paying. What a blessing to have a Christian dentist! We were also blessed to have a Christian chiropractor, Dr. John Whitmire. We had begun going to him when we were with the Salem YWAM Base. He did not charge us for the treatments. What a blessing!

John and Betty McCormick began meeting with our home church group in 1992. By 1993 we were meeting some at the home where they were staying. On Saturday, July 17, we all gathered to paint the outside of the house. It went quite well with Wendell's expert painting experience and leadership on the project.

In July we decided that we were, in fact, to be on Barnes Avenue. We began looking at manufactured homes. Jo and I began the process of clearing the lots of Scotch Broom, blackberries, and tall grass. And I started working on plot plan drawings to submit to the city. July was also a time of financial testing.

We got the first copies of the published *God's Simple Plan for His Church* book the first week of August.

On Saturday, August 7, several home church groups spent the day together at Champoeg State Park. During the day we laid hands on Chan and Martha Cathcart and recognized their role as fellow elders in our midst. They later shared with us that they sensed a greater freedom and anointing after that time.

This fall we began an annual process of putting up fruit and vegetables - can, freeze, dry, and store in a refrigerator in the garage.

August 21: Joanne flew back East to help with her sister Evelyn's wedding to Bill Allen. And she drove to Ohio to see my folks.

On Monday, August 30, I started a 16-day trip to Washington and British Columbia - contacts in Woodburn, Vancouver, Tacoma, Anderson Island, Bremerton, Port Orchard, Anacortes, Renton, Bellingham, Lummi Island, British Columbia, Kent, Portland, and home. It was a wonderful time of relationships and ministry.

Thursday, September 16: Jo and I went to the Coast to celebrate our 32nd wedding anniversary. "Thank you, Lord, for a wonderful wife."

Saturday, September 18: Kelly and Daniel (my grand-children) and I went to see hot air balloons being launched near Albany.

On October 9 I was on a Christian radio station in Albany talking about the home church concept and my book. This resulted in our meeting Mike and Cindy Wenger. He was in his car and heard the radio broadcast. He called me and shared their interest in home/relational church. This resulted in our subsequently starting another group in South Salem, which met some in their home.

Sunday and Monday, October 10-11, Jo and I spent two days at the Coast.

On Wednesday, October 13, I flew to Virginia for a House Church Conference. Rested and waited on the Lord on Thursday. The conference was Friday through Sunday, October 15-17. It was sponsored by a coalition of us that had been developing for several years - Hal Miller, Chris Smith, Chris Kirk, Barry Steinman, Rob and Julia Banks, others, and me. We had a conference every year or two in a different part of the country - Massachusetts, Virginia, California, Northern Indiana, Oregon, etc. These were wonderful times. This conference was held at a Mennonite College with more than 200 participants.

After the conference I spent time with Gerry and Wenda in Glassboro, NJ; and Lindsay and Tracey Reed and a house church group in Elizabethtown, PA.

In December Bob Fitts and I did some traveling together in the Northwest. And some of us in Salem produced a Christmas tract together for distribution as the Lord led.

Saturday, December 25 Je: "What a wonderful day we had with Greg and Beth and their family."

December 26 Je: "Life will soon be over - what have I accomplished?
1   Raised a 'preacher.'
2   Raised a delightful, musical woman of GOD.
3   Been a blessing to our grandchildren.
4   Released my wife to find her plan in GOD, including the writing of her book.
5   Written a number of books.
6   Helped pioneer personal evangelism.
7   Reached a few people in Chicago.
8   Been a witness to holiness people of the Charismatic Renewal.

9   Been a voice to YWAM relative to the local church.
10   Been a voice for 40 days of prayer.
11   Developed a team that had 5-Day Prayer Gatherings.
12   Been one of the voices/pioneers for home church.
In conclusion, I have obeyed GOD - and been His witness, prophet, and pioneer."

During 1993 Jo and I realized that we were in bondage to each other and spent some time releasing one another.

CHAPTER 16 - BEING A VOICE FOR HOUSE CHURCHES (Continued)

(House churches, US travels, a home again)
(1994 - 1995)

1994

January 5 Je: A word from Sandy Atwood: "There is a heavy anointing upon you, that goes wherever you go. You need to be at the right place at the right time. That anointing will be transferred to whomever you lay your hands upon. You are a man of peace, and spread peace wherever you go."

January 8-9: We had a Northwest House Church Conference in Washington hosted by Doug and Joyce Marsden. People came from WA, OR, ID, and British Columbia.

While on the trip to Washington we also saw Diana Blanchard, Darwin and Anne Newton with their family, Rick and Melissa Anderson and family, and Dr. Rody, our chiropractor.

On January 11 - I joined the YMCA to get more exercise, especially swimming.

By now there was a good-sized, functioning home church group: Barnetts, Bob Moran, Borbes, Dennis McGill, John and Betty McCormick, sometimes their sons John and Mat, Bob Iddings and his daughter Joanna, Yankuses, and us. We were beginning to sense that maybe it was time to start another home church group in South Salem.

I spent all day January 15 with John Lindell who wanted to build a Melaleuca business for us.

On Wednesday, January 19, we left for an extended ministry trip to Southern California.

219

We drove to the YWAM base in Chico, CA, and stayed overnight with Marcella Bracey, who had been Loren Cunningham's secretary when we were in Kona. The next day we drove 700 miles to San Diego and stayed with Jerry and Phyllis Mason. Spent the next day resting and waiting upon the Lord. GOD said to me that my message was to be "simplicity and release."

Saturday and Sunday, January 22-23, was a house church gathering at a state park east of San Diego, arranged by Jerry Mason. Jerry owned a brake and muffler shop and had a home church group in San Diego. There were people at the gathering from Mexico; Yucca Valley, Vista, Anaheim, San Diego, CA; and us from Oregon. We met Nolice and Marian Miller and Frank Smith for the first time - what precious people they are. Ted and Renie Faver came up from Mexico. Warren and Helen Peterson were there. And Bob Fitts. It was the beginning of some long-term relationships that we still have today.

On Monday we spent the evening and night with Darrell and Rachel Newhall. Rachel is Joanne's niece, the daughter of her sister Arlene. It was good to see them serving the Lord, although they divorced some years later.

On Tuesday evening we met with Ritch and Leslie Carlton and a home church group in San Diego. Ritch had written several booklets on the subject and we had been in touch by e-mail for some time.

On Wednesday I spent time with Wade Barrier, a house church brother, and Maynard Howe, who was an apostle to the Indians of Northern Canada, but was now retired and living in Southern California. We spent the evening with Hal and Claudia Ward. Hal had discipled me when I was a young Christian in the Navy in Texas.

On Thursday Jo and I took some time off and had lunch at the Coronado Hotel, a famous hotel in San Diego. In the evening we met with the group that Jerry Mason gives leadership to.

On Friday we drove to Mexico to spend some time with Ted and Renie Faver. On Saturday we spent time with their medical team, witnessing to those who came for medical help. I helped Martha, a local Mexican believer, lead her first soul to Jesus. In the evening we met with a new home church group.

On Sunday I spoke at Brother Luis' church - "Obey GOD." In the afternoon we spent time with Ted and Renie at the beach, where Ted baptized several. On Monday we drove back across the border to Bob and Joni Fitts' for fellowship and overnight. Also saw Ray and Maralyn Lyne, friends of Joanne's for many years.

On Tuesday early morning Don Hardy, Frank Smith, Bob Fitts, and I spent several hours together on the beach at the place where Bob and Joni were house sitting at Laguna Beach. It was a good time discussing how Brother Lee of the Local Church movement got off base and how we need to stay broken and walk in humility with those around us.

On Wednesday Bob Fitts and I spent time at the U.S. Center for World Mission and with Rob and Julia Banks at Fuller Theological Seminary. In the evening Joanne and I and Bob and Joni were with about twenty believers at Warren and Helen Peterson's in Anaheim. On Thursday Frank Smith, Don Hardy, Bob, and I were together again for several hours of sharing.

On Friday Jo and I spent two hours with Hubert and Rachel Mitchell. They are in their late 80s and failing. Hubert got out his accordion and played and we all worshiped the Lord. What a privilege to be with these great saints. Hubert had been one of my mentors since 1960.

Then we drove to Yucca Valley to be with Nolice and Marian Miller. We spent Saturday morning with them and with a group at their home in the evening. On Sunday morning we had further time with the Millers. This was followed by time with Joanne's two uncles and their wives, Uncle Orville and Aunt Ethis and Uncle Vernon and Aunt Esther. Later in the day we saw Joanne's cousin, Marlin Niesley, and his wife Mary Lou. We spent the night in a motel west of Los Angeles.

On Monday we had time with Al and Kathy VanDyk in Santa Barbara. Al is a prophet with a writing and publishing ministry, who had spent many years with Campus Crusade for Christ. We stayed overnight with Uncle Warren and Aunt R'Vene in their motor home parked at Pismo Beach. On Tuesday we drove to Antioch, east of San Francisco, and stayed overnight with Bob and Arlene Hughes. Arlene is Joanne's oldest sister. Wednesday evening we were with a home group in Sacramento. On Thursday, February 10, we drove home - we had been gone 22 days and traveled 3,644 miles!

On March 6 a new home group started in South Salem - ten people - very good time together. The group continued to grow - Renfros, Wengers, Jerry and Mary Christianson, Sandy Atwood, Ken Bentz, us.

John and Betty McCormick lived with us March 4-9, then left for a trip to Oklahoma.

March 15 we went to John Trachsell's funeral in Newberg and saw Joy May, who was his daughter and had been my secretary in the early 1970s in Marion, IN.

Greg and Beth moved to their new home on Barnes Avenue.

On April 20 we closed on selling the Cabin Court home for $87,000. We had purchased it for $55,000, so we made $32,000, which was split between Bachrans and us.

222

On April 29-30 we packed and stored our things at Sandy Atwood's big barn at his place in the country south of Salem and we moved to an apartment on South Liberty.

We spent the summer looking at manufactured homes - from Woodburn to Eugene - and trying to get a loan. We were also working on the lots - clearing, mowing, etc. And GOD kept giving us promise after promise that we would soon "dwell on the land" - Psalm 37, Isaiah 40, Jeremiah 42, Acts 17:26, Galatians 6:10, John 5:7-13, Genesis 26:3, 22; Exodus 2:24-25, 6:1-7, 15:13-18, 23:20-33; Leviticus 26:5, Numbers 23:19, Deuteronomy 8:1, Psalm 57:2, etc.

May 17-18:   We made a quick trip to Washington - chiropractor for Jo, Newtons, Seaburys, Marsdens, Kathleen McConnell, Holmbergs, brief time at Seattle waterfront.

On Sunday, May 29, our home church group gathered on our land and dedicated it to the Lord.

On May 31 we went to Kelly's graduation from middle school.

June 6, 1994: 50th anniversary of D-Day at Normandy - what a great crusade for the cause of freedom!

June 7: I had jury duty for the first time in my life. I continued to serve on a case until June 15 when it was a "hung jury" because I could not agree with the others - in my understanding there was reasonable doubt.

June 20-21: Bob and Arlene Hughes, Joanne's sister, came to visit us.

June 26: Kelly's ballet and tap recital.

July 19: I was on two Christian TV programs in Portland talking about home church and my book, GOD's Simple Plan.

On Sunday, July 31, we had a house church gathering with Rob and Julie Banks at the Fellowship Hall of the Free Methodist church. About 120 came from all over Oregon and Washington. The Banks were house church pioneers in Australia that had moved to the U.S. when Rob was on the faculty at Fuller Theological Seminary. Julie later died of cancer and Rob returned to Australia and later married again.

August 17-21 we took a little trip up the Oregon Coast and to be with Steve Seabury, Carl Mease, Mark and Laurie Sleeper, and others, at a retreat they held at a 4-H Camp near Shelton, Washington.

We had visited and made application at many loan offices in Salem over the past months. On Friday, August 26, we got word from the last one that they could not give us a loan. All of the companies either did not understand our "living by faith" income or they did not loan for manufactured homes. Our credit was very good and did not affect the loan companies' decisions. We were "dead in the water."

On Saturday, August 27, I noted in my journal: "GOD is good! I have my health, a mission in life, and a family that is walking with GOD, a wonderful wife, no debts, friends, and GOD Himself. If we are ever to have our own home again, GOD will have to initiate it."

On Sunday evening, at our weekly home church gathering, Ken Bentz, who had a manufactured home dealership called Santiam Homes, said he thought he might have something for us.

We met with him on Tuesday, August 30, and saw a new HomeBuilders Northwest home. HomeBuilders was a new company, and Ken had bought a number of homes to help them get started. He still had a couple of them left.

On August 31 Ken said he had gotten a loan for us and we signed a contract! (We found out later that Ken had co-signed on the construction loan with a company that he had sent a great deal of business to. What a dear friend he has been - we are so grateful!)

On Labor Day, September 5, I passed out 1,000 copies of a tract that I had especially written for the State Fair.

On September 7, my 59th birthday, we made some changes to the manufactured home layout and signed the final papers with Ken. What a birthday present! The next day Jo flew to New Jersey for ten days with Gerry and his family. GOD's timing on all of this was so amazing. Jo already had her ticket to go to Gerry's. She had to leave on the 8th. We also had to have her signature on the contract before HomeBuilders would begin the construction of our home. We had to sign on the 7th!

We hired a fellow to excavate where the home was to be and he began excavating on September 13. He ran into many large boulders, which meant he had to excavate several more days than we had originally planned.

Bill and Evelyn Allen came to visit us for a few days.

Because we were far enough away from the city water line, they gave us the okay to put in a well. The fees for the city water would have been $2,500. For another $500 we put in the well - 12 gallons per minute at 120 feet down. This meant we would have all of the water we would need for gardening, watering the lawn, etc., free.

I spent October trenching, putting in utilities, backfilling, and getting the gravel and concrete pads ready for the manufactured home.

I had much help from Dennis McGill, Ted Faver, Greg Bachran, Alan Yankus, Bob Iddings, Bob Moran, Wendell Barnett, and others. What a blessing they were!

October 16-26: We had a trip to Southern California for a National House Church Consultation, with a number of stops along the way. This included being on Christian TV with Ron Haas in the Bay Area regarding the house church movement and my new book on the subject. We even stayed in a Marriott hotel!

The manufactured home was scheduled to arrive on Monday, October 31, but a windstorm delayed it one day. So it arrived and was placed on the pad on November 1. Over the next two months another fellow and I built the garage and office addition. Joanne worked on the inside of the home, putting tile at the front doorway, for the wood stove floor, and at the kitchen and bathroom sinks. She also did other interior decorating. We saw GOD perform many miracles each week.

November 28-29 I had a quick trip by plane to the Bay Area to be on Christian TV again with Ron Haas and several pastors - to talk about the changing church, although I was the only one for much change.

After the program I spent time with Dave Meier and met Gary and Caren Linden for the first time. The next day I rode with Harold Bredesen to the airport. He was one of the early leaders of the Charismatic renewal and he talked about the baptism of the Holy Spirit and prayed all the way to the airport!

On December 20 Ray Brimhall from Washington sheet-rocked the entire house addition of large garage and two offices in one day - unbelievable! On December 21 Lyle Remmick started taping the sheet rock.

On December 21, we also moved into our new home. There was no electricity yet except an extension cord through our bedroom window!

On December 22 PGE hooked up the electricity, the phone was turned on, the well pump was wired up, the sheet rock joints got a second coat, and we finished moving from the apartment. On December 24 I put up towel racks and we got the bathroom organized.

On December 25, Greg came home from the hospital and we had a brief Christmas time with all of them. Greg had become very ill as a result of a staph infection he picked up. We almost lost him. This all happened during the time that GOD was doing a deep work in his life. We believe it was a clear attack from the devil. But, praise GOD, He brought him through.

And we organized our bedroom and closet. On Monday, December 26, we rested all day - didn't even get dressed!

What a year - the sale of the Cabin Court house, a place to store our stuff, an apartment for an eight-month stay, the provision of a manufactured home and loan, a garage and office addition built, and our moving into our own, permanent, probably final, home on this earth! GOD is so good and faithful!

1995

Much of the early months were spent getting the house finished - office and study, garage, painting outside, gutters, drain lines, and grading.

January 19: I moved into my study - what a blessing!

We had a quick trip to Washington January 20-23 - spent time with Seaburys, Sleepers, Shineoffs, Dave Woodrum, Rod and Ayako Billups. We had a Sunday meeting on January 22 at Seaburys - as part of the day we prayed over them, recognizing them as elders.

January 24: Closed with GE Capital on a 30-year, $65,000 permanent home loan. "I believe you, Lord, to pay it off."

February 4: Garage door opener installed and we began to park our car in the garage. Also an evening of fellowship with Knochs and Harry and Jan Ahler.

Feb. 5: We met with a group at Brian and Johanna Hewitt's.

Feb. 7: Began special 40 Days time - to be prepared for our next assignment from the Lord. He gave me the simple two-page writing *New Wine and New Wine Skins.*

Feb. 8-10: A trip to Washington - picked up George Bolduc at the Portland airport to travel with me. Dinner and gathering at the Sleepers. We spent time with Rod and Ayako, Seaburys, and Andersons.

Saturday, Feb. 11: We went to *Under His Wings*, a musical about the *Book of Ruth* in which Beth played the lead role, the part of Ruth. - "Beth did a fabulous job!" We are so proud of her and so thankful to GOD for all of her many giftings.

Sunday, Feb. 12: GOD spoke to me - He is going to renew my calling - a prophet to the nations - Jeremiah 1.

February 28 Je: "I am a prophet to the organized church and an apostle to the house churches."

March 1, 6-8 a.m.: Prayer time at Bob Morin's - the Holy Spirit was poured out in a mighty way - I walked out drunk in the Spirit.

Saturday, March 11: Met with a group of eleven in Albany.

Sunday, March 12: Met with a group in Woodburn.

March 14 Je: "GOD's people need a revelation - <u>they are</u> the church - they don't need to go anywhere or do anything - but enjoy/walk with/obey GOD - that's all!"

Began meeting monthly at Alger Marsh's for fellowship and prayer - he, Wendell Barnett, Dan Mayhew, Brian Hewitt, me.

<u>March 29 - April 25 - trip to Southern California - Jo and me.</u>
I am including some of the details to give an idea of our traveling ministry:
March 31-April 2: A three-day conference at Max Applegate's place in Carpenteria - teachers included Frank Smith, Bob Fitts, Max, Al VanDyk, Jo and me.
April 5: Spent the day with Bob and Joni Fitts.
April 6: Time with Bob and Frank Smith. Wonderful gathering in the evening at Petersons'.
April 7 - To San Diego and Mexico.
Saturday, April 8: Spoke to about 40 Mexican pastors - "New Wine and New Wine Skins." Went to a new area with Ted Faver, met with a couple, Foustino and Tomasa, at their small, dirt-floor home and taught them about home church. They said that that was what they wanted so we prayed over them - and planted a church in 30 minutes!
Sunday, April 9: Spoke at a Mexican church.
Monday, April 10: In Ensenada with pastor and his wife, Daniel and Mariane Navarro.
Time with Ted en route to San Diego. Time with Jerry Mason.
Tuesday, April 11: Time with Rachel and Darrell, Hal and Claudia Ward.
Wednesday, April 12: Time at Green Oak Ranch - Frank Smith, Ray Bringham, Maynard Howe, Ritch Carlton, Barry Steinman, Bob Fitts, Favers, us, four others. Wonderful time! In the evening - great time with Masons.

229

Thursday, April 13: Took the day off - Mason's group in the evening.

Friday, April 14: Swam at YMCA, time with Wade Barrier, time with Ray Bringham, with Frank Smith and a group in the evening.

Saturday, April 15: At a home in Indio - the Gospel was preached outdoors, and people were baptized. In the evening we went with Petersons to an ex-local church group where we met John Engles.

Sunday, April 16: With Carusos and their home church.

Monday, April 17: Went to Local Church bookstore in Anaheim. Met with Cook Barela and two other couples in the evening.

Tuesday, April 18: Joanne flew home. I had a good three hours with Jonathan Campbell in the afternoon. Met with Bob Fitts and a group in Riverside in the evening.

Wednesday, April 19: With Jonathan and Jennifer Campbell - while we were having breakfast we saw on TV that the Federal Building at Oklahoma City had been bombed.

I did research on tax-exempt status at Loma Linda University library in Southern California and saw the book on the court case about giving to Christian workers without a 501(c)3 - "A Federal Court Acknowledges Christ's True Church," District Court of U.S. - So. CA - Hon. Alfonso J. Zirpoli. This was encouraging to us in that people give to our ministry and we do not have a 501(c)3. When we left YWAM we were going to incorporate, but GOD told us that we were to have no connection with the government because of future days of persecution from the government.

I spent time with Lowell and Darla Ritchey - Darla is a distant cousin on Mom's side. Stayed with Fred and Elsie Johnson.

Thursday, April 20: I spent the day with GOD in the California mountains.

Friday, April 21: At Wm. Carey Library book ministry at U.S. Center; at Fuller Seminary; to Nolice and Marian Miller's home.

Saturday: Spent the day with Nolice at Yucca Valley and Joshua Tree Monument.

Sunday: Wonderful meeting at Miller's.

Monday, April 24: To Fitts' - Three hours with Bob and Barry Steinman on house church magazine vision. We all worked on it and it became a reality. It was called *House to House*. Barry Steinman did the editing, Jerry Mason handled the finances, and Petersons mailed it out. House2House, done by Tony Dale in Texas, later replaced it. Also went swimming with Bob; time with Matthew Ferrari.

Tuesday, April 25: With Frank Smith and Bob Fitts on the beach. With Frank and two brothers, then to the airport, and home.

Sunday, April 30: A wonderful day with about 50 house church people at Champoeg Park in Oregon.

Fri., May 5: Met with a group in Albany.

Sat., May 6: Spent the day with Tony and Kathy Mader who stopped by for a visit. Masons while in California gave us a fax machine - first fax sent on May 6.

Sun., May 7: House church gathering at our place.

May 11: Planted 80 tomato plants, hoping to sell tomatoes. We had a good garden and did sell some.

May 11-13: Ted and Renie Faver came for a visit.

June: Putting 1-3 Bible study booklets into a single book, *Basic Bible Studies*.

Trip to Mexico and Texas - Jo and me.
June 16-18: In Mexico with Bob Fitts, Saturday, June 17 - all-day seminar with Mexicans.
June 18-19: Resting at Masons back in San Diego.

June 22-25: House Church Conference in Austin, TX. Joanne and I stayed with Bernie and Sally Boureaux. Bernie had invited us to come and participate. After we got there and they learned of our understanding of the equality of women with men, they limited our participation in the conference. But people were asking for our ministry so they did allow us to have a workshop session, which was packed. GOD is faithful!

July 2: GOD is speaking to me about traveling less - concentrate on writing, Christian Leadership University, and people coming to us. Over the next months GOD brought many to visit us.

July 10-11: Painting outside of addition with Wendell Barnett. Jo and I did the trim.

July 13: Gutters installed, worked on drain lines.

Sunday, July 16: Good gathering at Yankus' - brunch and worship - about 30 people.

July 17: To the Coast with Beth and kids - "one of the funnest days of my life!"

July 22: Deliverance and inner-healing session with Lee Thompson.

July 25: Hiked to Marion Lake with Beth and kids.

July 27: Lyle did final sheetrock taping in the garage.
August 3: Wendell painted the garage interior.
Aug. 8: City gave us a six-month extension to finishing the house.

Aug. 11-13: Three-day gathering at Hewitt's farm - about 50 participated.

August 12: To Vancouver, WA, to marry Andy McCormick and Diana.

Aug. 17: Bob O'Connor's funeral.

Friday, Aug. 18: Steve Seabury came to visit - we had a group of 10 who gathered to meet him.

Aug. 20-23: Visit from Bob and Arlene Hughes.

Aug. 24: Rock garden built with rocks from excavating for our home.

Aug. 29 - Sept. 12: Visit from Mom and Dave. We did a lot of sightseeing - State Fair, Newport, Mount Hood, Northern Oregon Coast, and Mt. St. Helens. It was a wonderful time. But they had some airplane connection problems going home and never came out again!

September 7: 60th birthday - bought myself a CD player.

Sept. 13-17: Jo and I spent five days at the Coast celebrating our wedding anniversary. We stayed in a trailer at Seal Rock.

Sept. 22-25: A visit from Gary and Caren Linden - they met with our Sunday group. We met with Alger's group in the evening. Word from Gloria to me, "GOD is not through with you - you are to father many!" Word from Kathy Mason - "You are an apostle - to father fathers."

Sat., Sept. 25: Jo and I went to the Hood River area to glean apples and pears from the ground.

CHAPTER 17
CHRISTIAN LEADERSHIP UNIVERSITY
AND WRITING

(Christian Leadership University, started biography,
home finished and paid for, trip to Israel,
started on Dad's books, hand accident, US travels)
(1995 - 1997)

1995 (Continued)

In September we were given an opportunity to become part of Christian Leadership University, founded by Mark and Patty Virkler, preparing courses based on our writings. In late 1995 and January of 1996 I was busy preparing ten courses including Joanne's *God's Release of Women* and my nine - *Foundational Studies About the Christian Faith, New Testament Survey, How to Study the Bible, Personal Evangelism, Qualities GOD is Looking For in Us, What GOD is Saying to the Church Today, Getting to Know GOD, House Church,* and *Leadership-Servanthood in the Church.* This has been a wonderful ministry with the mentoring being done over the internet. By 2013 we have had 150 students on every continent except South America.

September 30 - October 2: Diana Blanchard and her children visited us. Diana was a student at Willamette University, attended New Life Fellowship when we were pastoring there, and became like a daughter to us.

October 3-4: Don Hawkinson visited us. Don and Ruthie are our closest friends from YWAM Kona days.

Friday, Oct. 6: Time with Tom Baker - he stopped by about once a month when in town on his vitamin business. We had great times of fellowship.

Sunday, Oct. 15:   More than 40 at house church gathering from 10 to 3.

October 16:   A visit from Georgia Penniman, which brought closure on the 5-Day Prayer ministry.   Georgia had been in our YWAM School of Evangelism and part of the 5-Day Prayer team.

This month - I wrote a *Workbook* for Jo's book on woman.

October 23:   Put in the attic stairs.   November 2-3:   John McCormick used a dozer to grade our yard.

This week: Sent 20 *God's Simple Plan* to Bob Fitts' overseas contacts in Papua New Guinea, the Philippines, the Solomon Islands, and six nations in Africa at his request.

Oct. and Nov.:   Made several trips to Lebanon to help re-modeling work at Meg and Ruby's home.   They were house church people.

Thursday, December 7:   We started a Bible study group - 10 people - studied 1 Peter.

December 22 Je: "How blessed we are to be part of a group of believers that:
1   Doesn't want buildings.
2   Doesn't want a one-man leadership.
3   Doesn't want a structured meeting.
4   Does want GOD's will - deep commitment.
5   Holy Spirit guidance.
6   True Spirit-led worship."

December 24 Je: "Am sensing that CLU is a major part of our future, encouraging the next generation, multiplying what GOD has taught us. It will also provide some income."

During 1995, we got involved in using and selling Melaleuca products through John Lindell. Joanne is also involved in selling JewelWay.

This year: GOD spoke "give no thought" (Matthew 6:31-32) regarding our finances to Joanne and me within a few weeks of each other. So we are attempting to fully trust GOD to provide our every need and not give any anxious thought regarding our finances.

This year we saw Hubert Mitchell, Bob O'Connor, and Hans Schnabel all go to be with the Lord. Hubert was one of my mentors when we lived in Wheaton and Chicago. He had been Youth for Christ's first overseas representative, to India, then Sumatra. His wife died in Sumatra, World War 2 had begun, and Hubert returned to the states. His sister was also a missionary in India, working with Rachel, a lady from Norway. In time Hubert and Rachel began corresponding and were engaged before they saw each other. They both have been such an example and blessing to us.

We knew Bob and Genevieve O'Connor in YWAM in Hawaii and Oregon. Bob was a precious brother in the Lord.

We attended Hans' funeral on October 21 in Portland. He died quite unexpectedly. I often got together with him whenever I was in Portland. We had good times of fellowship although he was quite confrontational.

This year I started this biography. I also started slowing down and traveling less.

1996

January 1: McCormicks stayed overnight.
I got eleven boxes of firewood from scraps at various construction job sites today.

I saw Mao Nguyen and prayed with him. Mao was a refugee from Viet Nam. I saw him several other times in the coming weeks.

January 14: Performed Mat McCormick and Melina's wedding. (They later divorced.)

To Vancouver: Saw Maders and Andy and Diana McCormick.

Sunday, January 28: Released from the northern house church group to concentrate in South Salem area.

Sunday, February 4: Everything was frozen - couldn't go anywhere. Bachrans came up for waffles and worship - Jamie led the Lord's Supper - Daniel passed the bread and juice. What a precious time it was!

Monday, February 5: Surprise birthday party for Jo on her 60th birthday.

February 8: Willamette River - flood of the century. We went to the Coast for two days free for seeing a sweeper demonstration. Saw Keiko the whale at the aquarium - awesome!

Sunday, February 11: New house church group started - 17 - Ken Bentz, John and Betty McCormick, Stan and Maria Pierce, Bob Iddings, Sterling and Pat Borbe, Joan Kerns, us, etc. - great time! As group solidified we met some at our place, some at Bentz's, and some at Joan's.

Feb. 12: Jeff Snyder poured our concrete driveway and sidewalks.

Feb. 14: GOD said that we were to prepare for hard times and also make the property like the Garden of Eden as much as possible. So we started an orchard - planted apple and pear trees.

238

In the coming weeks, we planted roses, figs, lilacs, rhubarb, grapes, and blueberries. And when all of the planting was finished over several years we had figs, grapes, blueberries, huckleberries, yellow plum, Brooks plum, sweet light and dark cherries, strawberries, Marionberries, raspberries, honeyberries, gooseberries, Braeburn and Fuji apples, and four varieties of pears.

February 15: Started building our front porch with John McCormick.

Feb. 19: Joanne and I started going to Vancouver to meet weekly for Bible study with Andy and Diana McCormick.

Feb. 28: March 1 - Josh Bentz dug the trench and I put in water and electric lines to the garden area. It was quite muddy, Josh's back hoe kept sliding, until we had prayer, then all went well!

March 7 Je: "I am too old to travel much - I need to write and disciple the next generation."

March 13: Final inspection on our house - we passed - PTL!
March 18: I designed and started building our back deck.

The Tuesday evening Bible study continues to go well - during the year we studied 1 Peter, 2 Peter, Jude, and 1 Thessalonians - participants included Mike and Janet Long, Joan Kerns, Al and Charlene Knoch, Melveena Hawks, Jerry Gorman, and us.

April: I raked our new yard and planted grass seed.

I had my first CLU student - Jaime Lenuso from New Windsor, NY. She took the *New Testament Survey* course.

Solid Rock Books closed down so we moved the supply of *God's Simple Plan* from Woodburn to our garage.

Closed on new GE Capital loan at 7 3/8 per cent.

May: Maders came for lunch and gave us $1,000 – they didn't know it but we had gotten behind on some of our bills and $1,000 was exactly what we needed! They also told us that they hope to pay off our home mortgage by December!

Monday, June 3: Beth and kids went with us to see the Iris fields north of Keizer and have a picnic.

June 4: Decision by Bible study group to do study and write a book on the Attributes of GOD.

Monday, June 10: To Portland for the day. We saw the Navy ships leave that were here for the Rose Festival and we saw Carol Preston.

I built shutters for the house as Jo desired.

June 21-30: Trip to Southern Oregon and Northern California - stops at Ahlers at Coos Bay, redwoods, Lindens and others, San Francisco, Lou and Sandy Thorpe, Niki Pickthorn, Charlene Malouf, Bob and Arlene Hughes, Don and Beverly Deadmond, and McVickers.

July 11: Day of Prayer - Micah 7:11-12 - we cannot travel as much but people will come to us.

July 7-13: House finished and ready for Gerry's visit.

July 14-26: Gerry and Wenda and gang arrived on Sunday p.m. for a visit. We did a lot of sightseeing - seeing Keiko at the Newport Aquarium, Cape Kiwanda beach at Pacific City, and Mt. St. Helens. With Beth and her tribe living so close the cousins had a lot of fun together. One of the highlights was praying over each grandchild. We also had professional photos taken of the family.

240

July 27: Don and Ruthie Hawkinson arrive for a visit.

July 28: August 3 - $1,400 provided for trip to Israel.

Sunday, August 4: Wonderful house church gathering - 8 people - 9:30-1:30.

Monday, August 5: Hosea 1:10 - "GOD again promising that my book (*GSP*) and other writings will touch people around the world - thousands of house churches all over the world - if I stay hidden, humble, broken." Hosea 2:18 - "I am to have some years of peace."

Aug. 7 Je: "Hosea 6:1-3 - 'Then shall you know if you follow on to know the Lord' - I should spend the rest of my life knowing Him."

Aug. 10: Clayton and Lois Moon, Joanne's cousin, stopped by for a visit.

Sunday, August 11: Great gathering - fifteen, including Tom and Teri Baker from Everett, WA - at Joan Kern's new manufactured home.

Sunday, August 18: Great time at Brian Hewitt's - about thirty including George Bolduc, a missionary to the Caribbean, whom we knew from Wheaton days when he was part of the house church that met in our living room. (He went home to be with the Lord in February 2013.)

Aug. 20-23: Vacation time with Jo at a house on the Coast at Yachats, OR.

Aug. 25-31: Good Sunday gathering - eighteen people. The Bible study on GOD is also going well - Gerry Gorman and Melvena Hanks are to coordinate the writing project. More than $400 came in for the Israel trip.

241

September 4: I am leaving for 6 1/2 weeks - Gerry's, Israel, Ohio, and Indiana. Jo was not part of this trip.

Sept. 6 Je: "My whole life has been centered around obeying GOD - vision, projects. Now GOD is calling me to concentrate more on people - relationships, enjoying people. I can't do it! But He can! 'Oh, GOD, help me!'"

Sept. 7 (61st birthday) Je: "My days of travel are over. Spend my last years - in prayer, writing, being a resource, being a blessing to my wife and those around me, 'be' instead of 'do.' "

Sept. 10: I am not feeling well, but believe that I am to go to Israel anyway. Flight from Newark to Israel - Boeing 747-400, the largest, holds 480 people, 700 mph, 37,000 feet altitude, minus 70 degrees temperature outside. Jews everywhere! Beautiful view of Alps, Italy, Greece, and Turkey.

Am now in Israel. Went to the House of Prayer to see Carol Preston. Went to the Guest House managed by Bob and Emyle Rabe from Burlington, WA, and had dinner with them and stayed there two nights.

Sept. 11-12: Sightseeing on my own in Jerusalem - what fun!

Sept. 13-22: Attended the Prayer Conference organized by Tom Hess. I was sick some of the time and was ministered to by my roommate, Choul, a Black refugee from Southern Sudan - what a humble servant he was!

Monday, Sept. 16: Derek Prince was at the Prayer Conference - and remembered me! - what a blessing. Things he shared - John 4:34 - Many Christian workers have good beginnings, few have good endings. Fasting is very important - one day per week.

I was able to give a *God's Simple Plan* to key leaders - one to Europe (Belgium), two to Asia (India and North Korea), one to Africa (Sudan), and one to a worker who goes into Morocco. Also a *Church Triumphant* to Seychelle Islands in the Indian Ocean. I was also able to share publicly at one of the sessions that GOD was raising up a new wineskin, but few were able to receive it.

Je: "The conference was a wonderful time of repentance, reconciliation, and prayer. But there is a lot of the old wineskin: control, all flowing from the top down, leaders having to be up front, only leaders pray (with a few exceptions), not really trusting the Holy Spirit." I left a few days before the conference was over due to lack of funds to pay for additional days and in order to have some time alone in Israel.

Monday, September 23: The Jewish Day of Atonement. I am staying back at the guest house with the Rabes, am spending the morning in prayer, and reading *Jeremiah*. Went to the Old City in the afternoon and to a CMA Messianic service in the evening.

Tuesday, September 24: To the Garden Tomb, Gethsemane, and the Via Delarosa. Arabs also mugged me for money while walking from the Temple area to the Mt. of Olives.

Wednesday, September 25: To Bethlehem in the morning and on to Tel Aviv in the afternoon where I stayed with a couple from Ghana.

Thursday, September 26: Visited Ben-Gurion's home in Tel Aviv - saw his marked-up New Testament (that might have been given to him by Nate Scharff). I providentially met a house church couple from Perth, Australia, while there. In the afternoon I went to the Mediterranean seashore. Then to Joppa - saw where Jonah sailed from, and the home of Simon the Tanner (Acts 10:6-8).

One evening in Tel Aviv I went to a little prayer meeting. A lady from Europe whom I had never met slipped me some money (I was almost broke). GOD is so faithful!

Friday, September 27: Flew to New York and on to Detroit, then drove to Fostoria.

Sept. 29 Je: "Jeremiah 13:16 - 'You hope for light, but GOD is sending darkness.' - Clinton to be re-elected."

In Fostoria: Saw Dad, who was now at a retirement center; had dinner with Skip and Jan Dunfee. Next day - breakfast with Kirians (gave them *The Way to GOD* booklet). In the afternoon I took Dave on errands, saw Gary McPherson and his niece, Diane, who was visiting and is a believer; also Norman Gibat; spent the evening with Bill Ramsey.

Thursday, October 3: Stopped at Stanley Tam's factory to see him; spent two hours with Mase Bailey in Lima; called Marion Noll; got settled with Dave and Linda Castro in Northern Indiana.

Friday - Sunday: House Church Conference in Northern Indiana. I stayed with Castros. The conference was very good and being with Dave and Linda was a great blessing. Dave was my best man at our wedding. Whenever I saw him I told him that he was still "my best man." (He has since gone to be with the Lord.)

Saturday, October 5: A word I had for the conference - "I want to exhort you that we each will see GOD's fruit in the greatest quality and quantity if we will concentrate on walking in humility, being broken, dying to self, walking in mutual submission with others, being hidden, being weak."

Sunday, October 6: Drove to Marion, IN, stayed with Bill and Evelyn Allen and watched the presidential debate on TV with them.

Monday, October 7: Lunch with Ben Medows; saw past neighbors - Carters, Bunches, and Haleys in the afternoon; Jack and Winnie in the evening.

Tuesday, October 8: Saw Milford Adams in the morning; Wayne Pence and Kyle and Doris Smith in the afternoon; Mayer and Mabel David and Maurice and Madeline Andrea for dinner; Glen and Betty Martin in the evening.

Wednesday, October 9: In the morning I went by our past home at 4001 S. Boots; saw Rob and Donna Oatis, Ginger Rittenhouse. Traveled to Fostoria in the afternoon. Watched the vice presidential debate on TV with Mom and Dave in the evening.

Thursday, October 10: Took Mom shopping in the morning, rested and read in the afternoon, saw Dad with Mom and Dave in the evening.

Friday, October 11: Drove to Lake Erie and saw Roy Swartz and Chuck and Carol Bixler.

Saturday, October 12: Rested, saw Jim Tucker, a friend and school classmate since the fifth grade.

Sunday, October 13: Attended Nazarene Church with Mom and Dave in the a.m. Saw Norman Gibat and Norm and Shirley Kniesley in the afternoon; Nancy Slaymaker in the evening - gave *Way to GOD* to all.

Monday, October 14: To Upper Sandusky to see Loren and Lois, Bob and Annie and Dick, and Dan and Barb at Loren's home. In the evening got word of Joanne Moser's home going - she and George lived in Eastern Ohio - she was a bold witness for Jesus for many years and used our Bible study materials to disciple people.

Tuesday, October 15: Bible reading and prayer with Mom and Dave in the morning. Afternoon - met with Clarence Pennington and George Gray to discuss putting Dad's writings into book form. Evening - went to a Gideon's dinner with George Gray.

Wednesday, October 16: Had breakfast with the Nazarene pastor in the morning. Went to town and met with George Gray, Mel Murray, and Dave to discuss the book. Evening - reported on Israel prayer conference at the Nazarene church; watched the last presidential debate.

Thursday, October 17 - Breakfast with Jimmy Johnson, a high school classmate who had become a Jehovah's Witness. Also saw Ray Dell and phoned Norman Gibat. In the afternoon Ron Griffin, a high school classmate, took me to Detroit. Went to a prayer meeting in the evening.

Friday, October 18: Time with Dave Grice in the morning; time with Ernestine Stewart and Michael Sumpter in the afternoon; flew home in the evening.

Saturday, October 19 Je: "What a wonderful six and one-half week trip - to New Jersey, Israel, Michigan, Ohio, and Indiana. GOD led, provided, and opened doors, blessed - daily. 'Thank you, Lord Jesus, for the privilege of knowing You!' "

Sunday, October 20: Home church group met at Bentz's home - seven of us - good time.

Monday, October 21: Started on the book(s) of Dad's writings about Fostoria, Ohio.

Tuesday, October 22: Kelly's 10th birthday.

Wednesday, October 23: Shared Israel trip with Bible study group.

Rest of week: Worked on Dad's book.

Sunday, October 27: Good home church meeting at Joan Kern's - ten of us.

Wednesday, October 30: Good Bible study - working on book on GOD's attributes.

November 8-18: Trip to WA state - time with Maders, Andersons, Sleepers, 3-day prayer retreat, Debi McPherson, Bob Penton, Dave Woodrum, Darwin and Ann Newton, Rosemary Lambert, Kathleen McConnell, Rod and Ayako Billups, Tom Isenhart, Dr. Rody, Doug and Joyce Marsden and Ray and Lynn in Kent, Tom Baker, others. Met with various home church groups and other gatherings.

November 22: First meeting of a new group we are calling Advisors, who will give oversight to our lives and work. This group included Greg and Beth Bachran, Jay and Carleen Ferris, Robert and Joni Fitts, Bob Lund, Alger and Gloria Marsh, and Frank Smith. Later Arne Jensen, Gerry and Wenda Krupp, and Dave and Janice Woodrum were added.

Nov. 28: Thanksgiving with Bachrans.

Sunday, December 25: Family Christmas with Bachrans.

November and December: Continued work on Dad's book; good Sunday home church meetings; good Bible study meetings working on GOD's attributes book; time with people, etc.

1997

January 2 Je: "Jeremiah 35 - Joanne and I have obeyed GOD for 35 years - and GOD is blessing us - brought us to the beautiful Willamette Valley, to the city of peace; given us a lovely home, yard, garden; is giving us friends; and a worldwide ministry, 'a mother of nations' and 'all families of the earth to be blessed'! What a GOD! And our children are serving the Lord - and our grandchildren and their descendants are to serve the Lord - Jeremiah 35:19."

January 3-4: Trip to Portland/Vancouver - Saw Alger Marsh, Steve Seabury, John and Betty McCormick, Jerry Thurston, Maders, Hampes, Lee Thompson, and Ron Rohman - and called Dan Mayhew.

Jan. 20: Tony and Kathy Mader handed us a check for $64,000 to pay off our home mortgage. What a miracle!!

February 8: Mike Wenger came by for one of his occasional fellowship visits.

Feb. 18: Met for five years for a weekly Bible study with Al and Charleen Knoch, Michael and Janet Long, Joan Kerns, Jerry Gorman, and Melveena Horst. The first year we studied a number of shorter books of the New Testament. The next two years we wrote *Getting to Know GOD*. The next two years we wrote *Qualities GOD is Looking for in Us*. These were wonderful years of fellowship, Bible study, and prayer. And Jerry and Melveena met, courted, and got married!

Feb. 19: I did a study on "rebellion" for Joanne Bachran. I discovered that the Bible does not talk about rebellion in relation to spiritual leaders, as is often mentioned in today's church world - it talks only about rebellion against GOD.

248

This week I started a 40-day period of being quiet before GOD, with some fasting. These were also weeks that I was helping Joanne with some final editing on her book. There was also a very good Sunday group that met from house to house. These were also months when I was planting fruit trees and enlarging our garden area.

Sunday, March 9: About fifty home church folks gathered together at Rob and Jean Moule's - we did this every so often - they were always wonderful times.

Tuesday, March 11: I had a saw accident - a piece of wood slipped that I was cutting and a Skil saw took a hunk out of my left hand. Joanne rushed me to the emergency room - they did temporary surgery that day and the final, permanent, 3 1/2-hour repair work the next. On Tuesday night Joanne stayed with me all night at the hospital at my request - what a wonderful wife!

I was back in the hospital, in ICU, the next week with a blood clot that had moved to my right lung. We found out that a group was at Brian and Johanna Hewitt's home praying that Tuesday evening. GOD showed Johanna in a vision that the death angel had come to get me, but the group through prayer pushed him back! Those who came to see me in the hospital included Mike Wenger, Meg and Ruby from Lebanon, Alger Marsh, Wendell Barnett, Brian Hewitt, Dan Mayhew, Melveena, Ken Bentz, Joan Kerns, and Al Knoch came by every day - bless his heart! This surgery was followed by weeks of therapy and the blood clot was followed by months of blood thinner.

April 10: I met with "the renewal pastors" at their regular prayer time. GOD gave me "a word" for them, that there was more "new wine" and "new wineskins" to come. The word came with great anointing. The word was received by one or two but rejected by most. Two pastors later called me a false prophet from their pulpits.

249

John Carney later told me that many of these pastors had decided a few weeks before I brought the word that they were not open to prophets. GOD help us! (I believe that the word did come to pass.)

April 16-19: We sponsored three days of fasting and prayer. We met at the Christian Church campgrounds in Turner - about 35 people came - it was a wonderful time. During one session we read out loud through the entire book of *Revelation* - and then went to prayer - it was a powerful time! The retreat included praying at the state Capitol on Friday

June 2 Je: "Jamie's 8th grade graduation - she is such a delight!"

Sunday, June 8: About 60 from various home church groups gathered from 10 a.m. to 5 p.m. at the Grange Hall west of Salem - it was a wonderful time!

June 10 - July 13: Trip to California, Mexico, Arizona - Joanne and me -
Tuesday, June 10: Drove down I-5, stayed with Bob and Arlene Hughes.
Wednesday, June 11: To Southern California - stayed with Mike and Juanita, Glenn Wilcox's sister.
Thursday, June 12: Went with Tim Munyer, Vic and Ina's son, to their gravesite - Vic had been part of LEI and was like a father to me; on to Rachel's in San Diego.

Friday, June 13: Met with Petersons and Seong. Seong was from Korea, but is a missionary to Israel - we met at the Prayer Conference there - he has a house church understanding and is part of our team going to Mexico. On to Ensenada, Mexico, with a team of Petersons, Seong, and us, with Ted and Renie Faver, missionaries to Mexico.
Saturday, June 14: Wonderful time of teaching, dialogue, and fellowship - 18 adults - quite an international group - English, Spanish, Korean, Hebrew, and Indian.

250

Sunday, June 15 - Traditional service at Faver's. Afternoon - baptisms in the ocean by Ted. Evening - captain's tour of Logos 2.

Monday, June 16: In San Diego - with Hal and Claudia Ward; and Rachel Newhall, Joanne's niece.

Tuesday, June 17: Not feeling too well - rested. "I hope this is the last trip like this." Evening with Jerry and Phyllis Mason.

Wednesday, June 18: Time with Frank Smith and Barry Steinman.

Thursday, June 19: "My ministry is to be behind the scenes, releasing others." To San Bernadino - Afternoon - With Darla Ritchey, my cousin, and her husband, Lowell. Evening - With Stanley Swartz, my cousin and Darla's half-brother, and his wife, Jan. Darla was the daughter of Ernest Eckert, who was killed in an aircraft training accident during World War 2. His wife, Lucille, later married Roy Swartz, and they had three boys, Stanley being the oldest. We stayed with Darla.

Friday, June 20: Afternoon with Uncle Orville and Aunt Ethis. Evening with Uncle Warren and Aunt R'Vene. These were Joanne's uncles, brothers of her father, Harold Sheets.

Saturday, June 21: 9 a.m. to 4:30 p.m. - A gathering of about 40 house church people, mostly leaders.

Sunday, June 22: Evening gathering of about 25 at Caruso's home.

Monday, June 23: Traveled to Phoenix - stayed with Lance and Holly Craw.

Tuesday, June 24: With Don and Merrily Hardy in the morning; Nesbitts in the afternoon; and met at Peter and Eve Englebrite's home with 12 house church leaders, of a network of three groups, in the evening.

Wednesday, June 25: An extended lunchtime with Bill and Barbara Mallen and the Hardys; with a group of 12 at Craw's in the evening.

251

Thursday, June 26: Had an extended lunchtime with Nate and Betty Scharff - Nate was the man who led me to the Lord. He and Mary had divorced (tragically) and he married Betty, a believing medical doctor he had met in Israel. It was so good to be with my dear father in the Lord - this was our last time together before he went to Glory.

In the evening we spent time with Phil Hughes, Joanne's nephew, and his new wife, Jandy. We left with a heavy heart - Phil once walked with the Lord, but not now.

Friday, June 27: Breakfast with Lance Craw and his friend, Jim Evans. Time with Lance, Holly, and their daughter, Naomi. Time with Dave Bradshaw. Trip to Safford, in Eastern Arizona to be with Bill and Pat Parker.

Saturday, June 28: A day to rest and prepare for Sunday. We saw some beautiful birds out Parker's patio door, birds I had never seen before. I noted this in my bird book, which I always took with me on trips. In the evening their pastor and another brother joined all of us for dinner.

Sunday, June 29 - In the morning I spoke on the five things that I believe will characterize the end-time Church - revival, restoration, unity, world evangelization, and end-time persecution - to about 120 people at the church Parkers are part of. The evening was an open, Body meeting of about thirty, which I introduced and facilitated. The time in Safford also included meeting a Jewish family with the last name of Krupp!

Monday, June 30: In the morning we made some stops in Safford; in the afternoon we visited historic Tombstone, AZ; and spent the evening with Carl and Anna Jackson in Tucson.

Tuesday, July 1: We traveled north from Tucson to Lake Montezuma for an evening meeting with a group of about 25 arranged by Bob Girard. Bob was the author of *Brethren, Hang Loose*, one of the first books written about a new church paradigm. Bob was pastoring a Wesleyan Methodist church in Phoenix when GOD began to show him new things. They formed into several house churches and gave the building back to the denomination! We kept in touch with Bob for a number of years - he was a great encouragement and a dear friend. He and Audrey are now both home with the Lord.

Wednesday, July 2: We drove to the Grand Canyon - what an awesome sight! In the evening we arrived at Joyce and Cody Cull's in Las Vegas. They were dear friends from Marion, Indiana, days.

Thursday, July 3; A day of rest and fellowship with Culls, including their daughters Sara and Amy.

Friday, July 4: We went with Joyce and Cody to the Las Vegas strip. At Caesar's Palace there was a production that said, "Caesar is Lord," - something in me rose up and I shouted out, "Jesus is Lord!"

In the evening we all had a picnic at Culls and watched 4th of July fireworks in the distance.

Saturday, July 5: We traveled to the Carson City area.

Sunday, July 6: Sightseeing at Virginia City. (We never took many vacations or did much sightseeing, except in connection with our ministry travels, but the travels took us all over the world, so we did visit some very wonderful and unusual places.)

Monday thru Sunday, July 7-13: We spent time with a number of people in various places in Northern California - Rick and Rockly Harris at El Dorado Hills, Cheryl Moore, Mark and Michele Beer, Brother Ma at Santa Cruz, Johnson and Wall at Scotts Valley, a group in San Francisco, and with folks in Nevada City. The most significant time was with a college friend, Spencer Harris, who prayed a prayer of "start" with Jesus.

253

On Sunday, July 13, we headed for our home in Oregon. We were both quite tired and ready to get home, but it had been a significant trip of encouraging house church groups and seeing other contacts in California, Mexico, Arizona, and Nevada. We had been gone 34 days, traveled about 5,000 miles, slept in 19 beds, and spent time with 16 house church groups - we praise the Lord for His faithful leading.

Monday, July 21: Went to the Coast with Beth and her three - what fun we had playing in the sand and water with our grandchildren.

Wednesday, July 23: Greg baptized Daniel in their outdoor, portable swimming pool. We are SO thankful that our six grandchildren are all following Jesus.

Sunday, July 27: Good time with Honans and Pierces.

July 31 - August 3: Spent time relaxing at Black Butte at Ken and Janet Bentz's vacation home.

Friday, August 22: A wonderful day at the Oregon State Fair with Kelly and Dan, our grandchildren. Going to the State Fair became an annual event for me, sometimes with the grandchildren, sometimes with Jo, and sometimes alone. I enjoy so much the animals, the produce displays from every county, and all of the new merchandise at booths. What a joy to live here at the state Capitol.

Sunday, August 24: Home church group at Beth's - 24 people.

August 29 - September 1: Ernestine Stewart and Michael Sumpter came from Detroit, MI, to visit us. We had a wonderful time of fellowship and sightseeing on the Mt. Hood loop and at the Coast. Ernestine was a convert to Jesus and a friend since Chicago days and Michael was her friend. On Sunday they went with us to a home church meeting of more than 30 at Wenger's home.

Sunday, September 7: My 62nd birthday - spent the day at Cape Kiwanda on the Coast with Bachrans, Honans, Michael Long, and Joan Kerns.

Thursday, September 11: Final release by Dr. Austin after my hand accident and therapy.

Tuesday, September 16: Our 36th wedding anniversary. How I thank GOD for my wife! We celebrated on Monday - shopping in Portland and dinner at Red Lobster.

Sunday evening, September 21: About 25 at our place - sharing, worship, Lord's Supper - really good!
Wednesday, October 1: Time with Alger Marsh and Dan Mayhew, house church leaders in Portland. We got together about once a month. Sometimes Wendell Barnett and Brian Hewitt joined us. These were good times of fellowship and prayer.

October 3 - 11: Traveling with Bob Fitts. Bob arrived by plane on Friday morning. Friday evening we met with a group in Portland. Saturday was a group at our home in the morning and about 40 at Rob and Jean Moule's in the evening. Sunday afternoon and evening was a gathering of about 25 at Pruitt's near Albany.

Monday we drove to British Columbia, Canada, and had a meeting with folks in Surrey. We stayed overnight with Dave Gemmell in Pitt Meadows. He had been a pastor of a traditional church. He and others left that situation and began meeting in several homes. Then they were led to stop all scheduled meetings and gather only out of relationship as the Holy Spirit led. We spent some extended time with Dave the next morning. Some of the things he shared included:
When you give up your turf, the whole turf will become yours.
Quit doing anything for GOD - cease from our own works, to see His works.
We are not to follow a pattern - we are to follow a Person.

Tuesday evening we met with about 15 in Ferndale, Washington.

Wednesday we saw Jim Keenan in the morning, had lunch with John and Lee Bermingham, and met with Dick Burke and a Bible study group of thirteen in the evening.

Thursday morning with Joe McIntyre, afternoon with Hylan and Rita, and a meeting with 25 to 30 at Brimhall's in the evening.

Friday we traveled by ferry to Anderson Island and met with Andersons and Wonderlys, who are doing home church together.

Saturday we went back to the mainland and had morning time with John Cook and Steve and Linda Mercer; lunch with Dave and Janice Woodrum. Then a brief stop with John and Betty McCormick in Vancouver, Washington, and home to Salem. It was wonderful traveling and ministering with Bob.

November 7-30: Trip to Midwest and East - Jo and me
Friday: Flew to Detroit.

Saturday: With a home church group in Warren, Michigan.

Sunday: Joanne and I were doing draperies for Ernestine - she did the sewing and I did the hardware.

Monday: More drapery work in the day; dinner with Michael Sumpter, his sister Shirley, Ernestine, and Joanne and me.

Tuesday: More drapery work in the day; evening with Bob and Betty Siefert. Bob was the one who got me involved in student government at Purdue - he influenced me to run for sophomore class president when he ran for student body president.

Wednesday was a day of rest and with the Lord.

Thursday: Michael let us use his Lexus for our upcoming travel! Thursday morning we were with Dale Cryderman and Bob Marsten in Spring Arbor, Michigan. They were both important relationships from our LEI days. Dale was district superintendent in the Free Methodist Church in Michigan and opened many doors for us. Bob was the chairman of the very fruitful citywide Lay Evangelism Crusade that we had in Battle Creek, Michigan.

Thursday afternoon we spent time with Chris and Lori Kirk, house church leaders in Sturgis, Michigan, and Northern Indiana. Thursday evening and night we were with Joanne's sister, Evelyn, and husband, Bill, in Marion, Indiana.

Friday I drove to Indianapolis and saw Don Laker, a friend from Purdue days - had a great time witnessing to him - he and his wife are good Methodists, but don't seem to know the Lord. Friday evening was back in Marion with Marvin and Hazel Hinds.

Saturday morning we were with Kyle and Doris Smith, who have supported our work for years. In the afternoon we were with Glen and Betty Martin, friends since we lived in Wheaton - Glen is head of the History and Political Science Department at Marion College (now Indiana Wesleyan University) and a teacher in YWAM schools all over the world. We spent the evening with Bill and Evelyn.

On Sunday, November 16, we drove to Fostoria to see my mother and my brother, Dave, who lives with her. (Dad was 92 and in a rest home in the late stages of Alzheimer's.) Had Sunday dinner with them, rested in the afternoon, and spent the evening with them.

Monday I had lunch with Bill Ramsey and Gary McPherson. Gary is my cousin and Bill is a long-time friend and strong believer.

Tuesday morning I met with some key men in Fostoria to discuss putting my Dad's weekly newspaper column on Fostoria history into book form. Joanne and I had lunch with my cousin Nancy.

Wednesday we took Mom and Dave shopping at Findlay and had lunch at Red Lobster - they seemed to really enjoy it. In the afternoon I spent time with high school classmates, Bob and Marilyn Hauser. In the evening more time with Nancy.

Thursday morning we traveled to Upper Sandusky to have breakfast with Loren and Lois Dillon and Barb and Dan Reed. Loren and Barb are my cousins, children of my Dad's sister, Ruth.

In the late afternoon we saw Helen Widener and her friend Mac in Lancaster, Ohio - Helen is a distant cousin.

We spent the evening and overnight with Gary and Beth Miltenberger in Morgantown, West Virginia. Gary had been our shipping clerk when we had the LEI office in Marion, Indiana, and they have supported us for years.

On Friday we traveled to Shippensburg, Pennsylvania, to meet with Don Nori of Destiny Image Publishers - they had published my book, *The Church Triumphant at the End of the Age* - and were considering doing Joanne's book on women.

We traveled on to Glassboro, New Jersey, to be with our son, Gerry, and his family, arriving in time for dinner. We were with them for a week - rest, fellowship, Thanksgiving, a day in New York City - a wonderful time.

On Saturday we drove to Eastern Ohio and saw Paul and Dorothy Smith, associates from LEI days.

On Sunday, November 30, we drove to Detroit, saw Gar and Rachel Darnes, returned the Lexus to Michael Sumpter, and flew home to Oregon.

We had traveled more than 2,100 miles by auto from Michigan to Indiana, Ohio, Pennsylvania, New Jersey, and back to Detroit.

December was spent getting caught up in the office, seeing many people, having Bible study and home church meetings, and having year-end and Christmas festivities with family and friends.

For many months GOD had been speaking that the coming years were to be those of less travel, more writing, and beginning to slow down (age 62).

CHAPTER 18
PUBLISHING, TO AFRICA

(Team to Ghana, Africa; Dad's books,
Preparing the Way Publishers, U.S. travels)

(1998 - 1999)

1998

January 9-12: Joanne and me - trip to Washington State:
Friday: Sightseeing in Tacoma, lunch with Dave and Janice Woodrum; Dr. Rody, chiropractor; to Marsdens.
Saturday: All-day conference on house church in Seattle sponsored by Fuller Seminary. I was part of the teaching team.
To John and Lee Berminghams. I witnessed to John in 1958 when we were both at Kingsville Naval Air Station in Texas - he was a student pilot and I was a CEC officer. He later came to know the Lord. While in the Navy in Vietnam he met and married Lee who is a dynamic Christian. While giving his testimony at a CMA church in Burlington. WA, he mentioned my name as one who had witnessed to him. Mutual friends, Bob and Emyle Rabe, who heard him mention my name, got us reconnected. We have spent a number of wonderful fellowship visits with them since.
Sunday: Further fellowship with Berminghams.
Monday: An ice and snowstorm blew in - we traveled home at 30 mph - it took 16 hours!

January 17 Je: "Things church leaders need to repent of:
1   Dividing the One Church by:
    a.   the clergy-laity division.
    b.   denominations.
    c.   local churches rather than the church-of-the-city.
    d.   male-female unbiblical teaching.
2   Not allowing the Holy Spirit to move.
3   Control."

January 31, Saturday: A Day of Prayer - 25 people from Salem and Portland.

Week of February 8-14: Joanne went to be with Gerry and his family to help them get settled in their new home in Marion, Indiana, where he is to pastor more than 300 collegiate and young adults at the College Church on the campus of Indiana Wesleyan University. I am building brick columns for the driveway lights as a surprise for her. I had never done brickwork before, but got a book from the library and just followed the directions. The columns turned out quite nicely and Joanne was very pleased.

February: I am reviewing the manuscript of Bob Lund's book *The Way Church Ought to Be*. The Tuesday evening Bible study group has finished writing the study book *Getting to Know GOD* and is now starting *Qualities GOD is Looking for in Us*. On February 28 I started 40 days of prayer, with some fasting.

March: Several couples of us began meeting to pray and plan about a team going to Ghana, Africa. This continued for a number of months.

Also in March I spent time with Wendell Barnett, Ed Montgomery, Don Moser, Bob Lund, Mike Wenger, Maders; Maylon Macy and Hubert Thornberg in Newberg; Webbs, Andy and Melissa.

April 5-10: Began planting our garden - potatoes, garlic, and asparagus.

April 10-12: A number of house church people gathered at Christian Renewal Center for a Resurrection Celebration weekend, from Friday evening through Sunday afternoon. It was a wonderful time of worship, fellowship, and teaching.

April 17: Our neighbor, Dewey France, and I did trenching work for a sprinkler system for our yard.

Sunday, May 3:   Good meeting at Joan Kern's - Honans, Longs, Pierces, Bachrans, Krupps, and Joan.

May 14-17:   We went through the first HeartChange workshop, designed and facilitated by Alger and Gloria Marsh. It was a wonderful, life-changing experience dealing with emotional wounds, blind spots, demonic bondages, etc. My life motto was: "I want to increase in being a person of integrity, humility, purity, and steadfastness who does the will of GOD in childlikeness and teamwork." We began recommending HeartChange to everyone we knew!

June 1 Je: "My calling - the years I have left :
-    become more whole and Christ-like.
-    finish writing projects.
-    be a voice for new wineskins.
-    help Jo be a voice for releasing women.
-    be a blessing to Jo, children, grandchildren, relationships we already have."

June 9:   Had lunch with Dewey and Emma - they are wonderful Christian neighbors - we got together for lunch and prayer a couple times a year.

June 25-29: Trip to Washington State - Jo and me:
Thursday: With Tony Mader in Vancouver, seeing a $10 million home he is building. Lunch with Rod and Ayako Billups in Tacoma, who were friends from YWAM-Kona days. Spent a few minutes at Pike Street Market and the waterfront in Seattle. Had dinner with the Shornicks; spent the evening with them, Keenans, John Lindell, and Bob.

Friday, June 26, we drove across the beautiful North Cascade Highway; saw the Grand Coulee Dam; and spent the evening with Steve and Cindy Seabury in Colville, in northeastern Washington.

July 4: Spent time with others at Brian Hewitt's farm near Rickreall.

Word from Joanne Bachran for me: "Just like the wine at the wedding in Cana, GOD is saving the best for last in your life. You'll go out in a blaze of glory for Him - 1 Thess. 5:24."

July 17 - August 3: Trip to Midwest by myself:
Friday: Trip to Indianapolis.
Saturday: Sealed Gerry's deck.
Sunday: At College Church - saw a number of people we knew from when we had lived in Marion.
Monday: Breakfast with Ben Gray.
Tuesday: A day at Purdue University.
Wednesday: Geoffrey's birthday; time with the Noggles - Howard is 80.
Thursday: Gerry and I had breakfast with Joe Seaborn, pastor of College Church. Trip to Fostoria, Ohio.

Friday evening: 45th High School Class Reunion. "It was good to reconnect with so many, especially believers Roger Ferguson and Richard Rothgeb."
Saturday: Breakfast with Skip and Jan Dunafee, the folks' neighbors. I had the privilege of leading Skip to the Lord some years earlier and always looked forward to seeing him and Jan. In the evening - more class reunion.

Sunday: To Church with Mom and Dave. Dad was at a rest home, in his final year, with Alzheimer's, and is blind. Played checkers later in the day with Dave. It had now become a ritual that whenever I got to Fostoria, Dave and I would play checkers and drink Vernor's ginger ale!

Monday: Breakfast with Bill Ramsey. Later in the day with Norman Gibat, a neighborhood friend when I was growing up on North Countyline Street.
Tuesday: Drove Mom and Dave to Lake Erie.

Wednesday: Met with the Committee for Dad's Book - Mr. Pennington, Norm Gibat, George Gray, and Dave and I - "They seem to have it under control." Evening phone calls - Frank Kirian, Barb Reed, Loren Dillon, Nancy Slaymaker, Michael Sumpter, and Ernestine Stewart.

Thursday: Trip to Detroit - time with Michael Sumpter.
Friday: Phone calls to a number. More time with Michael.
Saturday: To Western Michigan to be with Roger Bulkley.
Sunday: Spoke at Roger's church; lunch with Roger, Sharon, and the girls; to Indiana.
Monday, August 3: With Bill and Evelyn Allen, flight to Oregon. Je: "It was a wonderful time of seeing people - and ministry - and rest - IN, OH, MI. Thank you, Jesus!"

During the time that I was in the Midwest Joanne's two sisters visited her in Salem for five days. They had a ball!

Sunday, August 16: We hosted a retirement party for Stan Pierce in our backyard.

August 21 - September 3: Trip to California and Southern Oregon - Joanne and me:
Friday: Traveled to Redding, CA - stayed with Doug and Kathy Morgan - and their large boa constrictor snake that they kept in a large glass cage!
Saturday and Sunday: A house church conference sponsored by Jack Russell - good teaching by Al Green, Petersons, Doug Morgan, Jonathan Lindvall, Jim Wehde, Alger Marsh, and me. Joanne also had a workshop on the subject of GOD's plan for women. Je: "House church conference was wonderful!"
Monday: Trip around Mt. Lassen - awesome. Time with Harold and Kay Apger - Harold is a distant cousin on my Mom's side.
Tuesday thru Thursday morning with Maders helping them build a home for their son. GOD provided $3,000 for another auto. Dinner Thursday with Beverly, Joanne's cousin.
Friday: With Bob and Arlene Hughes.

Saturday: Afternoon with Tony and Francis; to Antioch with Todd and Ronda Cox.

Sunday: Wonderful gathering in the park with a home church group led by Todd and Ronda Cox and Mike and Sandy Marchio.

Monday: Drove to San Francisco; rode the BART; rode the cable cars; had lunch with Spencer Harris at Fishermen's Wharf; took a boat ride - fun day!

Tuesday: Drove to Al Green's in Chiloquin, in Southern Oregon.

Wednesday: With Greens.

Thursday: To home.

Monday, September 7, my 63rd birthday: Went to the Oregon State Fair, which was an annual event, which I enjoy very much. During that week, GOD provided a 1990 Buick Century for $6,500.

Monday, September 14: We celebrated our 37th Wedding Anniversary (two days early) by going to Portland and getting new wedding rings, which Jo had been wanting to do.

Saturday, September 19: There was a good-sized gathering of about fifty people, put together by Mike Honan, for fellowship and to hear Dean Cozzens and John White from Denver, CO.

Saturday - Monday, September 26-28: A House Church Conference in Portland sponsored by Dan Mayhew, Alger and Gloria Marsh, and us. In spite of some problems that developed during the conference, it was a valuable time.

Monday, October 19: Jo and I went around Mt. Hood - picked up two boxes of pears off the ground. A trip to Mt. Hood area to glean apples and pears became a regular trip about every other year. What a blessing it is to live where there is so much fruit and vegetables.

Sunday, October 25: Ed and Vivian Montgomery started a home church group - 10 people the first time - a good start.

November 6-7: I took a trip to Portland and Vancouver and spent time with Dan Mayhew, Tony Tuck, McCormicks, Lee Thompson, and Rapozas.

November 9: Good African Team planning meeting. Also getting tickets and shots this week.

November 13-16: Trip to Washington - Jo and me:
Friday: Time with Gary and Donna Lawrence from Marion College days.
Saturday: House church conference, hosted by Doug and Joyce Marsden and Ray and Lynn Brimhall - about 50 people from all over Western Washington. Je: "Great time!"
Sunday: Fun day at Seattle waterfront and boat ride to Bremerton; evening with the Woodrums.
Monday: Lunch with Norm and Virginia Westly, from Hilo, HI, days; to home.

December: Good house church leaders' meeting; good December Africa Team meeting; good Bible study group meetings; good Sunday gatherings; Advisors' Annual Report out; Christmas letter out. Also did brick work on the front of the garage; took jelly and cookies to the neighbors;

Greg's birthday party; very cold - broken water line at pump house; Christmas with Bachrans; helped Bob Lund move.

This year we gave a New Zealand publisher permission to republish some of our writings for people in that part of the world.

1999

January 8 Je: "Ezekiel, Chapter 3 - a reminder from GOD - I am a prophet - I am to listen to GOD, then speak - I am not to be concerned whether they hear or not."

January 10: A house church gathering at Christian Renewal Center - 43 people - very good time.

January 17: Good Sunday p.m. home church gathering at our place - Ed Montgomery, Knochs, us.

January 23: Christians for Biblical Equality meeting in Portland - we talked to Catherine Kroeger regarding an endorsement for Joanne's book, which she later sent.

January 24 Je: "Wonderful gathering - 14 people - real life - themes of unity and ministry - prayed over Knochs regarding their trip to California; prayed over us regarding our upcoming trip to Arizona; prayed for Stan Pierce, who is battling cancer."

Tuesday, January 26: Word of Dad's passing. He was 93, born May 8, 1905. Another year and he would have made it to the new Century, 2000. He lived his entire life in Fostoria, Ohio, where he worked at the town newspaper and then at the Fostoria Pressed Steel.
Remembrances of Dad:
-      Dad got me a Lionel electric train one Christmas when I was about four - and he played with it a couple of years until I was old enough!
-      We didn't have much - they bought me a used bike from a neighbor one Christmas.
-      They gave me a Super Flyer sled one Christmas.
-      Gardening together in the summers.
-      He always got excited in the spring when he saw the first robins.
-      Two fishing trips as a family to Northern Michigan.
-      We went together with a Boy Scout group to Philmont Scout Ranch in New Mexico.
-      He was one of the adult leaders of our Boy Scout troop.
-      He took a carload of guys, including me, to a high school basketball game in Bowling Green, Ohio. On the way home we slid on ice and went off the road. Dad was able to control the car and bring us back on the road without stopping.

- He used to straighten old, used nails and reuse them – a result of going through the Great Depression.
- Dad, Dave, and I built a garage for the car at our home on Countyline Street during his two-week vacation one summer. He called me "wheel" and Dave "matie wheel." This was a real highlight.
- To Presbyterian Church together every Sunday as a family. He tried to revitalize the Sunday School by teaching an adult class.
- He helped me do a really nice report for Spanish class. I still have that report!
- Rides together when he took me to or from Purdue.
- He always encouraged Joanne and me in our ministry and helped financially whenever he could.

I had a wonderful Dad!!

January 26-30 - Trip to Arizona: Jo and me:
Tuesday: Travel and good home church gathering at Englebrite's home.
Wednesday: Lunch with Nate and Betty Scharff. Dinner with Craws and Archibalds.
Thursday thru Saturday: I spoke at a House Church Conference sponsored by Fuller Seminary. Joanne had a workshop on GOD's plan for women.
Saturday: We flew to Columbus, Ohio; rented a car; rendezvoused with my sister, Janet, at the airport; and drove to Fostoria.
Sunday, January 31: Dad's viewing at the funeral home - about 100 people came through.
Monday: Dad's funeral and time with family. Gerry and his family came from Marion, IN, for the funeral and Gerry conducted the graveside service.
Tuesday: With family.
Wednesday: Flew home. Beth had a fire built in our stove, bless her heart!

February 7-10: Further preparation for trip to Africa.

269

<u>February 11 - March 3: Trip to Africa - Jo and me and team</u>
Thursday, February 11-12: We were told at the Portland airport that our flight would be delayed for two hours, which meant we would miss connections in Minneapolis and in Amsterdam. We prayed - and ten minutes later the pilot announced we were leaving! (GOD answers prayer!) We had a rough seven-hour flight to Amsterdam. From there to Ghana, on another seven-hour flight, we saw the beautiful Alps, the Mediterranean Sea, the Sahara desert, and a beautiful sunset. We missed connections with Emmanuel Lartey at the Accra (capital of Ghana) airport and spent the night at a lovely Wycliffe Bible translators' guesthouse.

Saturday, February 13: We made connections with Emmanuel and traveled by bus to Kumasi, about 150 miles northwest of Accra. On that trip we saw some of the most primitive living we have ever seen - mud huts and filth everywhere. Our home for the next week was to be in a dorm room at the University of Ghana at Kumasi. This setting was quite primitive, too. It took quite awhile to get our room clean and livable. The students were on vacation, but a few were still there - some of them fixed their meals by building a fire out on the lawn!

Sunday: We both taught on Sunday morning at a new church that Emmanuel was starting.
Monday: A day of rest - and some more of the team arrived - Bob Lund; his daughter, Jessica; Michael Sumpter; our daughter, Beth; and her daughter, Jamie. My Dad had just passed away and we brought a duffle bag full of his clothes with us to Ghana, so we had four generations of Krupps represented in Ghana - Dad, me, Beth, and Jamie!
Tuesday: A day of rest and orientation.
Wednesday: Team planning and prayer in the morning. The Africans cleaned the auditorium in the afternoon and Alger and Gloria Marsh arrived, which completed our team of nine. The evening was more team time with Emmanuel.

270

Thursday, February 18: The New Wine Skins Conference began - about 20-30 Africans were involved. The conference centered on New Testament Church Life - wholeness, evangelism, 1 Cor. 14:26 paradigm, etc. The conference continued through Sunday with 40-50 involved. It was a wonderful time of sharing truth with these African brethren. The only downside was their asking for money and for various possessions that we had.

Monday, February 21: We traveled by bus back to Accra. Joanne was not feeling well.
Tuesday: A day of rest at the beach on the Atlantic Ocean and team debriefing.
Wednesday: Alger and I met with a YWAM leader in a town near Accra.

Thursday, February 25: The Lord told me to go to the president of Ghana's office to give him some books. When arriving, I discovered that he was out of the country, in the United States. But I was able to meet with his assistant, who was a believer, and gave him the books - *Woman, Church Triumphant,* and *God's Simple Plan for His Church.*

While waiting in the lobby for my appointment with the president's assistant, I learned about a women's conference going on in Accra. I took a taxi to where they were meeting, and learned of a change in the meeting place; so went there, and was able to give Joanne's book to key business and professional women from ten nations of Western Africa. While with them, the leader from Ghana mentioned to me that she was a Christian and wondered if Joanne could speak to the local Women's Aglow chapter. I was also able to get a copy of Joanne's book to the president of Ghana's wife, the wife of the vice president, and the office of the United Nations in Ghana. What opportunities we had that day!

Friday: Joanne was very sick in the night and was taken to a missionary clinic the next morning.

271

Saturday Je: "We went to a trade fair and were able to give *The Way to God* to people from Nigeria, Niger, Benin, Togo, Burkina Fase, Ivory Coast, Mali, Liberia, Guinea, Gambia, Senegal, and Ghana - 12 nations - PTL!"

Sunday: Alger and Gloria left Ghana for other ministry stops in Europe.

Monday: In the evening Joanne was scheduled to speak to the Women's Aglow chapter in the nearby town of Tema. The leader, whom I had met at the Business and Professional Women's Conference, said she would try to send a car for us. If she couldn't she said we should meet her at the Page Hotel in Tema. Joanne tried to phone her all day without success - the phones were down - they worked only part of the time each day. At 6:15 p.m. we both felt it was time to take a taxi by faith to the hotel. Less than one minute after we arrived, she walked in the door - GOD's perfect timing! She took us to the meeting where Joanne spoke to about 40 women and gave them the remaining copies of her book, still in the original plastic comb-binding format.

Tuesday, March 2: We spent the morning at the beach, packed in the afternoon, and flew toward home in the evening. We flew all the next day - Accra to Amsterdam to Seattle to Portland. We had wonderful ministry opportunities on the flights.

Sunday, March 14 Je: "Wonderful house church time at Beth's - Wengers, Bachrans, Pierces, Knochs, and us, seventeen in all."

Spring was here and I spent much of March doing outside work. We also began a monthly house church leaders' meeting suggested by Mike Wenger and Bob Lund.

Sunday, April 4: Spent Easter day at the Coast with the Bachrans.

272

Sunday, April 18: Joanne had her annual piano students' recital in the afternoon. After that we drove to see the tulip fields east of Woodburn. This, likewise, became an almost-annual event for us.

Saturday, April 24 Je: "Beth came in fifth in the Mrs. Oregon contest - we felt she should have placed 1, 2, or 3. We are very proud of her."

April 25-28 Je: "Under heavy attack - it broke on Wednesday when Jo prayed for me. PTL!"

Sunday, May 2: A gathering of 57 people from seven different home-church groups met at the Deaf School here in Salem, arranged by Alan Yankus.

May 28 - June 7: Trip to Northern California - Jo and me:
May 29-30: A House Church Conference in Redding, CA - a wonderful time with 20-30 - teaching, worship, fellowship.
Monday, May 31: With VanDyks, to Maders.
Tuesday, June 1: With Maders - GOD provides funds to start Preparing the Way Publishers, LightningSource to do the printing, beginning with Joanne's book. The name, Preparing the Way Publishers, had been suggested to us by Beth, based on Luke 1:17. It was to be a prophetic publishing house, preparing the way for the Lord's return. The evening was a prayer time - 10 of us.

June 2-3: Sheets Reunion - time with Joanne's cousins.
June 4: Time with Joanne's sisters.
June 5: Time with Spencer Harris.
Sunday, June 6: With Brother Mike Marchio and about 40 in the park.
Monday: Trip home via vineyards, redwoods, and Oregon Coast. Je: "Thank you, Lord, for a wonderful 11-day trip to California."

June 8-12: Office catch up including work on Joanne's book: ISBN application, LightningSource application, and Library of Congress application.

June 13-19: Watched Navy ships, there for the annual Rose Festival, leave the Portland docks; overnight with McCormicks; time at the VA hospital for a checkup; time with Marshes. Worked on Joanne's book. Worked on starting Boilermakers for Christ - this is something GOD had been speaking to me since 1985. It is to be a network of born-again Purdue students, faculty, staff, and alumni - for the purpose of fellowship and jointly extending the Kingdom of GOD.

July: Continuing to work on Jo's book, preparing it for PTW publication. Working on Dad's book No. 1. Working on Boilermakers for Christ.

July 30 - August 2: To Southern California - just me:
Friday: Flight down.
Saturday - House Church Conference in Orange County with Robert Fitts.
Sunday: Gathering of 25-30 in San Diego.
Monday: Flight home.

Saturday, August 7: Jerry Gorman and Melveena Horst were married - they met at our Tuesday evening Bible study.

August 9-24: Trip to Midwest - Jo and me:
Monday: Flight to Indianapolis.
Tuesday: With Gerry and family.
Wednesday: Saw Wayne Pence at the Kokomo bookstore; officially launched Boilermakers for Christ at Purdue.
Thursday: Went with Gerry and family to the Indiana State Fair.
Friday and Saturday: Jo's 45th high school class reunion - very nice.

Sunday: To College Wesleyan Church where Gerry is on staff. Saw many old friends. He spoke in the evening service on 1 Thessalonians 3:11-13 - very good!

Monday, August 16: To Ohio; lunch in Lima with Mase and Penny Bailey; to Fostoria; saw Mom at the rest home in the evening.

Tuesday: Met with Dad's book committee in the morning; went swimming at the Fostoria pool in the afternoon; saw Mom again in the evening.

Wednesday: Had a picnic in Upper with my cousins.

Thursday: Saw Mom in the morning; lunch with Norman Gibat and his wife; dinner with Bill Ramsey.

Friday: Saw Joan Godsey in Toledo; time with Ernestine Stewart and Michael Sumpter in Detroit.

Saturday: Saw Mom; with George and Carolyn Moser in Prospect, Ohio; to Dan and Brenda Beaty's in Columbus.

Sunday Je: "With a house church group at Beaty's - about 15 folks - wonderful time!"

Monday: Breakfast with Gary McPherson in Columbus; drove to Gerry's in Marion, IN.

Tuesday, August 24: Flight home to Oregon.

August 27 - September 1: Trip to Colorado - Jo and me:
We flew to Colorado Springs on Friday. Friday evening through Saturday was a time of sharing by approximately 20 leaders, called by Dan Root of Seattle.

Sunday evening: With a Generation X church started by Dean Cozzens.

Monday: Dean Cozzens and I saw a number of Christian leaders, including at the Navigators, AD 2000, Partners International, and Every Home Crusade.

Monday evening: With Jim and Bev Carver who had moved to the Springs from Salem.

Tuesday: Jo and I drove to Pike's Peak and saw where *America the Beautiful* was written.

Tuesday evening: a wonderful time with Len and Dori Funck and a group of more than 30 at their home west of Denver.

Wednesday: Trip home.

275

September 6: I went to the Oregon State Fair.
September 7: My 64th birthday.

September 8-22: Trip to Hawaii - Jo and me:
Wednesday, September 8: To Hawaii, saw Arizona Memorial and Aloha Tower area, stayed with Vern and Celia Kuenzi.
Thursday: Jo and I toured Oahu.

Friday: With Vern and Celia Kuenzi, discussing the possibility of publishing his book, *Restoring the Vision of the End-time Church.* Met Tom Kiyuna and his wife - Tom and I had become close friends while working together on the maintenance crew at Glen Eyrie in 1959. Also toured the Hawaiian Capitol.
Saturday: An all-day House Church Conference on Oahu, arranged by Vern.

Sunday: An all-day House Church Conference with Bob Fitts on Maui - about 30 people - wonderful time.
Monday, September 13: Jo and I toured Maui.

Tuesday: To Kona, on the Big Island. This is where we had been with YWAM in 1976-80. We stayed with Bob and Joni Fitts.
Wednesday: Jo and I toured Kona.

Thursday: On the YWAM Base - lunch with Ross Tooley and Howard Malmstadt. Ross was from New Zealand and had been with YWAM for many years. Howard was the provost for the new University of the Nations.
In the afternoon we searched for and found Amber Silva, with whom we had lived for two months during our SOE in the fall of 1976.
In the evening we had a wonderful time with Dave and Mary Sue Ross, whom we knew when we were with YWAM.
Thursday was our 38th wedding anniversary, but we were going to celebrate it the following Tuesday on Oahu.

Friday: Had a wonderful time in the morning with Rod and Alexis Wilson, who were YWAM leaders, and with whom we went through the SOE.
We spent the afternoon with the Bob and Joni Fitts.
In the evening we attended a YWAM meeting - Je: "What a wonderful time."

Sunday, September 19, we conducted an all-day conference on house church with Bob Fitts in Hilo with about 15 people.
Monday morning was with Bob Fitts. Monday evening was with Amber, her new husband, and her son, Delta.

Tuesday we flew to Honolulu, stayed in a beautiful hotel, and celebrated our wedding anniversary with dinner on the ocean. Greg's brother, Chris, who was in the hotel business, had arranged the hotel accommodations.

Wednesday, September 22: Flight to Oregon. Je: "Thank you, Lord, for a wonderful two weeks in Hawaii."

Upon arriving home we had catch-up work to do in the garden and orchards - harvesting and processing fruit and vegetables.

Saturday and Sunday, October 9-10: A two-day House Church Conference with Alger and Gloria Marsh at a facility they had arranged in Hood River, Oregon.

Friday, October 22: Jo and I went to Hood River area and gleaned boxes of pears and apples from the ground at several orchards.

Friday, November 6: GOD spoke to me that it is time to "retire."

The latter part of December was spent preparing for Y2K - storing water in empty gallon milk containers and having extra canned food. This was because it had been predicted that everything would shut down worldwide because computers were not prepared and programmed to make the transition from 1999 to 2000. Nothing really happened!

CHAPTER 19
WRITING AND PUBLISHING

(Dad's books, PTWP books, CLU, RV, fishing)

(2000 - 2001)

<u>2000</u>

On Monday, January 3, I started a 40-day period of partial fasting and extra prayer. Je: "May GOD have His way these forty days."

I spent quite a bit of time in January working on Dad's book(s). Bob Iddings helped on the initial downloading of the original newspaper columns.

Also spent time with people - Crittendens, two men from Kenya, Africa; Woodrums, John and Betty McCormick, Bob Iddings, Johnnie and Onna McCormick, Dewey and Emma France, Bachrans, Brian Hewitt, Missy Ferris in Bend, Carol Preston, Hawkinsons; Portland - Paul Rapoza, Jim Steeck, Masa; Maders.

January 3 Je: "GOD has spoken the word 'retire.' To me that means garden, fruit orchards, yard, fishing, more fun connected with travel."

January 4: We met with our advisers - Marshes, Bachrans, and Bob Lund.

Friday, January 14 - Je: "You have a little strength . . . I place no other burden on you . . . what you have, hold fast until I come. - Revelation 2-3." I took this to mean no other big assignments from the Lord.

February 5:   Jo's 64th birthday - dinner with Pierces, Montgomerys, and Bernie and Connie Quebemann.

March 3:   Our granddaughter, Kelly, played Annie in her school play. Je: "Did a marvelous job!"

March 10-28: Jo went to Michigan to do drapes for Ernestine - also stops in Ohio and Indiana.

Sunday, March 26:   House church gathering at our place - 1:30-6:30 - 18 people - really good time.

Sunday, April 2 Je: "We went to a meeting at Bob Lund's - GOD healed my back and spirit - PTL! - a wonderful time."

Friday thru Sunday, April 21-23:   Resurrection Retreat of house church people from Salem and Portland areas at the Coast - 39 people - good deepening of relationship - very good time.

Making progress on Dad's book, Volume 1.

May 11: All wood supply in for next year. We get wood by going around to job sites and getting scraps that they approve of us taking.

<u>May 12-23: Trip to Northern California - Jo and me:</u>
May 12: Trip to Redding, CA - stopped at Jacksonville, OR - beautiful Oregon scenery.
May 13: With groups in Redding.
May 14: With Jack and Jan Russell and others. Met with Al and Cathy VanDyk.

May 15:   To Roseville - good time with Bob and Arlene, Beverly and Don, Don's brother.

May 16-17: With Bob and Arlene. Good time with their son, Paul, in the evening of May 16. Arlene and Joanne went to San Francisco on May 17. Bob and I rested, swam, and played billiards at the lodge.

May 16 Je: "I think GOD is making it clear that this is our last trip of any consequence. We need to give ourselves to writing and publishing. People will come and see us rather than our traveling to them."

May 18: To San Jose - time with Spencer Harris over lunch - time with Gilmores in the early afternoon. To Santa Cruz - to bed early.
Friday, May 19: Lunch at San Francisco wharf.

Friday p.m. to Sunday, May 19-21 - House Church Conference at Santa Cruz - very good!

Monday: We traveled from Santa Cruz up Route 1 through San Francisco, through the California vineyards, through the redwoods to Brookings, Oregon, where we stayed in a motel for the night.
Tuesday: Brookings to Salem.

Early June: We signed a contract with Arcadia Publishing to publish Dad's book, Volume 1. They are a company from Great Britain, with an office in Chicago, that does books only on the history of towns and cities. We were very fortunate to get connected with them.

Sunday, July 2: Jo and I went to the Coast for the day - we had a wonderful time!

Tuesday, July 4: We watched July 4 celebrations on TV - Washington, DC; Boston, New York, and Cincinnati.

July 19: August 9 - Gerry and Wenda and family with us. We did fun things - to Pendleton Mills outlet, family cookout, hike to Pamilia Lake, to beach at Cape Kiwanda (everyone climbed the sand mountain except me), to Silver Creek Falls, watched Republican Convention on TV.

Thursday, August 13 Je: "I have been under attack (mental, emotional, physical, spiritual) for two weeks now. Why? Why is the enemy able to gain a foothold?"

Friday thru Sunday, August 18-20: Jay Ferris is with us. Things he shared included:
Jesus is Lord of relationships.
The Church should be structured according to life.
Nail your expectations to the tree.
Trust only in Him.
What does life teach us about relationships?

August 21: Got peaches at an orchard north of Keizer - ate some and dried some.

August 23: Proofed Vern Kuenzi's book with Beth.

August 27: A day at the Coast with Jo from Lincoln City to Newport - a wonderful time!
August 31: Jo and I went to the State Fair with Alger and Gloria on veterans' discount day.

September 8: Alger Marsh spent the afternoon with Jo and me attempting to help us work through some issues in our relationship.

September 9: I performed Robert and Gina Rapoza wedding in Vancouver. They later divorced.

September 12: Lee Thompson and I spent several hours regarding possible curses, judgments, and soul ties in my life - it was a very fruitful time.

September 15: I wrote the General Superintendents of the Wesleyan Church to try to bring about some reconciliation from when we had to leave over the Charismatic emphasis. They answered, in part: "It would be difficult for us, as the current Board of General Superintendents, to interpret or adjust what happened in 1975. We cannot make a judgment on the past. While we disagree theologically and doctrinally on the issues raised by the Charismatic and Pentecostal movement, such should not prohibit our Christian fellowship. We are sorry that you still feel uncomfortable being around Holiness people, especially Wesleyans.   However, we certainly do consider you a brother in Christ and trust that the barriers of the past can be replaced with bridges of understanding and forgiveness. May the Lord richly bless you and Joanne in your ministry for the Kingdom of God." It was a gracious letter and I thank GOD for that.

September 16: We had dinner at Red Lobster to celebrate our 39th wedding anniversary.

September 18: We spent the day with Marvin and Hazel Hinds of Marion, Indiana, going to Mt. St. Helens. Hazel is a friend of Joanne's from childhood. They bought us a Golden Age Passport, which we still use often when camping, fishing, or visiting national parks.

September 23: We are now working on Bob Fitts' book about house church with Clint and Judy Crittenden of Woodburn. Clint does the cover artwork and Judy prepares the manuscripts for publication - editing, formatting, and coordinating with the printer, LightningSource. They do excellent work and we greatly enjoyed working with them.

September 26: I have just finished the editing of all of the articles for Dad's book, Volume 1.

October 1: Have just read *The Five Love Languages* book - there are five ways we express love to others - words of affirmation, spending quality time, giving gifts, serving, and physical touch. It is a very helpful book (see Appendix 4).

October 3: We watched the first presidential debate between George W. Bush and Al Gore.

October 14: We have been looking for an RV for several weeks and have found a beautiful American Clipper in Tigard. We got a line of credit on our home to pay for it and picked it up on November 1. It was built in the 1970s and needed a lot of work. We replaced the old carpet, Joanne put up some wallpaper, made new drapes, etc. And we enjoyed camping with it in Oregon, Washington, and California for the next three years.

October 17: I started on Joanne Bachran's book, a Bible handbook, called *God's Word Puts the Wind in My Sails* - it is a wonderful reference book that everyone should have.

October 19: I finished reading *Men are from Mars, Women are from Venus*. Although not based on Scripture, I found much practical truth and help in this book.

October 25-26: Beth and I proofed Bob Fitts' book. We proofed several books together - it was such a blessing to do this with my daughter, was a great help to our publishing work, and gave them some extra income.

Also, that week I bought a used fiberglass boat, with trailer, electric motor, anchor, and oars for $400 from a man in Albany through a newspaper ad. What a deal! In the coming years I would fish a number of Oregon lakes: Hebo, Devils, Carter, Loon, Laurence, Timothy, Clear, Harriet, North Fork, Silverton, Freeway, Detroit, Foster, Green Peter, Smith, Big, Suttle, Blue River, Cougar, East, Lava, Little Lava, Crane Prairie, Odell, Henry Haag, and several others.

284

My favorites were Green Peter, Smith, Cougar, and Blue River. Sometimes I would really get away and camp in a tent for two nights and fish for three days.

November 3: Brandon Fogert helped me put in a sewer line from the garden area, where we parked the RV, to the house to empty the sewage between trips.

November 7: Election Day - the presidential election is too close to call between Al Gore and George Bush.

November 10-12: First trip in our RV - to West Winds, north of Pacific City; then to Tillicum Beach, south of Waldport. Je: "What a wonderful time we had in our new home. 'Thank you, Jesus!' "

<u>November 15 - December 11: Trip to Midwest to work on Dad's book - just me:</u>
November 15: To Chicago - time with Willie Douglas, Len and Darlene Harris.
November 16: Had a very good time with Arcadia Publishing in Chicago.
Toured Chicago - Grant Park, Marshall Fields, Pacific Garden Mission, 528 N. Lockwood where we once lived, the Laramie house-to-house witnessing area.
Toured Wheaton - saw inside 312 E. Lincoln, where we once lived; drove down Gunderson Dr. where all of the Christian ministry headquarters were; downtown, and Roosevelt Rd.
Went to the Salvation Army Halfway House, where Len Harris works, for supper and rest.
Then to Union Station and a joyous train ride to Fostoria where Skip and Jan Dunafee met me in the middle of the night and took me to the family home at 927 N. Main Street where David, my brother, still lived.
November 17: Rest, with my brother Dave, got organized for the coming days.

285

November 18: Met with Ray Dell, George Gray, Leonard Skonecki, and Dave and got most of the photos we needed for Dad's book.

November 19: To Church with Dave.

November 20: Wonderful time with Mom at the rest home.

November 21: Breakfast with Pastor Chew, lunch with Kiwanis Club, afternoon with Ray Dell getting photos for Dad's book.

November 22: Working on book.

November 23: Thanksgiving - With Dave, Joan Godsey, and Mom.

Je: "I am very thankful that I can come to the close of life with a sense of fulfillment and contentment. GOD has been so merciful, good, kind, and faithful!"

November 24: Worked on book. Dinner with Bill Ramsey.

November 25: Worked on book. Talked with Janet's pastor, Larry Hatfield.

November 26: Day of rest. Bush declared winner in Florida.

November 27: Saw my sister, Janet, swam at YMCA, worked on book.

November 28: Full day on book.

November 29: Met with seven ladies from my high school class who regularly meet - I shared Jesus with them - two may be believers. Worked on book.

November 30: Worked on book. Lunch with Mom. Dinner with Skip and Jan Dunafee.

December 1: Planned further Midwest travel.

December 2: Bill Ramsey took me to get George Moser's car.

Sunday, December 3: Went to Assembly of God Church in Fostoria - very good!

Monday: Book loose ends. Took Mom around town.

Tuesday: To Loren's, my cousin in Upper Sandusky, for dinner. Je: "My traveling days are over! - books will have to go in my place."

Wednesday, December 6: Drove to Marion, Indiana. Good time with Gerry - time with Bill and Evelyn Allen; Marla, Brooke, and Adam Rhoades.

December 7: Good time with Gerry and Wenda in the morning. Evening with Glen and Betty Martin.

December 8: Lunch with Bill and Evelyn and Marvin and Hazel. Afternoon and evening with Gerry and family.

December 9: Back to Fostoria.
Sunday, December 10: Time with my cousin, Nancy Slaymaker. In the evening we got the weather report that a blizzard was moving toward Chicago. I felt led of the Lord to go home NOW!
Monday, December 11: I took the train to Chicago - the snow was already piling up. Willie Douglas met me at Union Station and took me to the north side to meet Carrie at Arcadia Publishers. Then to the airport. When Willie and I got to O'Hare most of the flights had been canceled, but there was still a flight open to Seattle - I took it, and even got a first-class window seat! Took a flight from Seattle to Portland where my wonderful wife met me!

December 14: Finished Dad's book, Volume 1, and mailed it to the publishers today. It was entitled *Images of Fostoria, Ohio - as told by Paul H. Krupp.*

Sunday, December 24: Christmas with Greg and Beth and Jamie, Kelly, and Daniel - we had a wonderful time.

December 26-31: Six days at the Coast in the RV - Lincoln City, Waldport, Tillicum Beach, Florence - much rest, beach walks, time with Jo, and time with the Lord. We sure enjoyed our RV!

2001
January 1: Purdue played in the Rose Bowl.

January 16: Started Dad's book, Volume 2. When working on putting Dad's columns into book form, we discovered that there was enough material for two volumes, not one. Arcadia Publishers agreed to our putting out Volume 2 if enough copies of Volume 1 sold.

287

January 20: President George W. Bush is inaugurated our 44th president after a long ordeal of deciding who won the race, which was finally decided by the Supreme Court.

January 22: Tried out my boat at Willamette Mission State Park. Je: "Saw a large tree with many large branches, each bearing fruit. GOD said, 'This is my life - branches include - Kingsville, TX; Marion College; Wesleyans - personal evangelism; Lay Evangelism, Inc.; Chicago - Grant Park, inner city west side, North side Jewish area, and Wheaton; Living Water bookstore; YWAM; Foursquare Church; USA prayer - 5-day retreats, 40 days; home church around the world; publishing (PTWP) - our writings, others' writings.' Thank you, Lord, for seeing fit to use a nobody like me."

Tuesday, January 30: We started a Bible study group, with thirteen people, studying 1 Thessalonians, a chapter a week, using Bible study methods I had learned at the Navigators.

One big project for January through April was working on Dad's book, Volume 2.

February 5: Joanne's birthday - dinner at a Chinese place with Pierces and McCormicks.

February 9-10: We went to Bob Lund's seminar based on his new book *The Way Church Ought to Be*. Bob is certainly a key man in GOD's Kingdom. We love him like a son!

Sunday, February 11: We went to Lucy's home group.

February 16-18: We got away to the Coast, Lincoln City to Tillicum Beach, south of Waldport, in our RV. It was a wonderful time of rest - "thank you, Jesus!"

February 20: I went over the page proofs for Dad's, Volume 1.

March 1: Went to Kelly's musical, *Godspell* - wonderful.

March 5: The first copies of Kuenzi's book arrived.

March 10: Last look at Fitts' book before it was sent to LightningSource.

March 22: Willamette Valley house church leaders together from 9 to 3 - "wonderful time."

March 23-27: To North Coast in RV - Cape Kiwanda, Cape Lookout, Cape Mears, Oceanside, Netarts, Tillamook, Rockaway Beach, Cannon Beach, Seaside, Ft. Stevens State Park, Astoria, Ft. Clatsop. Spent time with Cal and Vi Ludeman. "Wonderful time away - thank you, Lord Jesus!"

March 31: Went to Salem citywide prayer meeting at the Armory.

March 31 - April 8: Greg, Beth, and family took the RV to Southern California because Jamie and Kelly's high school choir was performing there and also so Jamie could check out a college. Jo rode with them as far as Roseville to see Arlene. They picked her up on their way back home.

April 3: Worked on Joanne Bachran's book.

April 4: Gerry called - he was not chosen to be the senior pastor at the Marion College Wesleyan Church.

April 5: Dave called - Mom has decided not to have surgery.

April 11: Bob Fitts' proof copy arrived.

Sunday, April 15: Riverside Park Easter sunrise service with Jo. Dinner with Bachrans at our place.

Sunday, April 22: Jo and I drove 275 miles in the Cascades looking at various possible fishing spots for me.

April 24: Finished the rough draft for Dad's, Volume 2 - sent to Ray Dell for photos.

April 30: The first copies of Dad's, Volume 1, arrived - copies were sent to those who had helped.
Joanne had her annual piano recital with sixteen students.

May 4-6: To the Coast, Tillicum Beach, which became one of our favorite spots to camp, in the RV.

May 7: Maders came by for overnight and a time of sharing.

May 10: Willamette Valley house church leaders together - Stan and Maria Pierce, Bob Lund, Alger Marsh, Doug Alfred, and us.

Sunday, May 13: Mothers' Day. Jo and Beth were together in the morning. I called Mom in the afternoon and then went to the Iris fields north of Keizer with Jo.

May 18 - Finished the *Knowing GOD Series*, which Jerry Gorman, Melveena Horst, Al Knoch, and I had been working on for some months. This series includes *Basic Bible Studies, New Testament Survey Course, Mastering the Word of GOD and Workbook, Getting to Know GOD,* and *Qualities GOD is Looking for in Us.* (They are now being used around the world by our Christian Leadership University students and in Harvest of Jubilee Bible schools.)

May 20 - Je: "Matthew 13:57-58 - Our writings, publications, and influence will go around the world, but not in Salem. Matthew 14:20, 31 - GOD is going to do the marketing of PTW books - and He will be glorified."

May 26: Beth is second in Mrs. Oregon contest, but first in our opinion!

June 7: Johnnie McCormick and Paul Rapoza are developing a website for PTWP.

June 8: Jamie graduates from Sprague High School - we are so proud of our grandchildren.

June 11: I rode all day on a Navy ship from Portland to Longview, WA - they were in Portland for the Rose Festival - "what fun."

June 22-24: Dan went with Jo and me on a fishing trip to Timothy Lake - "wonderful time - caught eight trout." Dan caught his first fish.

June 27-28: Frank Smith and John and Dianne Gill were with us to discuss our publishing John's book.

July 3 - August 4: Trip to Midwest without Jo:
This was quite a trip - the beginning of a new chapter and the ending of an old. The new chapter was the distribution of Dad's writings in book form - the old chapter was the selling of the family home at 927 N. Main Street.
Flew to Detroit via St. Louis. Michael Sumpter took me to Fostoria.
July 4: 4th of July with my brother, Dave.

I was in Fostoria promoting Volume 1 of Dad's books. We had an article in the Fostoria newspaper. I spoke at Kiwanis Club, was on WFOB radio station, was at the Lion's Club and at a Gospel sing at Gray's Park. I signed books at Readmore bookstore, at Fostoria Museum, at St. Catherine's rest home, and at Wesley Village. Sold 240!

Worked on photos for Volume 2. I got some from Ray Dell, some from George Gray at the Museum, and taking some photos myself. I met with the committee - Ray Dell, George Gray, Norm Gibat, and Dave. Also met with the Fostoria mayor about writing the foreword for Volume 2.

On July 19 we put a "For Sale" sign out in front to sell the family home at 927 N. Main Street where Dave lived alone since Dad was gone and Mom was at St. Catherine's Rest Home. During the next week I was busy packing and shipping items to Oregon - dishes for Beth; china, mirror, and dresser for Jo. Dave and I were busy cleaning out the house - attic, basement, garage, etc. - what a job! On July 30-31 Gerry picked up items he wanted - a desk, freezer, etc. Also, Gerry, Wenda, their three, Janet, Dave, and I, had dinner together at St. Catherine's with Mom on the 30th - she was so blessed to have us all together. On July 27 the house sold - in only eight days - what a miracle!

Other family times included:
- time with Mom at St. Catherine's.
- a band concert on Sunday with Dave and our cousin Nancy (Adams) Slaymaker.
- had lunch with Mom and Dave on July 11, Mom's 70th wedding anniversary.
- on July 20 I met with 13 high school classmates.

On Sunday, July 22, Mase Bailey drove me to meet with a house church group in Columbus - we stayed overnight in a motel - had breakfast with Gary McPherson on Monday morning.

Tuesday, July 24, Dave and I took Mom to the Seneca County Fair in Tiffin - she had such a good time.

Also, while in Fostoria, I had lunch with Norm and Kathleen Gibat; and lunch with Ray Dell; time with Frank and Royetta Kirian and Lorraine; breakfast with Skip and Jan Dunafee; and lunch with Ethel (Kranz) Baruxes, my high school girl friend, who was traveling through. I went to church at Nazarene, Presbyterian, and Assembly of God churches. Had a cousin's reunion on August 1. Frank and Royetta took me to the Detroit airport for my flight home.

It was a very full and fruitful time getting the home place sold and emptied, selling Volume 1 of Dad's books, working on Volume 2, and seeing people.

August 19 - 27: Vacation trip in RV to Central Oregon - Sisters, Bend, Crane Prairie Reservoir, East Lake - fishing, sightseeing. I caught a 17-inch trout at East Lake, biggest fish I have ever caught - also other smaller trout.

August 20: During our time away I was wondering if GOD had used us in any way and He encouraged me with the following - Je: "Ways GOD has used me, an unprofitable servant:
-    witness at Purdue after my conversion.
-    witness to my family after my conversion.
-    witness at the Presbyterian Church in Oxnard, CA.
-    witness to my CEC classmates at Port Hueneme, CA.

Kingsville, TX -
-    witnessing and soul winning on the base.
-    sailors I discipled.
-    tract distribution.
-    being a blessing at Calvary Baptist Church.
-    leading the Southern Baptist youth organization in the area.
-    being a "preacher boy" in the area.

Navigators at Colorado Springs:
-    my story to them.
-    making order out of the chaos in the building program.
-    discipling Duane Redeker, who lived in Colorado Springs.

Marion College:
-    street witnessing, especially at Court House Square with Dave Castro.
-    trips with students to Pacific Garden Mission.
-    my emphasis on Scripture memory.

Soul Winning training:
-    Wesleyans
-    Free Methodists
-    holiness movement
-    LEI, NHA, NAE

Chicago:
-    soul winning at Grant Park, in the Westside projects, in the north-side Jewish neighborhood, in Wheaton.
-    working with Len Harris.
-    the Legion Hall church group.
-    the Austin-Oak Park house church.

Marion:
-    Witness of Charismatic emphasis to NHA groups.
-    Leffler Construction Company - witness and good manager.
-    Starting Living Water bookstore with others.
-    Assembly of God Church - soul winning and new converts' class.

YWAM:
-    good family example.
-    started School of the Bible and School of Church Ministries.
-    first Master's degree in Kona.

294

Salem:
- laid a new foundation at New Life Fellowship.
- 'praying pastors of South Salem.'
- citywide prayer emphasis.
- Convocation on Christian Unity.
- joint Bible school.

Tacoma:
- prophetic voice to the YWAM base.
- prayer networking.

Northwest:
- 5-day prayer retreats.
- 40 days of prayer - Washington, Oregon.

National Prayer -
- prophetic voice to National Prayer Committee.
- 40 days - Pittsburgh.
- 40 days - nation.

Salem:
- 40 days of prayer in Oregon.
- house church network.
- resource to house church movement worldwide.
- house church magazine.
- PTWP - our writings and writings of others.
- being part of SalemNet.

All of this is:
- being a witness to what GOD has done.
- being a prophetic voice.
- pioneering."

August 29 Je: "Mark 13:34, 'He has given to each one his task.' What is mine now? To be a prophet-teacher with regard to GOD's plan for His Church."

August 31: To the State Fair with Jo. I have usually gone each year to the State Fair for a day to enjoy the animals, new products, etc., and to witness. Some years I wrote a Gospel leaflet just for that fair and passed out hundreds throughout the day.

September 2: Got pears and apples at Jeff and Lisa Snyder's.

September 7: 66th birthday. Breakfast with Dewey and Emma. Called Mom. Lunch at downtown Subway with Jo. Dinner at China Buffet with Jo. Had birthday dinner the next day with Bachrans.

September 9: Jo and me to the Coast for the day.

September 11: Terrorists attacked the United States - New York City and Washington, D.C.

September 12 Je: "A word from GOD - 'My son, rest, relax, go fishing, do whatever you would like. You have been faithful to My call. Now you are to rest. I will provide.' "

September 13: Ed Montgomery, Stan Pierce, Doug Alfred, and I - wonderful time of fellowship.

September 16: Our 40th wedding anniversary.
September 17: Celebrated our anniversary - we went to Portland for lunch - ate outside at a waterfront restaurant that Jo likes - had some prayer time together. "Thank you, Lord, for my wonderful wife!"

September 21: Made 27 quarts of V-8 juice with produce from our garden.

September 23: New York outdoor service in the aftermath of 9/11 was on TV.

<u>September 29 - October 5 : Fishing trip to the Coast:</u>
September 29 - October 2: Jo and I were together in the RV at Tillicum Beach, south of Waldport. On Tuesday, October 2, she headed for home with the car and I went to Loon Lake with the RV. En route I met a Christian couple, Jim and Betty Bevers, from Springfield. They showed up at Loon Lake the next day. On Thursday morning I got my limit of five in less than two hours - lengths were 15, 15, 14, 13, 11 inches. Betty cooked them and we had breakfast together. They were a precious couple. They later became part of a house church in Creswell, south of Eugene, led by Art and Mary Prichet.

October 4 Je: "September 11 was a wake-up call:
- not worship our creations and money.
- return to GOD.
- return to patriotism.
- return to helping each other.
- fight terrorism."
Had a wonderful time of prayer that evening - the Lord healed my mind of what I thought were Alzheimer tendencies. GOD often met with me in significant ways when I got away for several days of camping and fishing.

September thru December: Working on Dad's, Volume 2.

Throughout October: met with several house church groups - at Knochs,' at Alfreds,' group in West Salem, men on Thursday mornings.

November 3: Fishing at Detroit Lake - caught the limit of five per day - 9, 10, 10, 11, 11 inches. "Thank you, Jesus!"

November 17: A meeting of home church people hosted by Wengers in Rosedale - 80 people - really good.

November 22: Thanksgiving Day - dinner with Bachrans.

November 27: Finished first draft of Dad's Volume 2.

December 1: Jo had irregular heart beats - I took her to the emergency room. They had to put her to sleep and shock her to get her heart regulated. She has had no recurrences of that, praise the Lord.

December 16-17: Nolice and Marion Miller in town.

December 17: Word from my brother Dave that Mom had died from a stroke - "a shocker!" The previous Friday she had told Dave, "I'm not going to be your Mom much longer." At the time neither of them knew the meaning of what she was saying.

December 18-31: Trip alone to the Midwest:
Tuesday: Trip to Detroit - I was met at the airport by Ernestine Stewart and Michael Sumpter, stayed overnight with Michael, and drove his Lexus for the next two weeks.

Wednesday: To Fostoria, time with my brother Dave.
Thursday: Viewing of Mom's body - "she looks so nice."
Friday: Mom's funeral. I moved to Nancy Slaymaker's home.
Saturday: Not feeling well - needed this day off.

Sunday: Day with Dave - Nazarene Church, cemetery, etc.
Monday: Bookstore signing for Dad's, Volume 1. Lunch with Norm and Kathleen Gibat. Time with Dave.
Tuesday - Christmas: I spent the day with Dave.

Wednesday thru Friday: to Marion, Indiana - time with Gerry and family; time with Bill and Evelyn; prayed for Glen Martin's healing from cancer. Glen got a kick out of my driving a Lexus!

Saturday: Drove from Marion to Detroit - lunch with Fred Copple, from Kingsville CEC days, in Lansing en route.

Sunday, December 30: A get together of Ernestine and her friend, Curtis; Gar and Rachel Darnes, Michael Sumpter. Got word that Jo had fallen and sprained her foot.

Monday - New Years eve: Flight from Detroit to Portland via Houston. I spent some time with my friend Lydia Beltran at the Houston airport.

CHAPTER 20 - SLOWING DOWN

(Dad's books, PTWP books, CLU,
Seabee Reunion, RV, fishing)

(2002 - 2003)

<u>2002</u>

January 1: Spent the day with Jo watching the Rose Parade and the Rose Bowl game.

January 4: Serviced my boat and went fishing at Detroit Lake. I froze and caught no fish, but it was fun to get away.

January 6: Jo and I reviewed 2001 and prayed for 2002 together.

Wednesday, January 9: House church leaders together from 8 to noon - Doug Alfred, Alger Marsh, Harold Behr, and me.

January 13: Worked on the antique chair together with Jo. The chair had been in my family since the 1800s and was passed on to us by my Mom's cousin, Helen Widener. It still had the original horsehair on it and was in really bad shape. We had it completely restored and it is now beautiful and can actually be sat on.

January 15: I wrote a CLU course for the *Qualities GOD is Looking for in You* book.

January 17: GOD spoke the Salem House Church Conference vision to me.

Sunday, January 21: We met with the Yankus home church group - 21 people - good group.

January 22: Jo went to Portland for Extras Only movie shoot. She did this over a several-year period and really enjoyed it.

January 27: We woke up to six inches of snow. Jo and I walked to WalMart and to Carl's Jr. for lunch.

January 28: Our new couch arrived. Jo wanted to make a change and we bought it with money from the sale of Dad's books, Volume 1.

January 28: Willamette Valley house church leaders together at Denny's from 6 to 9:30 p.m. - eight couples - Behrs, Knaupps, Yankuses, Bachrans, Lunds, Marshes, Alfreds, and us. Good time of getting acquainted and fellowship. We are looking at a retreat in April to get better acquainted. Decision to hold off having a conference until next year.

January 29: Lunch and prayer with our neighbors, Dewey and Emma.

January 30: Discussion with Doug Alfred on Ultimate Reconciliation subject, which he believes, but I don't.

To Corvallis to put Jamie's curtains up.

February 1-4: To the Coast in the RV - Jo and me:
Friday: Florence for lunch - Coos Bay overnight.
Saturday: Early morning walk on beach with Jo. Breakfast and worship. Coos Bay - myrtle wood factory, cranberry bogs. Bandon - Lighthouse, cheese factory. Overnight at Cape Blanco - the western-most point of the 48 states.

Sunday: Morning - walk to overlook at Cape Blanco - breakfast near lighthouse, went to animal farm where we got to pet a little lion cub.

302

Afternoon - Bandon - cheese factory, time downtown - drive to Winchester Bay - lunch at lighthouse overlook - drive to Tillicum Beach by Waldport. Evening - beach walk, sunset, dinner, dominoes, clear night - beautiful stars.

Monday: Morning - Beach walk alone, beach walk with Jo, breakfast and worship, final beach walk, drive to Newport. Afternoon - lunch in Newport by boats, walk along Newport shops area, drive home - 514 miles on this trip. Je: "Thank you, Lord, for a fun time away."

February 5 Je: "Jo is 66 - where have the years gone? She has been a wonderful person to know and be with - for over 40 years. 'Thank you, Jesus!' " That evening we celebrated her birthday with the Montgomerys, Alfreds, and Pierces with dinner together at the Mongolian Grill. The following evening we celebrated with Beth and Greg.

February 8: We got word from Arcadia that Volume 1 sales are at 1,281, over the 1,200 needed for them to proceed with Volume 2 - "Thank you, Jesus!"

February 12: Started on final edit of Dad's, Volume 2.

February 16: Thirty-two boxes of firewood from a tree our neighbor, Dewey France, cut down.

February 18: Purchased new English Standard Version Bible. I had used the New American Standard since 1968, but the ESV has now become my favorite Bible translation.

February 22-24: We were invited by Harold Behr to share at the Friends New Works Conference held in Redmond, Oregon. These new churches are mainly house churches.

February 25: Began proofing John Gill's book. Went to Kelly and Dan's choir concert at Sprague in the evening.

This week: Got fertilizer from a pile at Dewey's - spread it on fruit trees - and lime on the garden.

March 2: We picked up the antique chair. Got more wood - our supply is now 138 boxes - "GOD is so faithful!"

Sunday, March 3 Je: "Good time with Jo - Word, prayer, discussion, the Lord's Supper." Afternoon - Epsom salts around fruit trees - moss killer on yard.

March 4: With Jo to Portland and Salem looking for material to cover the antique chair.

March 7: Lunch with Jay Grimstead - "very good time."

The green chair and coffee table that we ordered from the Russian furniture company arrived. This was something special that Jo wanted for our living room and was paid for with Fostoria book royalty.

March 8: Kelly's play - *Guys and Dolls*. Je: "Real cute. Kelly was very good, as usual."

Throughout March: NCAA basketball tourney.

March 17: Called Betty Scharff on her birthday. Je: "Forty-five years ago today, I was born again - thanks to the faithful witness of Abraham David and Nate Scharff. How I thank GOD for His reaching down to this poor sinner!"

March 23: Genesis 15:1-6 - Je: GOD has spoken to me that my spiritual descendants will be as the stars of the sky!

March 24: We and Alfreds went to Creswell to meet with a house church group - Jim and Betty Bevers, Art and Mary Prichet, and others - a good time by all.

March 29: Ollie, Dan's dog, was put to sleep and buried. It was a sad time for their entire family. Greg dug a grave in the back corner of their yard for Ollie and put a little cross on the grave with Ollie's name on it.

April 1: Watched NCAA final with Greg and Dan.

April 6-9: Trip to Coast in RV - Jo and me:
Friday: To Newport, lunch at Yaquina Bay lighthouse - to No. 12 spot at Tillicum Beach, our favorite place to stay - evening beach walk with Jo, dinner, dominoes.
Saturday: All day at Tillicum Beach - resting, walking, reading.
Sunday: Morning - played Uno, beach walk, breakfast, to South Beach area of Newport. Afternoon - nap at ocean pullout by Depoe Bay, to Casino RV parking area at Lincoln City.
Monday: Jo at the Lincoln City mall. I went to library book sale that takes place every Monday. Lunch at kite place. Parked at northern beach area. I got mussles from the ocean. Home at 5:30 p.m. "A wonderful four days away! 'Thank you, Jesus.' "

April 12-14: Retreat of house church core group - Alfreds, Behrs, Lunds, Marshes, Ed Montgomery - getting better acquainted and talking and praying about a house church conference.

April 16: Steve Seabury called from Turkey to get our input on several matters.

April 18: Jo and I went to see the tulip fields near Woodburn.

April 19: Fishing at Green Peter Reservoir - got my limit of five trout.

April 22: Jo's annual piano recital.

305

April 23 Je: "Genesis 22:12 - GOD is pleased with my obedience - and I am now to enjoy the garden, fruit trees, yard, flowers, deck, RV, and boat. Others are now doing house church planting and networking. How long keep PTWP? How long Jo teach piano?"

April 23-25: Worked on our deck - cleaning, repairing, painting, which was an annual task.

April 26 - May 9: Jo went to Indiana to be with Gerry and Wenda and their three, her sister Evelyn, and others.

April 29: Fishing all day with Bob Iddings at Green Peter.

May 1: Dad's Volume 2 sent to Arcadia. It was entitled *Images of Fostoria, Ohio - Volume 2 - as told by Paul H. Krupp.*

May 4: Watched Kentucky Derby on TV.
Je: "Important things in my life:
- GOD
- family
- friends
- home church
- publishing
- writing
- enjoying life - garden, fishing, fruit trees, etc.
Order of importance - GOD is No. 1 - all others equally important."

May 5: A neighbor, Steve Duvall, and I tilled and planted the garden. We did a garden together for several years.

May 13: Frank Smith and Gills were with us overnight. Bob Iddings joined us for dinner. Stan Pierce came over in the evening.

May 14: Genesis 26:3, Psalm 37 - GOD gave us this land and we are to <u>stay here</u>.

May 16-20, Thursday thru Monday: Fishing trip to Detroit Reservoir. I took the RV - Jo came up for part of Saturday and Sunday. It was a wonderful time of fishing, resting, reading, giving out *The Way to GOD* to other campers. Je: "I need to pull back this summer as much as I can, and as long as it takes, to feel totally rested - and to begin hearing from GOD afresh."

May 22: Willamette Valley apostolic network - Harold Behr, Doug Alfred, Jo and I - decided to meet as couples monthly in various homes through the summer - conference put off until later.
Maders came for lunch - they gave us money for the deck roof materials - they have been so generous to us!

June 1: Medina wedding - saw Bobbie Young.
Shannon Wenger high school graduation party.

June 3: Finished building deck roof framing - put up with the help of Stan Pierce, Ed Montgomery, Dave and Mike Honan, and Bob Bowlin.

June 7: Finished deck roof.

June 10: Sent *Dad's Volume 2* page proofs to Arcadia.

June 12: WV apostolic leaders - 10 a.m. - 3 p.m. - Behrs, Montgomerys, Alfreds, Wyants, and us - "Wonderful time!"

June 17: Gill books came.

June 19: *GOD's Simple Plan for His Church, 2nd edition*, to Judy Crittenden.

June 27: Began working on a revised edition of *You Can be a Soul Winner - Here's How.*

July 4: Breakfast on the deck with Bachrans and Andrew. Andrew especially liked to have a meal on our deck. Jo and I went to the St. Paul Rodeo in the afternoon. Watched celebrations in Boston and Washington, D.C., on TV in the evening. "Thank you, Lord, for such a wonderful nation!"

Friday - Monday, July 5-8: Time in the RV at the Coast - Jo and me:
All the campsites were taken - we stayed Friday night at the Shilo Inn parking lot in Lincoln City, allowed because I was a veteran.
Saturday: At the Lincoln City mall - gave *The Way to GOD* to a German couple.
Lunch at the ocean pullout north of Depoe Bay. At Depoe Bay - *Way To GOD* to a WW2 Seabee and to a Vietnamese Navy officer at the Newport pier. We found a place to park at the Newport warehouse area because of my Seabee cap.
Sunday: Breakfast at Seal Rock. We spent the rest of the day at Tillicum Beach. *WTG* to a motorcycle couple, man from Pennsylvania, and WW2 vet.
Monday: Up the Coast and home. Je: "Thank you, Lord, for a wonderful time of rest on the Coast."

July 12-22: Jo went to Indiana to help Gerry and Wenda pack for their move to Wisconsin.

July 12-17: Fishing and RV trip for me. Fishing and RV at Takinitch Landing for two days. RV and rest at Tillicum Beach for three days. Fished at Olalla Reservoir on the way home.

Reading book, *Self Matters.*
Most critical choices in my life:
- going to Purdue
- NROTC
- Jesus as Savior and Lord

- Joanne to be my wife
- personal evangelism emphasis
- baptism in the Holy Spirit
- being with YWAM
- moving to Salem
- New Testament church
- Preparing The Way Publishers
- apostolic network

Hierarchy of Needs, from the *Self Matters* book, with the most important need listed first:
- survival
- security
- self-esteem
- love
- self-expression
- intellectual fulfillment
- spiritual fulfillment

July 27 - August 2: Seaburys were in the area sharing about their ministry in Turkey.

August 5: Exodus 3:10-18 - GOD has called me to lead His people out of bondage.

August 7-12: RV fishing trip with Jo at East Lake, near Bend.

August 18: Fixed breakfast for Andrew and Jamie.

August 19: Fishing at Olalla Lake with Bob Iddings.

August 21: Defining moments in my life:
- December 7, 1941 - beginning of World War 2.
- Working as a boy - garden, yard work, paper route, Krogers.
- Purdue.
- NROTC.

- Abe David and Nate Scharff - March 17, 1957 - turning my life over to Jesus.
- Navy time - Port Hueneme, Kingsville.
- Calvary Baptist Church, base outreach work.
- Hal Ward, the Navigators.
- Marion College, Howard Noggle, meeting Joanne, time in College Church basement reading my Bible and praying about my future.
- September 16, 1961 - marrying Joanne.
- LEI ministry days.
- Chicago ministry days.
- Charismatic experience.
- Break with Wesleyans.
- Living Water Christian Bookstore.
- YWAM and Loren Cunningham.
- Salem/Tacoma - prayer/revival.
- Move to Cabin Ct. in Salem.
- Move to Barnes Avenue - home church, PTWP.
- Dad's Fostoria books.

August 23: Jamie was rear-ended in an auto accident.

August 26: Word that Steve Dillon has been born-again.

August 30: To the State Fair for the day. Evening - Jamie's birthday dinner.

September 16-23: Fishing trip to Loon Lake - got some nice ones. Jo with me 20-23.

September 30: Started putting *Bible Outlines* book together. This is a compilation of notes I have made during my daily Bible reading times over a 40-year period.

October 15: Garden work with Steve Duvall - gave a *New Testament* to Andy, his son. On October 18 they took our RV and boat for the weekend.

October 24: Spent the day fishing at Smith Reservoir - got two 10-inch and two 11-inch - "wonderful time."

November 5: Elections - Republicans keep House, gain in Senate, keep some governors.

November 11: Veterans Day - Went to Albany Veterans Day parade with our neighbor, Dewey France.

Thursday, November 28: Thanksgiving Day - Extra time in GOD's Word in the morning - dinner at Beth's in the afternoon.

December 7: Jo and I went to Portland - she went shopping - I rode the trolleys and trains.

December 14: Took cookies to our neighbors. Heisman football award on TV.

Sunday, December 15: Began meeting on Sundays with Rick and Toni Shrout for a shared meal and Bible fellowship.

December 18: Sprague Christmas concert at the Elsinore.

December 19: Don and Ruthie Hawkinson were with us for Saturday and overnight.

December 21: Phoned Glenn Wilcox, who had worked with me during LEI days.

December 24: Christmas in the evening at Beth's.

December 26: Spent the day with Jo - shopping, meals out, *Big Fat Greek Wedding* movie.

New Year's Eve: Time together with Pierces, Alfreds, Knochs, and Shrouts - games, snacks, and prayer.

2003

January 4-6: We went to the Coast - Lincoln City, Depoe Bay, Newport, Tillicum Beach. Gave *Way to God* to Chinese student attending Oregon State University and to Alaskan fishing boat.

January 7: Called Carol Crenshaw - she was a new convert in Chicago through Willie and Millie Douglas and now lives in St. Louis, MO.

Wednesday, January 8: House church leader couples together at Alfreds'.

January 11: Spent some time with Ted Faver, who was up from their work in Mexico.

Sunday, January 12: New home church group started at our place - Shrouts, Pierces, and us.

January 13: Did research work on my biography.

January 14: Spent time with Al Knoch studying the Ultimate Reconciliation subject. He is very strong on the subject. His grandfather was one of the main proponents of the teaching in the 1930s. I wanted to fully hear Al on the subject to make sure that I had not missed something in my conclusion that it was a false teaching that I should resist and refute. My mind was not changed.

January 15: Began making plans for a Seabee Reunion for all former Seabees and Civil Engineer Corps officers living in Oregon. The twins are 12 years old today.

January 18: Bought a used iMac, laser printer, floppy disc drive, and cable for $545 - GOD had provided $550! It took awhile to get everything working properly - with help from Greg, Gerry via phone, and Alan and Aaron Yankus.

January 26: Darlene Wilcox called - Glenn went home to be with the Lord on January 22. He was conducting a seminar on soul winning at a church in Texas - he prayed the closing prayer and was gone. Glenn had been a part of LEI and had a passion for souls like few people I have known. I will greatly miss him! Darlene decided to gather funds and underwrite the re-publishing of our book *You Can be a Soul Winner - Here's How!*, which came to fruition in 2004.

January 27: At their request we sent copies of *Basic Bible Studies, GOD's Simple Plan for His Church,* and *Woman* to Jim and Joan Schnabel in the Washington, D.C., area, for them to take to a conference in the Middle East. They were distributed to key leaders from Algeria, Libya, Morocco, Tunisia, Sudan, Egypt, Bahrain, Qatar, Kuwait, Jordan, Lebanon, Malta, Mauritania, Syria, United Arab Emirates, and India. What an open door! From that contact, Joanne's book was published in Arabic by Prepare the Way Publishers in Egypt. It's interesting the similarity of name to our publishing - theirs is "Prepare," ours is "Preparing."

January 28: President Bush's State of the Union speech.

February 1: I was in Portland taking an Internet Marketing seminar. While there I saw Bridgett, Gina, and Leah Rapoza at the Lloyd Center ice rink. Also learned of the terrible spacecraft explosion as it was re-entering the earth's atmosphere and preparing to land.

February 5: Jo's birthday - we went to dinner in the evening.

Friday, February 14: Valentine's Day - we went to the Coast for the day - had lunch at Whale Cove. Je: "Great day with a wonderful wife!"

February 17: David Atkinson to send $500 for an upgrade on a computer for Jo.

313

February 24: I had been working on upgrading a number of our writings and was today able to take the masters to Chris at Lazerquick - they included: the *Workbook for Woman, Basic Bible Studies, New Testament Survey, Getting to Know GOD, Qualities GOD is Looking for in Us, Leadership-Servanthood in the Church, New Wine Skins, Mastering the Word of GOD,* and *Mastering Workbook.* Since they now had the masters we could place phone orders any time and they would deliver the books to our door.

February 25: Re-did all of our CLU courses.

March 1: Went fishing with Bob Iddings at Olalla Reservoir near Newport.

Sunday, March 9: GOD led us to an iMac with floppy and printer in Portland for $350 for Jo.

March 12: Monthly get-together of valley house church leaders - Marshes, Don Wyants, Behrs. Je: "Very good time."

Sunday, March 16, house church: Wyants, Pierces, Bob Iddings, Rick Shrout, us. Je: "Wonderful time!"

March 17: Bush speaks to the nation - "time has run out" regarding Iraq.

March 18: Phone conversation with John "Jamie" Jamison. Jamie was student body president at Purdue the year that I was speaker of the senate. This was the first contact I had had with him for decades. In fact, I had seen him only twice since we graduated. The first time was in August 1957, when I was en route from CECOS to Kingsville, TX, and he and Sue gave me a copy of *The Man Called Peter* book. The second time was at the O'Hare Airport in Chicago. He has had quite a life of leadership in various enterprises on the East Coast.

March 19: The liberation of Iraq has begun.

March 22-25: Jo and I to the Coast - Lincoln City, Depoe Bay, Newport, Tillicum Beach - overnights at casino parking lot, South Beach State Park, and Tillicum Beach. Je: "I am really tired! And so grateful for this time away! 'Thank you, Lord!' "

March 31: Jo and I went to see the tulip fields near Woodburn.

Sunday, April 13 (Palm Sunday): 27 people from eight home church groups together. Je: "Really good time - 'thank you, Jesus.' "

Sunday, April 20 (Easter, or Resurrection Sunday): Went to Methodist Sunrise Service at the Salem Riverfront Pavillion. Afternoon dinner at Beth's.

Monday evening: Fifteen people at our place for a meeting with Robert Fitts.

April 22: Fishing at Harriet Lake - caught four 10-11-inch - saw incredible beauty en route including four deer.

Sunday, April 27: I spoke at Word and Spirit Church in West Salem.

April 28: Joanne's annual piano recital.

May 2: Went fishing at Blue River Reservoir - "Beautiful place." It became one of my favorite fishing spots.

May 12: Jo had "High Tea" to honor Betty McCormick on her birthday.

Sunday, May 25: On TV - Indy 500 race during the day; Memorial Day concert from the Capitol on TV in the evening. Je: "Thank GOD for America!"

May 26: Memorial Day. Service at Arlington cemetery on TV in the morning. Jo and I went to see the iris fields north of Keizer in the afternoon. Bachrans up for barbecue in the evening.

May 29: Jo had surgery on her throat to have a benign cyst removed.

June 2-3: Fishing with RV at Laurence and Timothy lakes.
June 17: Fishing at Smith Reservoir.

Saturday, June 21: Seabee Reunion here in Salem for former Seabees and Civil Engineer Corps officers living in Oregon - more than 120 came including wives. Je: "Wonderful time! Excellent help! GOD is good!"

June 26: Fishing at North Fork and Harriet lakes. Je: "Wonderful time alone with the Lord."

July 9 - August 9: Trip to Midwest - by myself, then Jo came:
I stayed with Ray Dell.
July 11-12: Glass Festival at Fostoria. Friday - spoke on WFOB radio about Dad's books, signed books at Readmore Bookstore, signed books at Museum.
Saturday: Book signings at R&L Glass, Glass Works, and Glass Museum.
Sunday, July 13: To church at EUB with Dave - followed by lunch at Wendy's with Kirians. In the evening Kirians, Dave, and I went to a Veterans' band concert.
Monday thru Saturday: Working on a foreword for a book by Frank Viola, checking on book supply at various locations, time with Gary McPherson, Ray and Mary Dell; much time with my brother Dave.

Sunday, July 20: With Dave and Nancy Slaymaker to a Dillon reunion.

Monday: Breakfast with Norman Gibat, evening with Bill Ramsey.

Tuesday: Spoke at Kiwanis on the theme: "It is safe to put your life in GOD's hands" with stories from my life.

Wednesday evening: took Dells and Dave out to dinner.

Thursday: Picnic with Loren and Lois - Jo arrives safely in the late evening.

Friday: Jo and I see refurbished 927 N. Main St. home - it is beautiful! My High School 50th Class Reunion fellowship at Black Cat in the evening.

Saturday: Class reunion banquet in the evening. They had me pray the closing prayer. I prefaced it with an exhortation to know GOD and be ready for heaven.

Sunday, July 27: We stop to see Joyce and Cody Cull in Northern Indiana on our way to Marion.

Monday - Wednesday: Time with Bill and Evelyn Allen, Marvin and Hazel Hinds, Glen and Betty Martin, and Doris Smith.

Thursday: Trip to Ottawa, Illinois.

Friday: On Christian TV at Ottawa.

Saturday thru Wednesday: At Gerry's in Wisconsin - staying at a cottage on the lake.

Saturday: Took a boat ride, rode a go-cart with Geoffrey, played checkers with Allison.

Sunday: Church and day with Gerry and family at their place in town.

Monday: Fishing with Gerry in the morning, took grandkids to lunch at McDonald's, fishing with kids in the evening - caught 19!, picnic supper at our place with everyone. Tuesday: Took Alex and Allison to breakfast, we all went to the Wisconsin State Fair, fishing off the dock in the evening.

Wednesday: Geoffrey to breakfast, lunch with Gerry and Wenda, dinner with everyone at Gerry's.

Thursday, August 7: Trip to Detroit, MI - stopped by Wheaton, IL, where we once lived. Ernestine had us in a beautiful motel suite.

Friday: Rested all day.

Saturday, August 9: Flight home to Oregon.

August 21: Bob Morin's funeral. Bob was a dear brother who was part of a house church in Salem for several years.

August 26: I finished writing *Bible Outlines*, a book that gives an outline for every book of the Bible and a title for each chapter. It is the result of notes I made during forty years of daily Bible reading.

August 27: The RV has been a delight to own, but we decided that it was time to sell it - and have parked it at WalMart.

August 29: Helping Greg, my son-in-law, put in his sprinkler system.

September 1: Jamie's 20th birthday celebration in the evening.

September 3: Fishing at Silverton Reservoir.

September 7: My 68th birthday - Jo gave me breakfast on the deck.

September 10: We went to a home in West Salem and picked plums.

September 12: Fishing at Smith Reservoir.

September 14: We sold the RV. We had it for three years and enjoyed it immensely.

September 15: Jo and I had lunch in Portland on the Columbia River to celebrate our 42nd Wedding Anniversary. The next day, the actual day of our anniversary, we had dinner at Izzy's in Salem.

September 19-22: Spencer Harris came to visit us. He is a dear friend from Purdue days who lives in the San Francisco Bay area. I have shared often and pointedly with him about a relationship with Jesus. Saturday he and I spent the day at the Coast. He went with us to our home church on Sunday and left on Monday.

September 30 - October 2: Fishing trip to Loon Lake - got nine nice ones during two days there.

October 18: Trip around Mt. Hood with Shrouts to get fruit.

October 23: Rick Shrout and I went to the SalemNet breakfast. This was my further attempt to relate to the Salem leaders - the Lord said that I should give it one more try. We were warmly received. Je: "Thank you, Jesus!"

October 25-28: Niki Turner was with us. We knew her and Wil, who are now divorced, during our time with YWAM.

Sunday, October 26: Home church with Shrouts and Pierces - spent the time affirming one another. Je: "Wonderful time!"

October 27: A day with Jo - Independence, Monmouth, and Amity.

October 28 - November 3: Writing various high school classmates with a Christian witness as a follow-up to our 50th reunion.

November 6: I passed out in the bathroom. I hit my nose on the heat register, which required eight stitches at the emergency room.

November 11: House church leaders together - Pierces, Knochs, Ed Montgomery, and Doug Alfred.

November 12: I have become weary of going to non-believing doctors. Every time I mention GOD, prayer, or healing they look away or make some negative comment. So I did some research and found a Christian doctor team, Drs. Oscar and Lerma Quijano. They became wonderful doctors and friends for both Jo and me until their retirement. Then we both switched to Dr. Terry Young, also a wonderful Christian doctor and friend.

November 30: We just received word of Andrew's brother's death in a car accident. He was Andrew's only sibling.

December 10: My first visit with Dr. Quijano - Je: "Wonderful Christian doctor."

December 13: Joe Palmer's funeral in Newport.

December 14: Saddam Hussein captured.

December 24: Christmas with Beth and family.

December 26-29: Trip to Washington state - Jo and me:
Spent time in Tacoma, Seattle, and Everett. Spent time with Laurie Sleeper, who is doing well without Mark; Tom and Teri Baker, and their home group including Shine and Edel; and Dan and Diana Blanchard, where we stayed for two nights.

CHAPTER 21
INVOLVEMENT IN SALEM

*(SalemNet, PTWP books, CLU, bookstores,
Retired Ministers' Prayer Fellowship,
House Church Conference, RV, fishing)*

(2004 - 2006)

<u>2004</u>

January 15: Thanks to Dave Adams, Rainbow West book stores began to stock our books at several locations. I would go and service the stores three or four times a year.

Sunday, Jan. 18 Je: "Shrouts, Pierces, us - wonderful time!"

Jan. 26-28: I went to my first SalemNet Prayer Summit. On Tuesday GOD spoke to me that we are to relate to the whole Church once again. Gordon Bergman asked me to lead a weekly, leaders' prayer time in South Salem. I was reluctant, but in the night GOD said, "Yes."

February 6-8: Joanne and I were guests of Holladay Park Plaza, a luxury retirement center in Portland. They were trying to entice us to retire in their facility. We were not ready for that and couldn't afford it if we were. But we had a lovely couple of nights there.

Feb. 13-23: Trip to N. Carolina at Jay and Carleen's invitation - Jo and me:
Sunday, Feb. 15: Spoke at a Clover, SC, church. Jo spoke in Sunday School on the Woman's subject. Lunch with the pastor and his wife.

Tuesday, Feb. 17: Joanne and I both spoke to about 60 at the Shepherds' annual banquet. This was a group of spiritual leaders in Charlotte, NC, that Jay had been relating to. Joanne spoke on the Woman's subject and I spoke on "The Church in Transition," giving a copy of our New Wine Skins booklet to each one.

On Wednesday Jay and I met with Methodist pastors in Morgantown.

On Thursday the four of us had lunch at "The Good Ole Boys" - I met "Cussin" Russ (more on this later). Also Mr. Walker, General George Patton's aide. He shared some interesting things about the general with us. In the evening we went to Charlotte for a meeting at Thomas' home - about 30 were there - it was a good experience of Body ministry. We stayed overnight at Alice's large home.

On Friday we spent several hours in a meeting dialoguing with about 20 from the Shepherds' group.

Saturday was a day of sightseeing - Biltmore House in Ashville; Billy Graham's Cove, where we left some of our books; and Ridgecrest, the famous Southern Baptist retreat center, where we also left books.

On Sunday I went to Russ's home and presented him with GOD's plan of salvation - I prayed with him, but I'm not sure if he truly repented or not. Then to the Sunday gathering at Ferris'. Several prophesied over us that GOD had more travel for us, even overseas. (This has not happened yet, and I doubt it if will.)

Monday: Traveled home. Je: "Thank you, Jesus, for a wonderful trip!"

February 27: Jo and I went to see The Passion of the Christ, a movie produced by Mel Gibson - very graphic!

March 5: GOD provided a very nice refrigerator for the garage for $30.

March 8: I painted the deck and picnic table.

March 9: I had lunch with Greg, my son-in-law.
March 10: Lunch with Dewey and Emma.

March 13: Gathered 15 boxes of wood for our stove.

March 18: Greg, Beth, and Dan came for dinner - I taught Dan the Navigator "Wheel" illustration.

April 1: 22 boxes of wood from a tree Dewey, our neighbor, had cut down.

April 4: Jo and I went to Woodburn to see the tulip fields.

April 9: Fishing at Smith Reservoir. In the evening Kelly sang *The National Anthem* at her school. Je: "What a voice!"

April 11: Easter Sunday - I read all of the biblical accounts in my *Harmony of the Gospels*. We went to the SalemNet Sunrise Service with Rick Shrout. Bachrans at our place for Easter dinner.

April 15-16: Don and Ruthie Hawkinson were with us overnight.

April 20: I was nominated for Purdue NROTC Hall of Fame. I found out later that I was not selected, but it was a great honor to even be nominated.

April 22: Tom White spoke at SalemNet breakfast - excellent - "Need to add apostles, prophets, and entrepreneurs to the mix of pastors for GOD's success in prayer movements." I totally agree.

April 26: Jo's piano recital - I gave her a dozen roses to honor her twelve years of teaching.

April 28: We bought an additional three feet on the eastern boundary of our lot from Greg and Beth.

April 29: I went fishing at Silverton Reservoir.

April: Proofing *You Can be a Soul Winner* and *Bible Studies for Soul Winners* for republishing.

GOD began to speak the "Reaching Cities" vision to me.

May 6: We went to the National Day of Prayer in Salem with Al and Charleen Knoch. We stopped to see Sterling and Pat Borbe afterward.

May 7: Gave *You Can . . .* and *BSSW* to Dewey and Emma to take to Africa on their hunting trip to give to believers there.

May 8: Dad's birthday - Je: "I miss him!"

May 9: Jo and I went to see the iris fields.

May 24: Rick Shrout and I went fishing at Olalla - got our limit!

May 26: Kelly's choir concert - she got the music scholarship and was named one of six "outstanding students."

May 30: Word of Glen Martin's passing.

May 31: Memorial Day cookout with Bachrans.

May: Spent time with Dewey's brother, Ken. I began stopping occasionally and witnessing to him.

June 1: Fishing at Silverton Reservoir.

June 4: Kelly graduated from high school.

June 5: President Reagan died. State funeral at Capitol June 9, California funeral and burial June 11.

June 6: 60th anniversary of D-Day.
Graduation open houses - Kelly Bachran and Candace Wenger.

June 13: I visited Dewey's brother.

June 14: Jo and I went to see the Navy ships leave Portland.

June 19: I went to garage sales with Jo - new tent for $20; chair for my study for $15.

June 21: Began spending time with Ed Tornberg.

June 22: New edition of *YC and BSSW* arrived.

June 25: Fishing at Smith Reservoir; checked out Blue River Reservoir.

July 9: 9:30-10:30 a.m. - got my limit at Smith!

July 13: Prayed with Ken, Dewey's brother, for salvation.

July 15-18: A visit from Jay and Carleen Ferris.
July 16: We took them to the Coast for the day.
July 17: 4-10 p.m. - Ten people were here for a meeting with Jay and Carleen.
July 18: We took Jay and Carleen to Detroit to rendezvous with Missy from Bend.

July 20: Spent time with Ken France, now a new believer.

<u>July 23-27: A trip to bookstores in Eastern Oregon - Jo and me:</u>
Friday: Stops in Bend: Christian bookstore, Missy Ferris, lunch in the park where we witnessed to a hippie couple from Indiana. To Burns: Three stores; with Janet Long to her cabin.

Saturday: To Sumpter and Baker City - two stores; wonderful dinner at an old hotel.

Sunday: Oregon Trail Interpretive Center; Hells Canyon and Joseph Rodeo; to Christian Retreat home for the night - deer came up in the yard and ate right out of our hands.

Monday: To Joseph, Enterprise, and La Grande - sold $500 of books at one place in Enterprise and $100 at another place. Stayed at a nice Motel Super 8 in LaGrande; spent the evening with Michael and Priscilla, Allison Laurence and Abbey. Allison had translated my book on home church into Spanish.

Tuesday: At Eastern Oregon State University and Christian bookstores in LaGrande; stopped at the Indian Center en route home. Je: "Thank you, Lord, for a wonderful trip! 1,100 miles."

Sunday, August 1: 10-2 - with Shrouts - wonderful time!

Tuesday, Aug. 3: Spent the day fishing at Smith Reservoir.

Aug. 4: Jamie got engaged to Andrew Palmer. We were so delighted!

Aug. 8-10: Retreat with Rick and Toni Shrout at Big Lake. Beth and her gang joined us on Sunday, the 8th.

Aug. 13: With Chieko and her father - I gave him a *New Testament* in Japanese. He was in the Japanese military toward the end of WW2 and is a delightful gentleman.
326

Aug. 16: I met with Ken France - Je: "I really believe he has met Jesus." The next day I shared this with Dewey and Emma - Dewey wept. Ken went home to be with the Lord soon thereafter. There was a remembrance time at Dewey's on September 5.

August 17: We had an hour-long talk with Woodrums about their possibly taking over PTWP.

Aug. 19-31: Jo went to Indiana alone for her 50th High School Reunion. She was asked to make appropriate remarks and give the benediction at the final banquet. The Lord gave her a wonderful opportunity to witness to her classmates before she prayed. This was something she had been wanting to do for years. She felt the Lord's help and freedom and that He gave her just the words to say.

Aug. 24: These great Christian leaders died within two weeks of each other - TC Cunningham (Loren's father), Kenneth Hagin, Bill Bright, Howard Malmstadt, and Derek Prince. It must be "a changing of the guard."

Aug. 31: I spent time with George and Joyce Wilde in Vancouver en route to get Jo at the airport. I had many phone calls and time with people while Jo was gone.

Sept. 7: My 69th birthday - free breakfast at Denny's - fishing at Smith - free dinner with Jo at Mongolian Grill. Birthday fellowship in the evening - Knochs, Dunbars, Bachrans, Ed Montgomery, Rick Shrout.

Sept. 11: One-by-one we are getting rid of responsibilities: Fostoria books, High School Class Reunion, Boilermakers for Christ, Willamette Valley house church net-working, traveling, writing, house church national leadership. Yet to do - pass off PTWP and write my biography.

Sept. 15-16: Frank Smith was with us overnight.

September 17: Saw Graham and Treena Kerr briefly for a wonderful reunion when they were speaking at an event here in Salem.

September 20: Jo and I to Portland to celebrate our wedding anniversary.

Sept. 27-29: Fishing at Loon Lake.

Sept. 30: Harvested Anjou pears and Braeburn apples from our trees.
Considered doing real estate - buying fixer-uppers, fixing them, selling or renting them - but GOD said, "No."

Sundays: We have begun meeting weekly with Tornbergs. These were wonderful times.

October: I am now marketing the PTWP publications at Western Baptist library and bookstore, Salem Bible College, Good News paper, prison chaplain, Molalla bookstore, Salem Academy, Newberg bookstore, George Fox bookstore, and Friends' Yearly Meeting.

One of the special feature editors came to our house and interviewed us for an article in the *Statesman Journal* newspaper about house church.

November 1-2: Diana Blanchard was with us overnight.

Nov. 3: Bush wins a second term. We bought a new freezer for the garage.

Nov. 7: 4-7 p.m. - House church at Tornbergs. Je - "Better all the time."

Nov. 14 and 18: Jo went to Jamie's wedding showers.

November 19: Fishing at Smith - got four.

Nov. 22: $200 from Willie and Millie Douglas, $500 from Jay and Tammy Martin. We are so thankful!

Nov. 26: Day with Hawkinsons.

Nov. 27: Andrew and Jamie ask me to do their wedding ceremony.

December 2: Shared my story at the SalemNet breakfast.

Dec. 4: Spent several hours with John and Amy Meyers.

Dec. 8: Started working out at Apollo.

Thursday mornings - weekly prayer times - Arne Jensen, Ed Tornberg, Steve Kilpatrick, others, and me.

Dec. 18: Jamie's wedding. It was a wonderful occasion. I was honored to do the ceremony. Andrew, Jamie's husband, is a wonderful, Christian young man. He grew up on the Coast, at Newport, where his father is a dentist. Joanne made the three bridesmaids' dresses.

Dec. 20: We took jellies around to the neighbors.

Dec. 22: Sunday gathering - Alfreds, Knochs, Coxes, Jay and Carleen Ferris, Tornbergs, us.

Dec. 25: Christmas with Bachrans.

2005

Sunday, January 2: 4-8 pm - At Tornbergs - wonderful times every Sunday.

I spent time with Stan Pierce, Ed Tornberg, Dave Wyant, John Roth, Wendell Barnett, and Bob Lund this month.
Had CLU students work. Went to see the doctor at the VA. Went to bookstores in Salem, Silverton, and Molalla.

Prayer times: Arne Jensen, Ed Tornberg, Jim Ware - Thursday 7-9:30 a.m. - sometimes Keith Churilla, Steve Kilpatrick, Ricky Faircloth, and Lee Gilkison.

Thursday, Jan. 20: Bush's Inauguration.
SalemNet breakfast.

Sat., Jan. 22: Spent the day with Dave and Janice Woodrum, John and Amy Meyer, and Bob Lund discussing PTW marketing.

Jan. 24-26: SalemNet Prayer Summit - Arne and I went and roomed together - on Wednesday Jerry Sloan prayed for me regarding healing from Wesleyan Church rejection.
Jan. 28: Dinner with John and Becky Roth.

February 1: Fishing at Olalla Reservoir near Newport.

Feb. 5: Jo's 69th birthday - lunch and bowling with Bachrans.

Feb. 8: Met with the local YWAM leaders - they prayed for us regarding what we had gone through at the Salem Base.

Feb. 11: Jo and I toured the Aviation Museum in McMinnville and saw the Spruce Goose.

Feb. 21: We purchased a 2004 Buick Century, with 30,865 rent-a-car miles on it, at Larson Motors in McMinnville.

Feb. 26: A meeting of home church groups at Bethel Church in the country, sponsored by Mike Wenger. About 40 people were there.

In February: 21 boxes of wood from Dave Wyant - 15 from Dewey.

March 4: Lunch with Dewey and Emma.

Thurs., March 10: I had the privilege of praying at the opening of the Oregon State Senate. Oregon was experiencing a lack of rain so I prayed for rain, which came in abundance throughout the Spring. GOD is faithful to answer prayer!

March 14: Lunch with Alger and Gloria Marsh.

16: Lunch with Greg Bachran, my son-in-law.

20: Psalms 81:10-16, Proverbs 29:26 - GOD to provide for us, not man or our doings.

22: Tornbergs bought us a new lawn mower.

April 5: The publisher in Egypt is going to translate and publish *Woman* in Arabic.
Lunch with John and Betty McCormick in Vancouver.

11: Fishing at Freeway Lakes.

17: Spent time in the afternoon with John and Amy Meyer.

25: Joanne's annual piano recital.

27: South SalemNet prayer to move from our home to Arne's nursery.

30: Gardening with Rene Tornberg at our place.

Spring each year - repair and paint boat, clean and paint deck, moss killer on yard, lime and Epsom salts on fruit trees, lime on garden, start garden plants inside.

May 22: I officiated at Mat and Michelle McCormick's wedding.

June 1: How we limit GOD - sin, unbelief, and disobedience.

3-6: Jo flew to Sacramento to see her sister Arlene.

9: Distributed tracts with Arne Jensen in the vicinity of the Rose Parade ships in Portland.

10: Breakfast with Beth for Father's Day. She usually took me to breakfast or lunch for Father's Day. These times alone with my daughter meant so much to me.

15: Fishing at Blue River reservoir - four 11-12-inches.

This year - throughout the year we were working with Clint and Judy on Stella Patterson's book, *Calling Forth the Remnant*. It was the most radical book we ever published, but very true and needed.

June: Dan and I replaced the bottom trim all around the house because some of it was rotten. Then Jo put a fresh coat of paint on the house and we hired Wendell Barnett to do the same on the garage/offices addition.

June: Spent time with Mike Lesh, Don and Mindy, John Roth, Dewey France, Keith Churilla, Ricky Faircloth, Terry Cox, and Sterling Borbe.

July 1: My call is to be a watchman to the Church - Ezekiel 3:5. Kelly sings the *National Anthem* at a soccer game. What a granddaughter!

July 4: To Molalla for parade and rodeo - we went only for the parade, but they were giving out free passes to the rodeo, so we were able to enjoy it, too.

July 10: Wonderful Sunday meeting - Tornbergs, Arne, Lunds, Meyers, us.

29: Fishing at Smith.

August 1: Beth at Beaverton hospital for surgery.

13: Jo and I took the day off and traveled around Mt. Hood.

25: Fishing at Blue River Reservoir.

September 7: My 70th birthday - breakfast with Beth, dinner out with Jo.
8: Fishing at Smith.

12: Celebrated our 44th wedding anniversary - saw Alger and Gloria, had lunch on the Columbia River - got a TV for our bedroom.

Sept 16-17: I was involved with Unity Fest with Ricky Faircloth. It was his vision to bring the churches of Salem together for this event, but few responded.

Picked apples and pears at Clara Welch's.

September 23 - October 9: Trip to the Midwest - Jo and me:
Friday: Flew to Detroit - rented a car and drove to Fostoria - went to Fostoria High School football game.

Saturday: Phoned Ray Dell and George Gray. Saw my brother Dave, sister Janet, Bonnie McClellan (Dave's girlfriend), Dave's new trailer.

Sunday: Church with my brother Dave and Bonnie McClellan, time with Bonnie Hanson (whom we stayed with), lunch with Bill and Gloria Ramsey, met George Gray at the Fostoria Historical Museum.

Monday, Sept. 26: In the morning we went to see Camp Berry, the Boy Scouts of America camp outside of Findlay, where I was on staff one summer. Wonderful afternoon with Dave, Janet, Jo and me; evening with my cousin Nancy Slaymaker.

Tuesday: a.m. - With my cousins in Upper Sandusky; lunch with George and Carolyn Moser; evening time with Kelly Downing.

Wednesday: a.m. - checkers and Vernors ginger ale with Dave; family lunch at Wendy's; dinner with Bonnie Hanson, time with Royetta Kirian.

Thursday: Dave and we went to Lake Erie for lunch with Chuck and Carol (my cousin) Bixler; dinner with Bonnie Hanson and Kelly Downing.

Friday: To Detroit - time with Gar and Rachel Darnes, Ernestine Stewart.
Saturday, October 1: Ernestine's retirement party where Jo and I shared briefly about our friendship of many years.
Sunday: Breakfast with Ernestine's family; rested.

Monday: Train trip through Chicago to Wisconsin.
Tuesday - We stayed at a cottage on the lake. We had a little groundbreaking ceremony with Gerry and Wenda on the land where they were getting ready to build their home. Then we helped them put the retaining plastic all around two sides of the land. It was wonderful to be able to help them even that little bit. They did much of the work on the house themselves and with donated labor.
Wednesday: Sunday - with Gerry and Wenda and the grandkids.
Sunday, Oct. 9: Flight home.

Oct. 12-13: Maders were with us - John and Amy Meyer came for dinner and John had a prophetic word for Tony.

October 14: We spent time with Jan Jones, a missionary to Japan.

22: Kelly's 19th birthday party.

31: $2000 provided for an Egyptian publisher to put Jo's book into Arabic.

November 7: We had a luncheon to honor retired ministers in the Salem area - 13 came. They wanted to meet again, which developed into a monthly prayer-and-luncheon time together for several years.

18-20: Jo flew to Southern California for a big Thanksgiving family celebration hosted by her Uncle Warren.

18: My first time with Mark and Dena Brehm - they came by to talk about home church.

24: Thanksgiving with Bachrans.

27: Jo had shingles, which pretty much incapacitated her for five weeks. She got up only to teach her piano lessons and spent the rest of the time in her chair in her sewing room. But we praise the Lord that she did completely recover with no residual effects.

December 23: I passed out Christmas tracts that I had written, at the mall.

December 25: Christmas with the Bachrans. Beth is on the road about one week a month traveling all over the country (even into Quebec) with Supra, an affiliate of GE Security, training real estate agents in the use of their lock boxes and other products. (She did this from 2000 to 2010, when they moved to Hawaii.)

Greg had a Carpet Brokers business for about 15 years. He sold carpet, ordered directly from the factories, and hired others to do the installing. They started the business in their home and later moved the showroom to a warehouse location.

Jamie and Andrew are about to complete their first year of marriage - still so much in love. Jamie completed her undergraduate work in business accounting at Oregon State University last April and will walk to receive her diploma with her husband when he receives his in March. Then they are off to Southern California where Andrew will be doing graduate work in architecture.

Kelly is a sophomore at George Fox University and on the worship team. Daniel is a junior in high school. Music is very much a part of all of their lives. It won't be long before Beth and Greg will be empty nesters. All the grandkids love Jesus - what more could we ask?!

Gerry and Wenda are busy with their ministry at the Wesleyan Church in Mukwonago, WI. They are finally able to get started on their new home and are racing with the weather to get it enclosed. Geoffrey is a senior in high school - so full of music. The twins, Alex and Allison, are freshmen this year - all three are in the high school orchestra. We were able to sit in on one of their orchestra classes during our visit in October - what fun!

December 31: Promise for the New Year - Hebrews 13:5 in the Amplified Bible - "I will not in any way fail you nor give you up nor leave you without support. I will not, I will not, I will not in any degree leave you helpless, nor forsake nor let you down, relax My hold on you. Assuredly not!"

Evening: New Year's Eve time with Jensens, Brehms, and Daniel Markoya - it was a wonderful time.

2006

Thursday, January 5: Arne, Ed, me - wonderful prayer time. Evening - House Church Conference committee - Tim Davis, Daniel Markoya, us.

Jan. 6-7: Working on a House Church Conference.

10-12: Visiting bookstores - Salem and Albany.

13: John Lindell here overnight.

15: Dinner with Bachrans and Dr. Mark and Gerry Palmer, Jamie's husband's parents - a wonderful time.

18: Jo and I are looking at possible conference facilities.

19: SalemNet breakfast; working on Stella's manuscript. Afternoon - with Daniel Markoya who is starting a conference web page.

20: Working on Chuck Tooman's manuscript for his book, *Richness in Christ*.

Sat., 21: All day in Portland with Jo - saw Bridget, Leah, and Danni Rapoza at the Lloyd Center skating rink.

23-25: SalemNet Prayer Summit - Arne and I roomed together again.

Jan. 31: Lunch with my son-in-law, Greg Bachran.

Sunday, February 5: Jo's 70th birthday
4-9 pm - House church group at Tornberg's - best yet!

Mon., February 6: Retired ministers' prayer and luncheon - more than 20 participated - 11:30-2:00 - wonderful time.

Saturday, February 11: Jo's 70th birthday luncheon and zip line at YWAM attended by Bachrans and a friend of Kelly. Greg made a DVD for Joanne. Such fun for the "old" lady!
Sun., 12: To Lincoln City and Depoe Bay with Jo for the day.

Feb. 15: 1 Chronicles 17:7-9 - GOD is with us - we are to move no more - see entire 1 Chronicles, Chapter 17.

Sat., Feb. 18: Trip to Castle Rock, WA, to share with about 40 intercessors. We shared about New Wine Skins, the up-coming House Church Conference, and the woman's issue - wonderful time.

Mon., 20: Evening with Brehms - good time.

24: Trip to Bend to see Jeff and Missy Stolasz.

March 10 - 21: The hose on the dishwasher leaked and ruined the kitchen floor, so I had to put down a new laminate floor. It turned out real nice and Jo was thrilled.

March 13: Word of Sterling Borbe's death.
14: Sterling's memorial gathering.

Sunday, March 19: First meeting at Brehm's - more than 60 people. GOD had spoken to me a few weeks earlier that it was time to start meeting there. I called the Brehms to share that with them, and, before I could share, Dena said the Lord had spoken the same thing to her. When she called Mark, who was on a business trip to Seattle, she discovered that the Lord had spoken the same thing to him that morning. So GOD had spoken to all three of us, we all put the word out, and more than 60 showed up!
Sunday, March 26: Twenty-eight people at Brehms for their second house church meeting.

Started working on John Sweetman's book, *The Unleashed Church*.

338

March 29: John and Amy Meyer visit us with a bouquet of roses, bless their hearts. They are like a son and daughter to us. I call her "Kid" because she is some years younger than John.

April 1: At Rick and Toni Shrout's new home in Lyons.

Sat., April 8: I officiated at Travis and Kendra's wedding. Kendra is Arne and Caren Jensen's daughter.

14: I am believing GOD to heal Joanne's shingles.

14-15: Jay Ferris visit.

Sun., April 16: Brehm's - about 35 people - Robert Fitts and Jay Ferris shared.

Thursday and Friday, April 20-21: A Retreat at Debi Wyant's home for those who will be teaching at the House Church Conference.
Saturday and Sunday: April 22-23 - *New Wine and New Wine Skins Conference* with teaching by Jonathan Campbell, Tim Davis, Jay Ferris, Robert Fitts, Maurice Fuller, Nate and Joanne Krupp, Gary and Caren Linden, Bob Lund, Daniel Markoya, Alger and Gloria Marsh, Frank Smith, and Dave and Janice Woodrum. More than 100 people participated - from California, Florida, Idaho, Michigan, North Carolina, Oregon, Texas, Washington, and Canada - and missionaries on furlough from Cambodia and Burkino Faso in West Africa. It was the most awesome conference we have ever been involved in - GOD truly met with us.
Mon., April 24: We took Toomans, Fullers, and Pattersons, who had participated in the conference, to the Coast for the day.

April 25-26: I worked on my boat - this was an annual task of cleaning, patching, and painting to get ready for the coming fishing season.

339

Fri., April 28: Fishing at Smith and Blue River.

Mon., May 1: Retired ministers' prayer and luncheon.

May 2-6: Arne helped me put in a sprinkler system for the upper orchard and garden area.

8: Jo and I took the day off and drove up the Washington side of the Columbia River.

10: We got word that Ed Tornberg had cut his arm on some broken glass and we rushed to the hospital to be with him.

19: Jo went fishing with me at Blue River. We did not catch any fish and it was her first and last time to go fishing with me!

May 22: I asked the Lord what else He had for me to do. He said, "Nothing, My son - just rest, relax, and enjoy My presence. Pass PTWP on to others that I will show you."

May 31: Psalm 61:6 - GOD to prolong my life.
9 a.m.-3 p.m.: Beth went with me to the Coast for an early Father's Day - it was a wonderful time!

June 5-6: Loon Lake - camping and fishing.

Sun., June 11: House church group at Arne's - wonderful time!

Monday, June 12: Jo and I went to Portland to see the ships leave.

Sunday, June 18: Andrew and Jamie's graduation from Oregon State University at Corvallis. We are so proud of them both!

<u>June 20-28: Trip to WA - Jo and me:</u>
We stayed with Art and Mary Prichet Tuesday thru Sunday - spent time with them and saw John and Lee Bermingham, Al and Charleen Knoch, Don and Ruthie Hawkinson, Denny Gunderson, Tom and Teri Baker; met with a group at Art and Mary's; and toured the Everett Boeing plant.
On Monday we moved to John and Lee's in Anacortes, spent time with them, had a meeting with Rabes, Hawkinsons, and Berminghams; and took a boat trip for one day to Victoria, B.C.

July 1: We spent more than an hour on the phone with Dave and Janice Woodrum and made a decision to turn PTWP over to them. We spent three hours with Darwin and Anne Newton in the afternoon.

Sunday, July 2: Home church group at Jensen's – baptized Rachel Bustamonte in the outdoor pool.

July 4: Spent time with Greg, Beth, and Dan.

Friday, July 7: To the Coast with Jo.

July 8: I spent three hours with someone who wanted our home church group to become part of a church he hoped to start. After subsequent meetings with him GOD told me, "I was not to walk with him."

Tuesday, July 11: Frank and Betty Smith came through - we had an evening meeting - 18 people - wonderful time.

July 12: All day PTWP transition meeting with Janice Woodrum.

July 15-30: Spent time at Jensen's getting their place ready to sell.

July 18: I went fishing at Smith Reservoir while Jo painted the living room and dining room. She is the painter in the family and my getting out of her way is a big help.

Sunday, July 23: Went to the HeartChange Sunday meeting with Arne and Caren for Mark Brehm and Henry and Rachel.

Monday, July 24: To Mt. St. Helens with Jo for the day.

July 30: Word that my brother Dave was in the hospital.

Monday, August 8: Retired Ministers' prayer and luncheon time.

August 11-16: Trip to Tacoma area. Stayed with Darwin and Anne Newton. Spent time with Rich and Cheri Carbone, Jack and Wilma Eads - Jack is going to do website work for us. Also Kathy Wolf, Bonnie McCullough, and Rick and Melissa Anderson on Anderson Island. We had an evening with Jim and Julie Vitzthum, Anne's mom, and Angelia, her husband, and three children; and had chiropractic treatments with Dr. Gordon Rody.

Aug. 17: Got peaches at our usual place north of Keizer.

Aug. 22: We had a visit from Steve and Cindy Seabury, missionaries to Turkey - had an evening gathering with 15.

Aug. 24: Fishing at Smith.

Aug. 25: Jo had her book at the Oregon State Fair and sold 50 copies.

September 9: Walt and Ruth Ann Hager spent four hours with us telling of their church ordeal.

Monday, September 11: Jo and I went to the Coast for my 71st birthday.

342

September 13: With Mark and Dena celebrating their 20th wedding anniversary and our 45th.

15: Benjamin Brehm is born.

16: Jo and I - Anniversary dinner.

September 20: Met Heinz Raudszus from Portland and had lunch - he carried the Nickel Ads paper in Salem. In the evening we picked up Gerry and Geoffrey at the Portland airport. They came for HeartChange. We went to their open worship time on Sunday and spent Monday together at the Coast, which was a really fun time.

Friday, October 6: Jo flew to Sacramento to spend time with her sisters.

October 12: Fishing at Smith.

October 20-23: Trip to Southern California for Uncle Warren's wedding with Sue.

Saturday, October 28: We spent the day displaying our writings with Oregon Authors at Independence, Oregon.

Sunday, October 29: The Salem and Dallas house church groups met together at Brehm's in Dallas - 25 adults plus many kids - to hear Arne's report on his trip to Pakistan with Dave Woodrum.

November 1: I visited bookstores in Salem, Albany, and Dallas with our books; saw Brian Hewitt.

November 2: A committee met to plan another House Church Conference - this was one of many such meetings to plan the up-coming conference in the spring of 2007.
In the evening we had a birthday dinner celebrating Beth's birthday.

Sunday, Nov. 5: We went to George Fox University to see Kelly on the worship team.

Monday, Nov. 6: Another Retired Ministers' prayer and luncheon.

Nov. 23: Thanksgiving with Bachrans - wonderful time!

Nov. 28: A group of us met to resolve a situation that had arisen in our home church group.

December 20: Greg's birthday dinner.

24-25: Christmas with Bachrans.

27: Jo and I went to the Coast for the day.

CHAPTER 22
FURTHER SLOWING DOWN

(2nd House Church Conference, Alaskan cruise,
PTWP to Woodrums, Neighborhood Prayer Groups, paper
routes, became great-grandparents,
house fire, Greg and Beth to Hawaii, fishing)

(2007 - 2010)

<u>2007</u>

January: House Church Conference Committee planning.

Jan. 7: Sunday meeting at Brehms' - very good.

8: MinhMan, our Vietnamese friend, called from California - it was so good to talk with her.

14: At Brehms' - I began teaching the *God's Simple Plan* book to this house church group.

We started making plans to take an Alaskan cruise to celebrate our 45th Wedding Anniversary. (We thought we might be too old to enjoy it on our 50th!)

February 2: Jo and I went to visit Sauvie Island outside of Portland, where we saw eagles.

10: Willamette Queen cruise with Jo on the Willamette River near Salem for her birthday.

Sunday, Feb. 11: Teaching at the Tornberg group on End Times from Matthew 24 - don't give in to fear or deception.

13: Went to Air Force Band concert with Jo.

February 19: I took Jo to her chiropractor in Aloha, we had lunch at Sweet Tomato.

March 5: Retired Ministers' prayer time and luncheon.

6: Fishing at Silverton Reservoir.

17: My 50th spiritual birthday - "thank you, Jesus!"

April 8: Easter Sunday - dinner with Bachrans.

April 20-22: Another House Church Conference, coordinated by Mark and Dena Brehm.
Friday, April 20: Conference speakers' retreat - "Wonderful!"
Saturday and Sunday: Conference - "Very good!" Sunday evening - time with Tony and Felicity Dale, who had stayed with us.
Monday morning: Time with Woodrums.

May 6-13: Cruise to Alaska to celebrate 45 years of marriage.
There were 3,000 passengers and a crew of 1,000. We were very "pampered" and it was so restful and fun. There were also many opportunities to witness throughout the cruise.
Sunday, May 6: Drove to Seattle and boarded the ship.
Monday: A day of rest at sea.
Tuesday: At Ketchikan, Alaska.
Wednesday: We saw glaciers at Tracy Arm Fjord in the morning. At capital, Juneau, in the afternoon. Saw Sarah Palin's governor's house - she was not yet famous.
Thursday: at Skagway.
Friday: I talked with a pianist performing on the ship who was trying to get back to GOD.
Saturday: A day of rest and travel to Victoria.
Sunday: Back to Seattle, home to Salem.
Rest, food, and scenery - what a wonderful time we had! "Thank you, Jesus!"

May 17-20: I had a plane trip to Wyoming for a Men's Prayer Retreat sponsored by Del Tinsley - at the famous 57,000-acre Willow Creek Ranch near Kaycee, WY. This was one of the hideouts of Butch Cassidy and the Sundance Kid. I shared the speaking time with Robert Hall from Texas.

24-25: A visit from Loren Dillon, my cousin, and his wife, Lois - we spent Friday at the Coast.

May 27-31: Trip to Wisconsin to see Gerry and his family - Jo and me:
May 27-29: We took a train trip from Portland, OR, to Milwaukee, WI, to spend six days with our son, Gerry, and his wife, Wenda, and their three. We slept in our seats the first night, but had a berth the second. We spent time with an Amish family on the train who knew the Lord - with twin girls, Mary and Miriam. The food and scenery were wonderful.

Geoffrey is looking forward to starting college this next year, and the twins, Alex and Allison, will be juniors in high school. It was a great joy to see and stay in the new home that Gerry and Wenda spent the past two years building. We spent time with Len Harris at the Midway airport before flying home.

June 8: Dan's high school graduation. He had a solo part when his jazz choir sang.

12: Fishing at Blue River Reservoir.

17: Father's Day - Mark Brehm called. He was like a son to us.

18: I had lunch with Beth to celebrate Father's Day.

Sunday, June 24: Seven people at David and Julie Farr's - it was a good beginning for a new house church group.

347

June 26: Fishing at Foster Reservoir.

27: Early morning prayer time with Arne Jensen, Daniel Markoya, and Mark Brehm.

29-30: Participated in a House Church Conference in Vancouver, WA, sponsored by the Dales.

July 4: At Bachrans for brunch.

Sunday, July 8: Finished teaching *GSP* at Brehms'.

July 10-12: Camping and fishing at Smith, Trail Bridge, and Blue River reservoirs - caught nine including a 14-inch brown trout at Smith. One can keep only five trout a day and have only a total of 10 in your possession.

22: We, along with Marshes, appointed Brehms elders with the Dallas group.

August 2: Went with Heinz on his Nickel Ads paper route.

August 6-8: Serviced Christian bookstores in Salem and Albany.

9-13: Stayed at Clint Preston's home on the Coast next door to Carol Preston's. We spent time with her and time on the Coast from Lincoln City to Florence.

16: I was a sub for Heinz' Nickel Ads paper route for the first time.

27: I spent a day at the Oregon State Fair.

August 3: Time with Woodrums - GOD provided $5,000 as a gift for our giving them PTWP.

September 17: Because of leaks, we had to have a new roof and skylight put in on our home, which cost exactly $5,000. GOD's faithfulness and timing are awesome!

This month: GOD gave me the concept of Neighborhood Prayer Groups throughout Salem.

Saturday, October 6: A new home church group hosted by Bob and Cathy Boudreau - 5:00 to 8:30 pm - 12 people - "good time."

19: Kelly's 21st birthday

We officially turned PTWP over to Dave and Janice Woodrum on October 26, 2007. Non-believing, unfaithful spouses left both Dave and Janice in 1991. They met through a prayer ministry in Washington State, and were married in 1994. They have a worldwide ministry of conducting evangelistic-healing crusades, organizing and teaching leadership training seminars for Christian leaders, and starting Bible schools to prepare Christian workers. Most of their work has been in Asia and Africa where they have 23 schools and use Joanne's book and seven of my writings in these schools. We hold them in high esteem. They moved PTWP to their home and office in Chehalis, WA. (See Appendices 5, 6, and 7 for more on the PTWP publications.)

November 2: Beth's 45th birthday party.

10: Jo and I went to a Blazers basketball game in Portland.

11: GOD provided a three-legged fruit ladder through Arne.

12: I went to the emergency room with blood clots and had to be on blood thinner for several months.

16: I took Jo to the emergency room with chest pains. It was pericarditis, an inflammation in the fluid around the heart.

November 22: Thanksgiving with Bachrans.
December 26: Family Christmas with Bachrans.

2008

January 1: I was called by GOD to a 21-day partial fast - juice, few fruits and vegetables, light breakfast, water, no TV or newspapers.

Jan. 5: Psalm 108:12-13 - Don't send a letter out regarding our financial needs - trust GOD, not man.

Jan. 7: Retired Ministers' Prayer Fellowship monthly gathering.

Jan. 15: I went for a heart stress test at the VA hospital in Portland - everything checked out okay.

Jan. 23, Wednesday: to CRC for the annual prayer summit - I went for just the one day.

Jan. 23: Al and Charleen Knoch came for an overnight stay - we always enjoyed our times with them.

February 4: Jo and I went to Portland to celebrate her birthday. 5: We went to the Mongolian Grill for Jo's birthday.

Saturday, Feb. 9: A work day at our place - Mark, Josh, and Gabe Brehm and Bob Boudreau, Bruce, and Duy - they split 70 boxes of wood and did some yard work.
Saturday, February 9: Evening - Home church group at Boudreau's - 11 people - wonderful time.

February 12: Colonoscopy at VA hospital in Portland - everything checked out okay.

Feb. 15: Byerlys, Brehms, Boudreaus, us - an evening of sharing - good time.

Sunday, February 17: We went to Ben Bentz' wedding.

Feb. 25 - March 4: Jo went to Wisconsin to be with Gerry and Wenda and to see Allison play in the musical *Wizard of Oz* during her junior year of high school - Jo said it was very well done. She also traveled to Indiana to see her sister Evelyn.

March 4-6: Frank Smith and his friend Robert visit - we had a Tuesday evening meeting at Arne's and went to Jim Morris's prayer breakfast on Wednesday.

March 18: We saw Dena's paper on hell - she begins her walk toward Ultimate Reconciliation.

March 21-25: Jo went to Sacramento to see Bob and Arlene.

March 22: Bob and Sherrill Hawley's first time at the Saturday house church meeting at Boudreau's.

March 26: I did Heinz' paper route.
Monday, March 31: I began to deliver the *Salem Monthly* paper to businesses in Silverton and Mt. Angel.
April 2: Did Heinz' route again.

April 7: Retired Ministers' Prayer Fellowship - we decided to discontinue as attendance was dwindling.

April 10: Isaiah 40:2 - "her time of service is ended" - the Lord spoke to me through this verse that it is time to retire.

April 13: A day with Jo at Lincoln City.

April 26: Kelly graduated from George Fox University.

May 1: I have added Woodburn to my *Salem Monthly* paper routes so am now doing Silverton-Mt. Angel-Woodburn (SAW) paper routes.

May 26: Neighbors together for fellowship and prayer in the evening - it was a wonderful time.

May 29: SAW paper routes.

June 20-25: We enjoyed a vacation at Marsh's cottage at Seaside - we had one day at Astoria, one day at Long Beach, and the rest of the time at Seaside - it was a wonderful time.
June 26: Heinz' route.
June 30: SAW routes.

July 14-16: Fishing and camping at Little Lava Lake and Lava Lake. GOD spoke Psalm 81:6 - "I relieved your shoulder of the burden" - it is time to retire.

August 1-3: Seaburys, missionaries to Turkey, visit – House church groups met with them at Bush Park.

Aug. 5: Neighborhood picnic party - 10 families - great success. This became an annual event - the neighbors getting together at our place for an evening of potluck food and fellowship.

Aug. 8 - 8/8/8: Tim Davis and Joy's wedding.

August 11: Fishing at Olalla.

August 15-18: Trip to WA - Jo and me - Spent time with Hamiltons, Hawkinsons, Jonathan Campbells, Woodrums, Dr. Rody. Meetings with people at Hamiltons on Friday and Saturday evenings.

Aug. 22: I went to the Oregon State Fair.

Aug. 27: Fishing at Blue River and Smith.

August 29: Added Dayton, McMinnville, Amity, Rickreall, Dallas, Monmouth, and Independence to my *Salem Monthly* paper routes.
30: SAW routes.

September 16: 47th Wedding Anniversary - evening dinner with Jo.

18-23: Jo to Wisconsin to be with Gerry, Wenda, and family.

20: Boudreaus got a new dishwasher and gave us their old one, but it was new for us and such a blessing. Bob even came and installed it!

25: Neighbors together for fellowship and prayer.

27: Uncle Warren and Sue came for a visit.

September: We started a series at the Boudreau group on *Knowing People* - motivational gifts, ministry gifts, birth order, temperaments, love languages, etc. - it was very informative and helpful. The teaching was shared by a number of us.

Sun., Sept. 12: Fruit run to Mt. Hood area with Hawleys, gleaning apples and pears.

October 22: Fishing at Smith.

October 27: I had a heart ultrasound, scheduled by Dr. Radzik - there was some blockage.

November 2: Beth's birthday dinner.

Nov. 4: Obama elected president.

December 25: Christmas with Bachrans.

353

2009

January 2: Good evening with Stan and Maria Pierce.

Sunday, Jan. 3: Our home church group - wonderful time - we each shared about our plans and hopes for 2009.

4: I saw the "Valkyrie" Hitler movie with Greg, my son-in-law.

4-6: Knochs with us.

5-6: SAW and MM (McMinnville to Monmouth) routes.

10: I phoned Frank Foltz - he is dying of cancer.

12: Phoned Harold Apger, Mase Bailey, and Marion Noll.

15: Went to the SalemNet monthly breakfast, serviced bookstores, and phoned twins on their birthday.

Tues., Jan. 20: I went to CRC for the prayer summit for the day.

February 3-4: SAW and MM routes.

February 14: Valentine's Day dinner at Great Wall Chinese buffet with our house church group - 16 people - good time. At the dinner someone gave me my first copy of *A Letter From GOD*. It is one of the best evangelistic tools I have ever seen and I now pass it out daily wherever I go.

17: We had Holly, my *Salem Monthly* paper route supervisor, for dinner. Her heart was healed in an Oral Roberts meeting when she was a young girl, but she is now very New Age.

19: Andrew and Jamie's first child, and our first great-grandchild, Audra Elizabeth, was born. She continued the Elizabeth name: Joanne's mother was Miriam Elizabeth, Joanne is Joanne Elizabeth, Beth is Elizabeth Ann, Jamie is Jamie Elizabeth, and Audra is Audra Elizabeth.

March 2-3: SAW and MM routes.

9: Neighbors together - five families.

12: Did Heinz' route.

17: Called Betty Scharff on her birthday - and my spiritual birthday. She prays for us daily - what a blessing!

19: Our neighbors, Salvador and Kim's two-year-old daughter fell out of the second-floor window onto their concrete driveway. She was taken to the hospital. The word got around and the neighbors were praying. When we went down the next morning Salvador answered the door and said, "It's a miracle! - she's okay." The neighbors were praying!

19: Did Heinz' route.

April 1, 3: SAW, MM routes.

6: I went fishing for the first time at Henry Haag Lake.

11: Easter brunch with Bachrans.

23: The Neighbor Prayer Group project for Salem was launched in April and May. Mona Edwards became the coordinator for this and put together a flier that she and I began distributing throughout Salem.

May 1, 4: SAW, MM routes.

May 7: Went to National Day of Prayer in Salem.

May 16: Bruce, a Chinese student at Salem Academy, living with Boudreaus, had given his heart to the Lord and was baptized.

17: Time at HeartChange with Ernestine and Carletta, who had come from Detroit, MI.

20: Fishing at Carter Lake.

25: We saw Audra for the first time.

29: With Palmers, Beth, Jamie, Audra, Kelly, and Dan.

May 30: Jo and I flew to Milwaukee
31: Alex and Allison's high school graduation.

June 3: At Purdue - we had lunch with Bob Truitt, who has made much progress with Boilermakers For Christ. Then I spent time with the NROTC captain, who is a believer - I shared how I had wanted to stay in the Navy, but the Lord said, "No," and he shared how he wanted to get out of the Navy, but the Lord told him to stay. Then I met with the dean of students, whose brother is a Baptist pastor. Evening: Dinner with Paul and Marla, Adam, Bill and Evelyn.

4: Lunch with Jack and Winnie, and Betty Martin.

5: To Fostoria - time with Mase and Penny Bailey in Lima en route.
Saturday, June 6: A family picnic with Dave, Janet, and our cousins.
June 7: Went to Janet's church with her, along with Dave, Jo, Bonnie and Kelly and Casey; Jo to Indiana, then Wisconsin, then home ahead of me.

8: Kelly and I went to a Christian bookstore in Findlay to get him a Bible, which he began to read.

356

June 9: Time with Norman Gibat and wife in Fostoria; Norm and Shirley Knisley in Tiffin.

10: In the morning I had breakfast with Bro. Chew; went by to see the Presbyterian Church where I attended as a boy; and met Brother Dixon, the new Nazarene pastor.
In the afternoon I had lunch at the country club with high school classmates Jim Tucker, Marilyn Hauser, and Ron Griffin; and saw Bob and Carolyn Etzinger, who were also there at another table. I also went by a rest home and saw George Gray. I also saw Amie and her family, and Ray Dell later in the afternoon.

June 11: I had breakfast with Jimmy Johnson, a high school classmate. Then Dave and I went to Lake Erie to see Chuck and Carol (my cousin) Bixler.
12: Royetta and Lorraine were having a garage sale and I went by and spent some time with them.
Saturday, June 13: I distributed *A Letter From GOD* in downtown Fostoria.

Sunday, June 14: I went to Marion, Ohio, and went to church with Steve Dillon. We had lunch together and then I moved to Loren's for a few days.
15: I had a bad cold and finally went to a nurse practitioner who Loren and Lois arranged for me.
16: I spent time with Bill Ramsey.
17: I spent time with Annie Bumgardner, George Moser, Barb and Dan Reed, and Loren and Lois.

June 18: I moved back to Bonnie's in Fostoria. Kelly prayed out loud with me for the first time!
June 19: Bonnie took me to Toledo to catch an early morning train to Chicago, then another train to Wisconsin.

19-24: I was alone with Gerry and his family - Joanne had already returned home.

June 24: Flight home to Portland.

26: We picked cherries from our two trees.

July 22-24: Camping at Olallie Campground and fishing at Smith and Blue River. GOD visited me en route home and I wept the entire way thinking about GOD's goodness.

August 4: Annual Neighborhood Block Party at our place.

7: Spent the day with Brehms - they are getting off base theologically.

9: Dan's birthday party.

16-19: Camped at Ice Cap and fished at Carmen and Blue River.

This year several of us considered an online Bible College, but after much prayer, we did not proceed with it because GOD said, "No!"

Aug. 28: A day with Greg and Beth - we went to Multnomah Falls and Bonneville Dam on the Columbia River. It was a wonderful time together with them.

September 7: I went to the Oregon State Fair on my birthday - passed out the *GOD letter.*

Sept. 16: 48th Wedding Anniversary - lunch with Jo.
21: To Portland to celebrate our 48th - lunch on 30th floor of one of the downtown buildings - quite a view of the city!

29: We had a heat pump installed at our home so we have air conditioning in the summer on hot days and inexpensive heat as a backup to our wood burning stove in the winter.

November 5: We got a new refrigerator for our kitchen - the old one was making strange noises.

6: The city cleared out blackberry bushes along our fence line - PTL!

13: I was in an auto accident (not my fault) and spent the next year seeing Dr. Whitmire, our chiropractor; and swimming and sitting in the Jacuzzi at the Court House Athletic Club, with the membership paid for by our auto insurance company, GMAC. When that membership expired we began paying for a continued membership. I continued daily swimming in the warm water pool. In 2013, I began swimming a quarter of a mile each day in the lap lanes pool.

November 21: We went to a Blazers basketball game with our friends Bob and Sherrill Hawley. She, being the generous hearted person that she is, cheered for both teams! We had fun teasing her.

Nov. 26: Thanksgiving with Bachrans.

December 8: We had an electrical fire in our garage. The garage and our two offices had to be rebuilt and there was smoke damage in the house.

ServPro did the cleaning and our neighbor, Barry Edwards, did the construction work. We were greatly pleased with all of the cleanup and construction work.

Our insurance allowed us to get a new mattress, cedar chest, camping equipment, shelving, tools, mower, tiller, freezer, refrigerators, new carpet for our offices, etc. - what a blessing! There was a refrigerator in one corner of the garage waiting to be sold. Everything around it was covered with smoke. The refrigerator was completely clean! We believe angels had protected it.

December 9: Jo was having heart pains. She called the ambulance since I was not home. She had a mild heart attack, but the cardiologist determined that there was no heart damage. Many were praying! She spent one night in the hospital.

14: Neighborhood Christmas Party at Dewey and Emma's. This became an annual event.

21: Kelly Downing called from Fostoria - he had been in Texas and had led Ron, his mother's boyfriend, to the Lord! Kelly had come to the Lord the previous May, had not yet been baptized and did not attend church anywhere - but was reading his Bible and leading people to Jesus!

23: We moved home from the hotel to our home, which had been cleaned and three rooms repainted. The work on the garage and two offices still had to be finished in the coming months.

_2010_

The first half of the year was spent getting resettled in our offices and garage after the fire.

Greg, our daughter Beth's husband, took a job in Hawaii in January. Beth is working on selling their home and hopes to join him soon. Their oldest, Jamie, is married to Andrew, they live in San Diego, and have a little baby girl, Audra, now a year old. Kelly was on American Idol television program, and now lives and works in Los Angeles. And Daniel has also moved to Southern California, currently lives with Jamie and Andrew, and has just gotten a job at an Apple computer store.

We continue to have wonderful times with our Saturday evening home church group that meets at Boudreau's and includes them, two high school students at Salem Academy from China and Viet Nam, Leo and Kelvin. It also includes Hawleys, Hagers, McCormicks, and occasionally Pierces, and their friends, Marta and Jerry.

I continue to trumpet the Neighborhood Prayer Groups with Mona Edwards. Also, a prayer team of she, Jerry Sloan, Arne Jensen, and I began sponsoring a monthly prayer time for revival at the Capitol Park Wesleyan Church.

January 26: I went to CRC to spend the day with the men at the annual prayer summit. These are always wonderful times of worship, sharing, and ministry to one another.

April 15: Barry Edwards finished the house remodeling after the fire.

20-26: Gerry and Wenda came to visit. They spent two days at the Coast and the rest of the time with us. Gerry and I went fishing one day at Foster Reservoir where we saw an eagle. We had some wonderful times of fellowship and prayer with them and Greg and Beth.

May 9: Joanne had to take me to the emergency room and I was diagnosed with diverticulitis.

June 14: We had a Neighborhood Prayer Group gathering, which included most of our neighbors, to rededicate our home to the Lord after the fire and rebuilding.

24-25: Bill and Gloria Ramsey came to visit us from Upper Sandusky, Ohio. Bill had been part of LEI and is a dear friend.

July 6-8: Camped at Olallie, fished Smith and Blue River.

14: I had a second diverticulitis attack.

361

July 22: Greg and Beth moved to Hawaii, where Greg grew up. We miss them! This was a huge development in their lives and ours.

After living so close to them for 20 years, their leaving has left a huge void, but GOD is helping us. And GOD assured me through the story of Jacob and Laban in Genesis that it was time for Greg to return home after being in Salem for 20 years (see Genesis 31:3, 38). They are renting their home in Salem until it sells.

It has been a very difficult move for Beth, but GOD, in His faithfulness, has given Beth a position as a Hawaiian Airline's flight attendant. This has made it possible for her to fly free to see their children and grandchildren in Southern California. And it's also allowed us to fly to Hawaii at a huge discount to see them.

August 3: Our annual neighborhood picnic in our backyard.

September 5: I officiated at the wedding for Aimee Boudreau and Rocky Krieger.

CHAPTER 23 - RETIREMENT

(Turned 75, CLU, MOAA Chaplain, paper route, gardening and orchards, fishing)

(2010 – July 2014)

<u>*2010 (Continued)*</u>

I turned 75 on September 7, 2010. On Saturday, September 11, I had a 75th birthday party at Bush Park. It was a potluck with about 40 friends from the Salem area participating. It was a wonderful time of thanking each of them for the contribution they had made to my life. We sang three of my favorite songs - *Now I Belong to Jesus, How Can I Say Thanks,* and *Great is Thy Faithfulness.* (Some of my other favorites include *The Old Rugged Cross, What a Friend we Have in Jesus, Onward Christian Soldiers, The Battle Hymn of the Republic,* and *GOD Bless America.*)

September 20-21: Lois and Clayton Moon, Joanne's cousin from Kansas, came for a visit.

Sept. 27-29: I went camping and fishing at Loon Lake, one of my favorite spots.

October 17: We went fishing at Henry Haag Lake with Bob and Sherrill Hawley. It was their first time fishing and Sherrill caught a nice 12-inch trout.

Oct. 21: I did my *Salem Monthly* paper routes for the last time. They began every other week, which was just too much for me to do. I also was increasingly uncomfortable with the paper's content.

November 5: I went fishing at Cascade Park in Salem. They recently changed the regulations and now allow small boats with electric motors.

363

November 6: Bob and Cathy Boudreau went with us to a Blazer basketball game at the Rose Arena in Portland.

Nov. 18: I was led by the Lord to go to my first MOAA (Military Officers' Association of America) luncheon. Joanne began accompanying me in December. I had been getting notices about these meeting for several years and in November the Lord made it very clear that I was to go to that meeting. As everyone was introducing themselves, and it became my turn, I shared that I wanted to stay in the military, but the Lord told me that He had another plan for my life, which ended up being 50 years of Christian ministry and missionary work with Joanne around the world. One of them, sitting across the room, hollered out "Now we have a real chaplain." The board approached me about becoming the chaplain for the group, which became official in January 2011.

After the Pledge of Allegiance to the flag I have about two minutes to share something inspirational from the Bible or from American or military history. (A list of the items I have shared is found in Appendix 14.) Then I pray. This is a wonderful open door to share truth, which I greatly enjoy. I also began spending time with some of the men one-on-one, having breakfast or lunch with them, or going to their home. These have been wonderful times of getting better acquainted and sowing spiritual truth into their lives.

Nov. 19: We had some excellent time having coffee with Roger and Rosie, our Jehovah's Witness neighbors.

November 23 - December 7: Jo went to Hawaii to help Greg and Beth remodel their condo.

December 6: We had our annual Neighborhood Christmas Party at Dewey and Emma's.

2011

I have had my fill of travel, people, vision, programs, projects, meetings, responsibilities, stress, etc. It is time to retire and "smell the roses." I look forward to doing only a few things, having more time to be with the Lord, tend to my fruit trees, go fishing, and be with my wife and family. I began pulling back from as much as possible. This included the Salem Neighborhood Prayer Group vision, praying for revival, SalemNet participation, and meeting with fewer people.

But we did continue several things:
Joanne and I continue having our daily Bible reading and prayer together after breakfast. (This is in addition to our personal time with GOD before breakfast.)

We continue to meet almost weekly with our home church group.

We continue to mentor Christian Leadership University students via the internet. From 1996 through 2012 we have mentored more than 150 students from every continent except South America. This includes Joanne's course on releasing women and my nine courses on various biblical matters. (See Appendix 8 for a list of courses.)

We continue to meet with our neighbors - in the spring with just the believers for prayer - and twice a year (a picnic in August and a Christmas party in December) with everyone. These have been wonderful times of bonding.

I continue to service two Christian bookstores in Salem several times a year.

I continue to go to the Court House Athletic Club almost every afternoon to swim and sometimes do the treadmill. Almost every day GOD has someone for me to talk to about the Lord.

Joanne continues to teach piano students, but is down to five students.

Joanne continues to go to the hospital each Sunday morning as a volunteer chaplain. She comes home with many interesting stories including leading some to faith in Christ.

I continue my MOAA ministry, which includes the monthly luncheons and spending time with various ones.

We continue to host various people who are traveling through the area, i.e., missionaries, relatives, etc, but we are cutting back on this some.

We hope to continue doing what we have been doing the past few years - as long as GOD gives us the strength to do so.

I am devoting more time to gardening, our fruit orchards, and camping and fishing.

On June 11, Jamie gave birth to their second child, Aaron Joseph.

On September 16, we had our 50th wedding anniversary. We celebrated by going to the Coast for an overnight stay. And we will celebrate further with a family reunion and celebration in June of 2012 in Southern California (more on this later in this chapter).

We also got word that Hal Ward, who discipled me as a young Christian, had gone to be with the Lord on September 16.

In September, I was led to discontinue regular participation in the weekly house church meetings as part of my retirement and getting rested up from the years of meetings and ministry to people. I still attend occasionally as GOD leads but no longer feel a great sense of responsibility.

In October the six chapters of MOAA in Oregon had a statewide convention. I was asked to be the chaplain at this event, which was quite an opportunity and honor. It included the attendance of an Army general, an Air Force general, and a Coast Guard admiral. I gave the invocation and explained that "invocation" means inviting GOD to come and be present. I encouraged all to invite Him to come and be with us at the convention - and to invite Him to have a greater place in their daily lives. At the noon luncheon I shared from Deuteronomy 8 on how GOD blesses or curses nations depending upon their obedience to Him. At the evening banquet I shared Joshua 24:14-15, "As for me and my house, we will serve the Lord," and explained that Joshua was a great military leader whose purpose in life was to serve the Lord. We concluded the convention by singing GOD Bless America, and sensed the presence of GOD in a very meaningful way.

In December we took a trip to Southern California to see Andrew, Jamie, Audra, and Aaron; Kelly, and Daniel; and to meet Kelly's boyfriend, Cameron. After only two days I became very ill with a kidney stone. I was in and out of the hospital twice, but we were finally able to fly home. During my time in the hospital I really connected with Cameron. He is a very wonderful Christian and we are very happy for him and Kelly.

During this year I got acquainted with Ola Elkanah and his wife, from Nigeria, Africa, who pastor The Redeemed Christian Church of God in Salem, and are our neighbors. Their daughter, Dara, began taking piano lessons from Joanne and Ola and I would often spend time together while she was having her lesson. He is a wonderful man of GOD and always has an encouraging word for me. I have spoken in their church a couple of times and they call us Grandma and Grandpa.

2012

2012 was quite an eventful year for us as a family.

The kidney stone that began to give me such pain finally passed on January 9, for which I praised the Lord! But on January 23 Jo took me to the hospital emergency room with pain in both legs, which they confirmed were blood clots, which probably developed because I was so inactive for weeks with the kidney stone.

This year Joanne and I began playing dominoes most evenings and sometimes briefly throughout the day when we had a few minutes. It has been a great way to relax and spend time together.

We had planned to take a trip to Hawaii to see Greg and Beth in January, but with my health issues the trip was delayed until March. We flew over on March 1 and home on the 7th. It was such a wonderful time to be with them in the condo they have worked so hard to refurbish. It rained much of the time and we got to see from their lanai all of the waterfalls, 21 in total, on the east side of the Ko'olau Mountains. We had dinner at a nice hotel one evening to celebrate our wedding anniversaries.

It stopped raining long enough on Tuesday morning that I went to see the battleship *Missouri* where the armistice was signed ending World War 2. I got there for the 9 a.m. tour, no one else showed up, and they gave me a private tour of the ship! I got one of the official photos taken of me with the ship in the background, which I passed around at the next MOAA luncheon.

Jo took a trip to Wisconsin and Indiana March 29 - April 3 to see Gerry and his family and to hear Allison give her Junior Vocal Recital at Indiana Wesleyan University.

In late March Ken Bentz came over and split 66 boxes of wood for our stove. He also got me signed up with a ministry out of the CMA Church that brings wood to people in need - what a blessing!

On April 14 Cameron Brier proposed to Kelly, our granddaughter - she was quite surprised and we all were very joyous.

June 15-20 we made a trip to Southern California. We stayed overnight with Rachel, Joanne's niece, and spent some enjoyable time with her and her husband, Steve, on the morning of the 16th. In the afternoon we were at Aaron's first birthday party.

June 17-20 was a family reunion that Gerry and Beth had put together, with some help on local details from Jamie. It was the first time that we had all been together for 12 years and included all of our children, grandchildren, Kelly's fiancé, and two great-grandchildren. We all stayed together in a large house a few blocks from the ocean in Oceanside, California. It was a wonderful time of fellowship, games, eating, prayer, family photos, walks, and time at the beach, and celebrating our 50th Wedding Anniversary.

On June 25 I went to the VA Hospital in Portland for an appointment at the Coumadin Lab. There was an elderly gentlemen playing the piano in the lobby. I found out later that he had spent 30 years playing, singing, and acting on Broadway. After my appointment I stopped by the piano and asked him if he could play *GOD Bless America*. He played it in a number of variations and when he was finished the entire lobby, numbering about 40 people, broke into spontaneous applause.

One day in July I got to talking to Liz, a lady at the Court House pool. I found out that her parents from Warsaw, Poland, spent WW2 in a German concentration camp, where she was born. They migrated to the US when she was four. What a story!

As I watched the opening ceremony of the Olympics on July 27 my heart was stirred afresh for the nations of the world. I don't know what this means, but I am at the Lord's disposal: "Here am I Lord, send me."

On September 7 (my 77th birthday) Cameron and Kelly were married at Hacienda de las Flores in Moraga, in the Bay area of Central California, where Cameron grew up. We drove down for this, spending two nights with Bob and Arlene Hughes. At the wedding reception the entire gathering sang *Happy Birthday* to me, which greatly blessed me.

We took two days to come home, enjoying the Golden Gate Bridge, wine country, large Redwood trees in Northern California, and the Oregon Coast.

September 22 I officiated for the wedding of Melissa Medina and Sean Jackson. Melissa was a little girl when we pastored New Life Fellowship. We met Sean, who is with ServePro, when we had the garage fire. It was such a blessing to do their wedding.

In September we were able to purchase a 39-inch flat screen TV with two financial gifts from the wedding. Over the next weeks Jo and I built a cabinet for it so that it can be closed off from view in the living room when we desire that. This was Joanne's idea and we worked together on designing and building it.

October 5-7 Joanne and I spent three days in prayer with nine other Christian workers, hosted by the Marshes at their House of Myrrh ministry center in Oregon City. (This was our last time to be with Jay Ferris, who went home to be with the Lord on June 13, 2013, after a two-year battle with cancer.)

All this year we watched the debates, leading up to the presidential election and on November 6 Barrack Obama was elected for a second term. We were very saddened at this, but know that GOD is ultimately in control.

In November Joanne and I made two trips to Chehalis, Washington, to teach in one of Dave and Janice Woodrum's missionary training schools. This was videoed for use in their 40-some other schools in Asia and Africa and is available to any who might want them. (See Appendix 7 for a list of topics and how to order.)

In December we had the usual Christmas correspondence and activities. On Christmas day we Skyped with Gerry and his family in Wisconsin and Beth and her family at Jamie's in Southern California. Also in December I did major pruning of all of our fruit trees.

Throughout the year we were busy with our usual work: CLU students for both of us; MOAA chaplain for me; hospital chaplaincy work for Joanne, and her piano students. Also, not long after I started attending MOAA, Joanne was invited to attend the Women's Military League chapter here in Salem. It is relationally, but not officially connected with MOAA. Not long after she began attending, they asked her to serve as the chaplain, which she has enjoyed doing. Also the usual yard, garden, and orchards work, and several fishing trips for Nate.

2013

Shortly after Thanksgiving, 2012, I began to have problems with a skin rash. Various over-the-counter lotions seemed to help some, but I was still having some small areas into May.

I spent several weeks assembling a songbook for MOAA, which was first used at the February meeting. It has three sections: the national patriotic hymns, the songs of the various military services, and a few Christian hymns. I look forward to our using this occasionally at future Officers' Call luncheons.

On January 21 we learned of Heinz' death and I was offered his Nickel Ads paper route. After an hour or so of prayer I took the route. It was 30 drops in Salem, Keizer, and West Salem, although I soon built it up to 48 drops. I would pick up the papers about 9:15 a.m. and finish the route around 2:30 p.m. They raised my income from $80 to $100 per week, which was a big help on our finances. I really enjoyed doing it and getting out around town.

We flew standby to Hawaii to be with Greg and Beth February 28 - March 8. We had one first-class seat going over, which Joanne insisted that I take - what a blessing! I spent the entire time in Hawaii reading a book about Johnny Appleseed, swimming once or twice a day, and resting.

One day Beth took me around the northern side of the island - we stopped at the pineapple fields, had lunch at a famous little stop in Haleiwa, spent some time at Sunset Beach watching the surfers, and stopped at the beautiful hotel at Turtle Bay. We also saw the Methodist Church at Kahuku where Roy Sasaki pastored and where Lee Thompson and I once had a series of meetings. It was such a fun day with my daughter!

Joanne spent quite a bit of her time working with Beth refinishing a small drop-leaf table Beth had picked up through Craig's List. Refinishing furniture has been a hobby of Joanne's for many years. Throughout our married life she has furnished our home either with unfinished furniture, which she would finish, or used items that needed refinishing, making them look like new.

It was so enjoyable to be with Greg and Beth for eight days. On the flight home Beth was one of the flight attendants so we got to see her on-the-job. Between her and the other flight attendants who knew we were her parents, we were truly pampered.

In the fall of 2012 I began to trim our fruit trees and also our big pine trees. I cut up the larger branches and got 18 boxes of firewood! Travis Stubbs, who does yard work for us occasionally, hauled off a huge load of the smaller branches on March 9. I performed Travis and Kendra Jensen's wedding in 2006 and it has been a blessing to get re-connected with Travis.

March 15-19 Jo got a ride with the Boudreaus to and from Sacramento to see her sister, Arlene, and husband, Bob. With their getting up in years, she always wonders if each visit will be her last chance to see them in this life.

April 23 - May 6 Joanne went back to the Midwest to be with Gerry and Wenda in Wisconsin, be at Alex and Allison's college graduation from Indiana Wesleyan University, and spend a few days with her sister, Evelyn. Allison majored in Bible, with a minor in Music, and Alex in Art. (Alex has done the artwork for the cover of this book.) She had planned to fly to Detroit to see Ernestine Stewart and Juakemo and Carletta Griffin, but she got sick and had to cancel that portion of the trip. I just was not up to this trip and did not go.

373

While Joanne was gone Greg and Beth came to Salem for three days to close on the sale of their home. This was the closing of a chapter in their lives. They had built the house and lived there for 20 years and raised their three children there. It was so wonderful to have some time with them. A lovely Christian family, Chad and Jessica Harvey and their three young daughters, purchased the home.

We have had a busy summer. On June 13 we got word that Jay Ferris had gone to heaven. He had battled cancer for two years. We both feel a great void in our hearts as Jay was a close brother in the Lord and an important part of our lives for close to 40 years. We remain in touch with Carleen.

I got the idea of our getting an Astro Van to use for fishing and camping, did a lot of research, almost bought one, but ended up feeling that we were not to do it. Maybe next spring - we'll see how GOD leads.

I worked with Alex, my grandson, on the cover for this biography. He did a marvelous job! And I went through the biography several times, making corrections and additions.

On July 3 I was honored, along with other veterans, at the Volcanoes baseball game in Keizer. The honoring of veterans is an annual event near the fourth of July. This was our first time to attend a game and we enjoyed it so much that we went four other times throughout the summer - Hawleys came with us once, Bentzes once, and Boudreaus once.

We had new neighbors, Ligali and Ekaette Harruna, move into the new, vacant home on the circle, Ligali is from Ghana and Ekaette from Nigeria. We love them a lot! I had the privilege of praying at their House Warming Party.

In July Jamie, Audra, and Aaron spent a day with us in connection with their visiting Andrew's parents in Newport and Andrew river-rafting with his dad. We took them to the carousel at the riverfront park, which they rode four times! They also enjoyed picking some of our blueberries. Audra is using words like "delightful." Aaron and I really bonded on this visit - as they were leaving our home, he told Jamie "more Papa."

Andrew was also with us for part of a day before they headed back to California.

It is such a joy to get to see them annually on their visit to Andrew's folks in Newport. But once a year is not nearly enough!

For several weeks we had problems with the Buick starting. We ended up putting in a new starter and ignition switch, which seemed to solve the problem.

August 1-5 Joanne rode with Brenda Waters, her friend from Australia, to Sacramento to spend a few days with Arlene and Bob, to help them pack, as they were getting ready to move to an apartment closer to their daughter, Charlene.

On August 1 I had an eye exam and learned that I need cataract surgery, which was scheduled for October 1.

Our sprinkler system stopped working on the lower level and we discovered that the solenoids needed replacing. I was able to find the replacements even though they were 20 years old.

On August 7 we had our Annual Neighborhood Picnic in our backyard - there were twenty adults and ten children - and we all had a great time.

On August 13 Ted and Renie Faver, our missionary friends from Mexico, stopped by for lunch together. They are doing such a terrific job with their orphanage, which they pioneered, and other activities.

Dave and Janice Woodrum now have more than 550 students in 39 Bible schools in 10 nations. Their curriculum includes 10 of our writings and some of our teaching on DVDs. It is such a privilege to have a small part in their wonderful, multiplying ministry to the nations.

On August 19 Jo and I went to the Portland Zoo. It was such an interesting time - seeing the very tall giraffe, the huge hippo, the baby elephant, the polar bears, etc. - but we were sure tired by the end of the day.

In early August I got word that the Nickel Ads paper was going out of business at the end of the month so this eight-month job is ending. In some ways I am glad, but it has sure been a blessing financially.

Our garden produced quite an abundance this year - beans, corn, tomatoes, lettuce, cukes, zucchini, and beets - and potatoes that came up from last year! Our orchards, likewise, produced a lot of wonderful fruit - the Bartlett and Asian pears are huge this year. So we are busy canning, drying, and freezing fruit and vegetables.

The two-hour drive to fish at Smith, Blue River, and Cougar seemed too far this year so I fished several times at Green Peter, Foster, and Detroit lakes, which are only about an hour away. I enjoy so much these times of getting away - to be alone with the Lord, to enjoy the beautiful scenery, and to, hopefully, catch some rainbow trout.

Beth arranged her travel in order to spend September 3 with us. It is always such a blessing to have a visit from our daughter!

Joanne and I celebrated 52 years of marriage on September 16 by spending the 16th and 17th at the Coast with an overnight at a motel in Newport. We had a wonderful, relaxing time.

On September 30 we got word that Uncle Warren was now with Jesus in heaven. He was one of Joanne's favorite uncles and the last living relative of that generation.

I had cataract surgery on my left eye on October 1 - everything went well and I will get my new glasses in early November.

Gerry and Wenda came to visit us October 22-25 and Beth was here October 21-22. We had a wonderful time, but missed Greg who was not able to join us because of his work schedule. The kids helped with some inside and outdoor projects and Gerry and I went fishing one day. And we had a retirement party lunch in my honor one day. The last time we were all together was in June 2012, but we keep in touch by frequent phone calls and occasional Skyping. We are so proud of our two children and their spouses!

In late November I turned my Christian Leadership University work over to our friend and associate, Mona Edwards. For 18 years I have greatly enjoyed working with students around the world who have taken my courses, but it is time to pass this work on.

I began passing out the *Letter from GOD* in 2009 and continue to give it to people as I go throughout the day as the Holy Spirit leads me. I have passed out well more than a thousand by now and have been turned down only a few times. I have had a number of businesses tell me that they have posted it in their lunchroom. I had a girl at a college follow me out to the car to thank me for ones I placed in their lounge.

I once had a worker at Lowes tell me that his daughter was murdered and his wife died - and he had been waiting for six years for someone to give him something like this! It is my deep conviction that many people are not too interested in church, but they are hungry for truth and a relationship with GOD. (You can download this wonderful piece of literature at FathersLoveLetter.com.)

2014 (January - July)

Greg and Beth found a very reasonable rental in Kaneohe that needed lots of TLC. They felt it was worth putting some of their own sweat and money into improving it. They moved in on January 1 and on January 2-20 Joanne went over to help with repairs. She loves to help her kids with projects on their homes whenever possible. Over the next several months, Beth and Greg continued fixing it up and it is now truly lovely. May 3-10 we both went again for a time of rest and being with them.

Joanne and I both felt the Lord was saying it was time for her to retire from teaching piano. So the end of May she concluded her over twenty years of teaching. After the garage fire in 2009, and the garage and both of our offices had been totally refurbished, she moved the piano from inside the house out to one end of her office. So one end was her office and the other end her piano studio. She felt that upon her retirement she was to sell her lovely Baldwin piano - which she hasn't played much for several years - and transform the end that was her studio into an additional guest area. She was so thrilled when a wonderful Christian family, whose four children had been her students, bought the piano. She found a futon on Craigslist to put in that room. Now we have a place for both our kids and their spouses to sleep when they are here together.

378

June 3-19 Jo went to the Midwest. She spent a week with her sister, Evelyn, and saw Alex in Indiana. Then she made a brief visit to Detroit to see Ernestine Stewart and Juakemo and Carletta Griffin. From there she went to Mukwonago, Wisconsin to visit Gerry, Wenda, Geoffrey, and Allison. Their front door and light windows on either side needed refinishing. She was so happy to be able to do that project for them. It turned out to be a much bigger job than at first thought and before it was all over, Gerry ended up doing as much as Joanne. Wenda, and Allison even got in on the project. It turned out beautifully. Upon arriving home, however, Joanne decided that was the last circuitous trip she was gong to take. From here on each trip would be a one-destination trip. She does love to travel, however.

On July 14, Andrew and Jamie had their third child, Tanner Owen Palmer. I can't help but give some of our great-grandkids nicknames. Since Tanner's initials are T. O. P., I like to refer to him as TOPs. And he is one precious little boy. His big sister and brother, Audra and Aaron, have accepted him into the family with all their love. Beth was there to help Jamie and Andrew welcome this third grandchild. Greg was able to join her for a few days. We are hoping they will make it up to Oregon to visit Andrew's parents in the not too distant future so we can meet Tanner. They always come and spend time with us on those occasions.

On July 11 Joanne had a bad fall in the kitchen resulting in a hairline fracture in her pelvic bone. She spent two nights in the hospital. I put the word out to our e-mail list requesting prayer - we were overwhelmed by the response from friends all over the country, and some overseas. We didn't know how much we were loved! As I finish this Biography, we are seeing GOD's hand at work as she is improving remarkably and we are believing Him for a full recovery.

As I finish this biography I must share that I am "all traveled out, all peopled out, and all meetinged out" - I can't stand the thought of traveling, seeing people, or going to a meeting. My days of ministry are over. I once had a worldwide vision and ministry, then it narrowed to the United States, then to the Pacific Northwest, and then to Western Oregon. Now it's not much more than our immediate neighborhood! It is time to retire. I rejoice in that which GOD has allowed me, with Joanne, to be involved in over the past 56 years since I met Jesus. As much of my life has been spent trying to discover GOD's plan for His Church, you are encouraged to see Appendices 9-13.

Although we are now "retired" we still give away copies of books that we have written. And we now have time to bless other ministries in various ways. And I can spend more time gardening, fishing, and being with family and friends.

I have been working on this autobiography since 1995 - 19 years! It is such a relief to finally bring it to a conclusion. It is time to pass the manuscript on to the publishers. This was done in the summer of 2014. Bob Hawley, our friend and brother in the Lord, took on this task, assisted by Gerry Krupp, Debi Renfro, Alex Krupp, and my wife. I am deeply grateful to them for their work.

I pray that this book will be a blessing to all who read it, and most of all, bring glory to GOD. And may He use it to raise up an entirely new generation of those who will "seek first HIS Kingdom."

CHAPTER 24 – CONCLUSIONS AND FINAL THOUGHTS

It has been an awesome honor, privilege, and joy to be a follower of our Lord Jesus Christ, with my wife, Joanne, for more than 50 years.

Following and obeying Him has taken me to every continent and resulted in my writing approximately 20 books. And I have been involved in pioneering several emphases including personal evangelism, extraordinary prayer, and home church.

I have had the privilege of being affiliated with the Navigators, Campus Crusade for Christ, the National Association of Evangelicals (NAE), the National Holiness Association (NHA), Youth with A Mission (YWAM), Christian Leadership University (CLU), and the Military Officers Association of America (MOAA).

Joanne has written a book on GOD's plan for women, which has been translated into Urdu and Arabic and has been used around the world. She has served as a volunteer chaplain at the Salem hospital and chaplain for the Women's Military League, and has had an extended ministry of being a friend and encouraging and counseling many. And she has been my partner and a tremendous encouragement and assistance to me.

We have had the privilege of knowing and working with some of GOD's choicest servants.

All of this would not be true without the help of many co-laborers, for whom we are extremely thankful. There are many who have prayed for us, encouraged us, worked with us, and supported us financially. We are so grateful to GOD for each of them.

Early in my Christian life GOD spoke to me that Matthew 6:33 would be an important truth in my life: *But seek first the kingdom of GOD and His righteousness, and all these things will be added to you.* This has certainly been true. We have attempted to put GOD and His Kingdom first in our lives - and we have spent our entire married life trusting GOD to supply our financial and other material needs and have been amazed at His faithful and abundant provision.

We are very proud and thankful to GOD for our children and their mates, Gerry and Wenda, Beth and Greg; and our grandchildren, Geoffrey, Alex, Allison, Jamie and Andrew, Kelly and Cameron, Dan; and our great-grandchildren, Audra, Aaron, and Tanner; and especially thankful for those who are walking close to Jesus. Even Audra, at age three, invited Jesus into her heart and often refers to Him as being an intimate part of her life.

My only regret is that my ministry sometimes was a higher priority than my family.

Our more than 50 years of serving Him together have been an awesome honor, privilege, and joy. Joanne and I are so very grateful to GOD!

APPENDICES

APPENDIX 1 - HOW TO BECOME A FOLLOWER OF JESUS, THE CHRIST

I (Nate) became a follower of Jesus, the Christ, on March 17, 1957, as told in Chapter 2. The following, taken from the booklet *The Way to GOD** explains how you, too, can become His follower.

Stop and Realize that:

GOD made us and planned that we should have fellowship with Him. GOD would be our heavenly Father - loving us and being constantly concerned with our best interests.

The Bible says:
"So GOD created man in his own image, in the image of GOD He created him; male and female He created them." Genesis 1:27**

"For the LORD is good; His steadfast love endures forever, and His faithfulness to all generations." Psalm 100:5

We in return were to love and obey GOD.

The Bible says:
"And now, Israel, what does the LORD your GOD require of you, but to fear the LORD your GOD, to walk in all His ways, to love Him, to serve the LORD your GOD with all your heart and with all your soul, and to keep the commandments and statutes of the LORD, which I am commanding you today for your good?" Deuteronomy 10:12,13

"And you shall love the LORD your GOD with all your heart and with all your soul and with all your mind and with all your strength." Mark 12:30

*This booklet was first published in 1973 and revised in 2012 by Nate Krupp, his son, Gerry Krupp, and his grandson, Alex Krupp.
**Bible quotations are taken from the English Standard Version with slight revisions.

3

Recognize that:

We chose to go our own way - to run our own lives - to try to work things out for ourselves without yielding our lives to GOD. The Bible calls this attitude and act of rebellion "sin." And we have all been guilty of this.

The Bible says:
"All we like sheep have gone astray; we have turned every one to his own way; and the LORD has laid on him the iniquity of us all." Isaiah 53:6

"For all have sinned and fall short of the glory of GOD." Romans 3:23

Sin separates us from God. It separates us from having fellowship with GOD in this life. That is why we have our fears, frustrations, and problems. It also separates us from being with GOD in the life to come.
The Bible calls this separation from GOD "death."

The Bible says:
"Behold, all souls are Mine; the soul of the father as well as the soul of the son is Mine: the soul who sins shall die." Ezekiel 18:4

"For the wages of sin is death, but the free gift of GOD is eternal life in Christ Jesus our Lord" Romans 6:23

Know that there is One Way:

In spite of our rebellion, GOD still loves us and sent His Son, Jesus Christ, to provide the way that we can be forgiven and can come back into fellowship with GOD. With this restored relationship comes peace of mind, joy, new purposes in life, and life forever with GOD.

The Bible says:
"But GOD shows his love for us in that while we were still sinners, Christ died for us." Romans 5:8

4

Jesus said, "I came that they may have life and have it abundantly." John 10:10

This gift of fellowship with GOD - in this life and in the next - is called "eternal life." And GOD offers it freely to every person.

The Bible says:
"And this is eternal life, that they know you the only true GOD, and Jesus Christ whom you have sent." John 17:3

"...but the free gift of GOD is eternal life in Christ Jesus our Lord." Romans 6:23

To Receive this gift of Eternal Life you must:

1. Turn from your sinful, selfish ways to GOD.

The Bible says:
"Whoever conceals his transgressions will not prosper, but he who confesses and forsakes them will obtain mercy." Proverbs 28:13

"Repent therefore, and turn again, that your sins may be blotted out, that times of refreshing may come from the presence of the Lord, and that he may send the Christ appointed for you, Jesus" Acts 3:19-20

2. And personally receive Jesus Christ as Savior and Lord.

The Bible says:
"But to all who did receive Him, who believed in His name, He gave the right to become children of GOD" John 1:12

"For everyone who calls on the name of the Lord will be saved." Romans 10:13

"Not everyone who says to me, 'Lord, Lord,' will enter the Kingdom of heaven, but the one who does the will of my Father who is in heaven." Matthew 7:21

5

A Review:

Let's review what we have learned:

1. GOD loves us and wants to have fellowship with us.
2. We are separated from GOD by our own sin.
3. Jesus Christ has provided the way back to GOD.
4. To respond, we must (a) turn from sinful, selfish ways to God, and, (b) receive the Lord Jesus Christ as our Savior and Lord.

Your Invitation:

Jesus says:

"Behold, I stand at the door and knock. If anyone hears My voice and opens the door, I will come in to him and have fellowship with him, and he with Me." Revelation 3:20

"All that the Father gives Me will come to Me, and whoever comes to Me I will never cast out." John 6:37

Your Decision:

Do you know of any reason why you cannot turn from your own way and personally receive Jesus Christ as your Savior and Lord?

Would you like to do this now?

You can receive this gift of eternal life now by sincerely praying:

"Dear Lord Jesus,
I know that I am a sinner and deserve to go to hell.
I cannot save myself.
I believe that You are the Son of GOD and that You died on the cross for my sins.
Right now I turn from my sins and take You as my Savior.
Please forgive me and save me.
I open my heart to You and invite You to come in.
I turn my life over to You.
Make me the person you want me to be.
Amen."

6

Assurance

For your assurance, complete the following:

1. Did you open the door of your heart and life to Jesus Christ and invite

Him to come in? _____

2. Did He come in? _____

3. Then where is He now? _____

The Bible says:

"And this is the testimony, that GOD gave us eternal life, and this life is in his Son. Whoever has the Son has life; whoever does not have the Son of GOD does not have life." 1 John 5:11,12

1. Do you now have eternal life? _____

Signed _____   Date _____

Finally:

To develop this wonderful life of fellowship with GOD :

1. Be baptized. Mark 16:16.

2. Read and obey the Bible for daily strength. Start with the *Gospel of John.* Matthew 4:4

3. Ask GOD daily for strength and guidance. John 14:13

4. Tell others about Jesus Christ. Luke 8:39

4. Fellowship, worship, and serve Christ with other Christians.
    Hebrews 10:24, 25

APPENDIX 2 - MAJOR SCRIPTURES THAT HAVE INFLUENCED MY LIFE

Through the years GOD has given me the following Scriptures as major "sign-posts" in my life.

Scriptures	When Given	How GOD Spoke
Mark 16:15	1957	My purpose in life - to evangelize the world.
Matt. 6:33	1957	Seek first His Kingdom - He will provide every need.
Mark 1:17,18	1959	A call to Christian ministry.
Matt. 4:4	1960	Be a person of the Word - master the Word
Jer. 33:3	1960	Believe GOD for great things.
Jer. Ch. 1	1960	GOD has called me to be a prophet.
Acts 24:16	from Hubert Mitchell:	Always have a clear conscience toward both GOD and people.
Lam. 3:21-23	1961	GOD is faithful - and will be to Joanne and me.
Jer. Ch. 18	1962	I am clay in His hands for Him to fashion me as He chooses.
Psalm 91		My favorite chapter in the Bible - I need to stay under the shadow of the Almighty.
Ezekiel 37:10	1962	Our ministry to result in an army of people.
John 17:4	1962	My two-fold purpose in life - to glorify GOD and to do what He has for me to do.

Habak. 2:2-3	1963	Writing to be part of my work.
Many Throughout the years		The importance of the Holy Spirit His filling, fruit, gifts, and leading.
Eph. 5:21-6:4	1965	Family, not ministry, is to be first priority.
Phil. 3:10	1972	Purpose in life - to experience Him, His power, and His suffering.
Revel. 19:6-7	1980	GOD reigns - a shift in focus from Mark 16:15 to helping the Bride be ready.
Many verses	1980	Move to the Pacific Northwest (Oregon).
No verse - the witness of Spirit	1981	Stay in the Northwest - revival is coming.
Matthew 8:9, 20, 25-28	1981-85	Be under authority, by a servant.
2 Chron. 7:14	1984	Major on being a person of humility, prayer, and holiness.
"From sea to shining sea"	1985	Our primary place of ministry is USA.
Galatians 2:20	1985	Rest in Jesus - anything significant that is done will be done by Him.
Matt. Ch. 5-7	1986	I am to live by the Sermon on the Mount.
Revel. 2:24-25	2000	GOD has no more major projects/truths for me to pioneer - just be faithful with what He has already given me.

APPENDIX 3 - PEOPLE WHO HAVE INFLUENCED MY LIFE

The following people have had a major influence on my life.
(These are in approximate chronological order.)

Dad and Mom Krupp - they laid the foundation for my life - hard work, belief in GOD, family values, patriotism, etc. We did a family garden together, but much of it fell on me, and there I learned the love of gardening. I was always close to Dad. I was close to Mom until my teenage years. Because of her insecurities and controlling manner, I pulled back from her at that time.

The Boy Scouts - I learned many basic skills from them, especially when working on my many merit badges - cooking, hiking, camping, fishing, boating, bird watching, stamp collecting, safety, forestry, etc.

Ira Cadwallader - I met with him only once, but it was very strategic, as he was the one who encouraged me to go to Purdue.

Purdue NROTC instructors - I was especially influenced by LtCdr Young (Navy) and LtCol Honour (Marine).

Bob Siefert - he got me involved in Student Government at Purdue. He was running for Student Body President and wanted me to be on his ticket as Sophomore Class President.

Abraham Zion David and Nate Scharff - these were the two men who led me to Jesus Christ on March 17, 1957. Abraham had prepared the way since September 1956 with his love and friendship. Nate led me to Christ. Both of them discipled me as a new believer. I owe them so much!

Brother and Sister Hoover - they were the pastors at the Lafayette Wesleyan Methodist Church and became my Mom and Dad in the faith the rest of my senior year at Purdue and in many years following.

11

Howard and Marie Noggle - at the end of my senior year at Purdue Abraham took me to Marion College where I met Howard and Marie. They became like a Dad and Mom in the faith for many years following. In 1959 Howard gave me the first books I had ever read about the Spirit-filled life. He introduced me to my wife in 1960. He was one of the most joyous and Christ-like men I have ever known.

Cdr. Robert E. Sparks - he was my senior Civil Engineer Corps officer for most of my two years at Kingsville NAAS. He was a very disciplined man who loved the Lord. From him I learned many basic procedures of efficient administration.

Lydia Beltran - Lydia was from Spain and an adopted daughter of the Sparks. She was also my girlfriend for about a year of my time in Kingsville and was like a big sister, challenging me in my walk with the Lord.

Christians at the NAAS in Kingsville - Paul Jackson, Jim Knutz, Rusty Reynolds, James Davis - these were some of the Christian enlisted men and civilian workers whom GOD used in my life during my two years at Kingsville.

Brother Bob Clemens - he was the pastor of the Calvary Baptist Church in Kingsville where I was active. He was very zealous for the Lord and for the lost. Also Bro. Chism, the head deacon, and other people at the church.

Hal Ward - was the Navigator representative for servicemen in the Texas area. He looked me up, visited me several times, taught me about having a Quiet Time, and discipled me at Kingsville and in the years thereafter.

The Navigators at Glen Eyrie - Jerry Bridges, Lorne Sanny, Bob Foster, Jim Downing, Chuck Farah, Clyde Lawson - these Nav leaders and others discipled me for fifteen months at Glen Eyrie, the Navigator headquarters. They especially emphasized Luke 16:10, being faithful in the little things, and taught me how to study and memorize the Bible. I still use things every day that they taught me.

Ford Madison - Ford owned a dairy in Colorado Springs, CO; was a zealous soul winner; and took me with him on visitation evangelism on several occasions. He used CS Lovett's basic method as presented in his book, *Soul Winning Made Easy.*

Hubert Mitchell - I first met Hubert when I was working at the front gate at Glen Eyrie and he came to spend time in prayer with Lorne Sanny and speak to the staff. I was drawn to him, looked him up in Chicago when I was on my way to Marion College, and spent time with him on various trips to Chicago. He was on the original LEI Advisory Board and became a great encourager and mentor to me for many years. He once told me, "Think BIG, but keep it SIMPLE." Joanne and I visited him and Rachel in Southern California just a few months before his home going.

Herb Jauchen - I met Herb through Nate Scharff. He was a vice president with Christian Life Publications and was instrumental in getting my testimony, *I Met Christ on the Campus,* published by American Tract Society.

Professors at Marion College - Leo Cox, Laura Emerson, Clarence Huffman - these instructors at Marion College had a profound influence on my life as I watched their godly lives and learned more about theology, speech, and Christian service.

Mayer David - it was Abraham David's younger brother who encouraged me to start seeing Joanne Sheets Brannon.

Joanne Krupp - no words can describe the influence that my wonderful wife has had on my life. She is an example of the Christian faith made practical and real. She has influenced my life much more than any other person.

Harold Sheets - Joanne's father opened the door for our ministry of soul winning training in the Wesleyan Methodist Church and later served as an advisor to LEI. He was like a father to me.

Billy Graham - Although I never had the privilege of meeting him, Billy Graham has had a tremendous influence on my life as a spiritual leader, a leader in evangelism, and a man of impeccable integrity.

Dave Castro - was one of my best friends at Marion College and the best man at our wedding.

Gene Edwards - was in soul-winning training a few years ahead of us and was a great encourager in our early days. Later he was greatly influenced by Watchman Nee's writings, especially *The Normal Christian Church Life*, and gave me a copy, which confirmed many things GOD was already showing me.

Robert E. Coleman - wrote the foreword for my book on soul winning and was a great encouragement during our early days of soul winning training.

Lyman Coleman - his writings were our first interest and experience with small groups.

Forrest Gearhart - was the pastor of the Wheaton Wesleyan Methodist Church and helped us to decide to move to Wheaton and became our pastor there.

NAE leaders - George Ford and Stan Mooneyham - these men at the NAE headquarters in Wheaton, IL, were great encouragers as we began LEI.

LEI associates - these co-laborers were a great encouragement as we labored together to call the Church to New Testament evangelism - Mase Bailey, Dave Cunningham, Gar Darnes, James Davis, Jay Ferris, Len Harris, Hugh Hedges, Tom Johnston, Glen Martin, George and Joanne Moser, Vic Munyer, Marion Noll, Art Prouty, Bill Ramsey, Paul Smith, Jim White, and Glenn Wilcox, and office staff Stan Hahn, Joy May, Jean Schuler, Debbie Ewick, Walter Simonds, and Gary Miltenberger.

Of these LEI associates we became the closest to Jay Ferris who became a confidant regarding GOD's plan for His Church.

The Charismatic Renewal - many in the Charismatic Renewal were able to influence and guide us as we entered this dimension of the Christian life.

Gary Henley - was a co-worker in our early house church experiment in Chicago. We went on to have an international ministry of reaching and discipling people. We have reconnected in recent years.

Ernestine Stewart was a convert to Christ in Chicago but later moved to Detroit. She has remained a close friend to Joanne and me, calling us Ma and Pa. And her daughter, Carletta, and husband, Juakemo, now call us Grandpa and Grandma.

Kathryn Kuhlmann - my back was healed in one of her meetings in Chicago in 1970.

Wayne Pence - we worked together to start the Living Water Bookstore in Marion, IN. He later took over the entire ministry, which expanded to also include a store in Kokomo, IN.

YWAM leaders - Loren Cunningham, Jim and Joy Dawson. Loren was a mentor during our time with YWAM Hawaii. Jim and Joy were like Dad and Mom to me during our YWAM years. I especially identified with Joy in a similar calling of prophet-teacher. After our time with YWAM we continued to enjoy contact with Don and Ruthie Hawkinson and Lee and Carolyn Thompson.

Revival leaders - Edwin Orr and Leonard Ravenhill - these men, both with whom I had the privilege of spending time with on several occasions, greatly influenced my life regarding the hope of a worldwide, end-time revival.

YWAM Washington leaders - Denny and Dodie Gunderson, Graham and Treena Kerr, Rod and Ayoka Billups - Our time with YWAM Salem was tumultuous and we received much healing from our relationship with the leaders in Tacoma.

Tom Isenhart was the pastor of Puget Sound Christian Center in Tacoma where we attended and were greatly blessed by our relationship with him.

Washington prayer leaders - Bob Penton, Al Gamble, Jim Watt, Dave Woodrum - these were some of the men who we had the privilege of praying and working with during our time of mobilizing prayer in the Northwest.

National prayer leaders - Armin Gesswein, Ray Bringham, Gary Bergel, David Bryant, Vonette Bright, Joy Dawson - these were some of the national prayer leaders who we had the privilege of knowing during our mobilizing prayer ministry days.

Carol Preston - was our secretary for more than a year in Tacoma and has continued to be a faithful friend.

Ken and Janet Bentz and Tony and Kathy Mader - it is because of their generosity that we have a home to live in!

Our Advisers - We have had a group of advisers who have given oversight to our lives and ministry for a number of years. They include Greg and Beth Bachran, Jay and Carleen Ferris, Robert and Joni Fitts, Arne Jensen, Gerry and Wenda Krupp, Bob Lund, Alger and Gloria Marsh, Frank Smith, and Dave and Janice Woodrum. Our advisers have been a great blessing to us in numerous ways.

Al Knoch - is a Bible teacher and friend who helped us with our writings.

Alger and Gloria Marsh - their friendship and HeartChange workshop have had a major impact on our lives.

Arne Jensen - Arne has become a good friend and prayer partner with whom I meet often. His deep walk with the Lord is a great challenge to me.

Gordon Bergman - GOD used Gordon to bring me into the fellowship of other spiritual leaders in Salem.

Many associates in the Northwest - GOD has given us the privilege of fellowshipping and working with many during our years in the Northwest. They are too numerous to name. But we are grateful for each one.

Our children - we have learned much from our children as they have become adults and taken on their own personality, family, work, and ministry. We are so grateful to GOD for them and their children (our grandchildren). And now I must add their grandchildren (our great-grandchildren!).

APPENDIX 4 - BOOKS THAT HAVE INFLUENCED MY LIFE

The following books have greatly influenced my life.

Publishers
The following addresses are given for publishers listed most frequently:
Baker = Baker Book House, Grand Rapids, MI 49516.
Bethany = Bethany House, Minneapolis, MN, 55438.
CLC = Christian Literature Crusade, Fort Washington, PA 19034.
Eerdmans = Eerdmans Publishing, Grand Rapids, MI, 49500.
Harper = Harper & Row Publishers, New York, NY,
Moody = Moody Press, Chicago, IL
Revell = Revell, Old Tappan, NJ 07675.
Tyndale = Tyndale House, Wheaton, IL
Zondervan = Zondervan Publishing House, Grand Rapids, MI 49506.

Bible and Christian Theology
Bible Study
The Bible. This has been my basic study since my conversion to Jesus Christ in March, 1957. In the Bible I have found the answers to all of life. The translations that I have found most helpful include:
Amplified Bible - this was my study Bible from 1957 - 1967.
New American Standard Bible - my basic study Bible from 1968 - 2007.
English Standard Version - it has become my favorite translation since 2007.

A Harmony of the Gospels: Stevens and Burton. Scribner's Sons, New York, NY, 1932. The classic harmony of the four Gospels.

A Survey of the New Testament: Gundry, Robert H. Zondervan 1970. The best New Testament survey book.

A Survey of the Old Testament: Archer, Gleason L., Jr. Moody, 1985. The best Old Testament survey book.

17

Halley's Bible Handbook: Halley, Henry H. Zondervan, 1965. A guide, along with my Bible, for many years.

Nave's Topical Bible: Nave, Orville. Associated Publishers, Byron Center, MI 49315. A compilation of Bible passages by subject, which is very helpful in topical study work.

The Greek-English New Testament: Zondervan, 1958.

Unger's Bible Dictionary: Unger, Merrill F. Moody, 1957.

Vine's Expository Dictionary of Old and New Testament Words: Vine, W.E. Revell, 1981.

3-Volume series: Baker. Necessary for in-depth Bible study.
    Gesenius' Hebrew-Chaldee Lexicon to the Old Testament
    Strong's Exhaustive Concordance
    Thayer's Greek-English Lexicon of the New Testament

Theology
A History of Christian Theology: Placher, William C. Westminster Press, Philadelphia, PA, 1983.

Foundations of Pentecostal Theology: Duffield, Guy P. and VanCleave, Nathaniel M. LIFE Bible College, Los Angeles, CA, 1983.

God, Man, & Salvation: Purkiser, Taylor, and Taylor. Beacon Hill Press, Kansas City, KS, 1977. A basic Arminian theology.

Life in the Son: Shank, Robert. Westcott Publishers, Springfield, MO, 1967. A classic on conditional security.

The Bible: Its Hell and Its Ages: McCrossan, T. J. Order from Clement Humbard, Youngstown, OH 44515. Refutes the Ultimate Reconciliation heresy.

Family Life
Beyond Sex Roles: Bilezikian, Gilbert. Baker, 1985. A releasing view of women in the church and home.

Dare to Discipline: Dobson, James. Tyndale House, Wheaton, IL, 1970. A classic on raising children.

Forever My Love: Hardisty, Margaret. Harvest House, Eugene, OR, 1975. A must reading for men, about women.

Men are from Mars, Women are from Venus. Gray, John. HarperCollins, New York, NY, 1992. About the differences between men and women.

Temperament and the Christian Faith: Hallesby, O. Augsburg Publishing, Minneapolis, MN, 1962. A classic on the four temperaments.

The Act of Marriage: LaHaye, Tim and Beverly. Zondervan, 1976. Sexuality from a Christian perspective.

Woman: God's Plan, not Man's Tradition: Krupp, Joanne. Preparing the Way Publishers, Salem, OR, 1999. The equality of women from a biblical perspective.

The Christian Life
A Treasury of A.W. Tozer: edited by Wiersbe, Warren W. Christian Publications, Harrisburg, PA 17101, 1980. A collection of Tozer's favorites.

Bodily Healing and the Atonement: McCrossan, T.L. Kenneth Hagin Ministries, Tulsa, OK 74150, 1982. A recent reprinting of McCrossan's classic on healing.

Christ the Healer: Bosworth, F.F. Revell, 1973. A classic on healing.

Deeper Experiences of Famous Christians: Lawson, James G. Whitaker House, New Kensington, PA 15068, 1998. About the Spirit-filled life.

In His Steps: Sheldon, Charles M., John C. Winston Company, Toronto, Canada, 1937. The fictitious story of a group of believers who determined to always ask "What would Jesus do?" in their daily lives and how it transformed their town.

Full Surrender: Orr, J. Edwin. Marshall, Morgan, & Scott, London, England, 1951. The believer's life of full surrender to GOD.

Peace With God: Graham, Billy. Doubleday, New York, NY, 1953. A classic on salvation.

Pigs in the Parlor: Hammond, Frank. Impact Books, Kirkwood, MO, 1973. About deliverance from demons.

Prison to Praise: Carother, Merlin. Logos International, Plainfield, NJ 07060, 1970. Thanking God "in all things."

Studies in the Sermon on the Mount: Lloyd-Jones, D. Martyn. Eerdmans, 1960. A classic, two-volume series on the Sermon on the Mount.

The Complete Works of E. M. Bounds on Prayer: Baker, 1990.

The Five Love Languages: Chapman, Gary. Northfield Publishing, Chicago, IL 60610. How we can express love to one another.

The Cross and Sanctification: Hegre, TA. Bethany, 1960. The best book I have found on the subject of sanctification.

The Latent Power of the Soul: Nee, Watchman. Christian Fellowship Publishers, 1972.

The Release of the Spirit: Nee, Watchman. Christian Fellowship Publishers, 2000.

The Transformation of the Inner Man: Sandford, John & Paula. Bridge Publishing, South Plainfield, NJ 07080. A classic on inner healing.

They Speak with Other Tongues: Sherrill, John L. McGraw-Hill, New York, NY, 1964. A classic on the experience at the heart of the Charismatic Renewal.

True Discipleship: MacDonald, William. Gospel Folio Press, Port Colborne, Ontario, Canada, 1962. Jesus' terms of discipleship. One of the most challenging books I ever read.

War on the Saints: Penn-Lewis, Jessie. Thomas E. Lowe, PO Box 1049, Cathedral Station, New York, NY 10025, 1973. An unabridged edition of this classic on spiritual warfare.

Church History and New Testament Church Life
Church History
A History of Christianity, Volumes 1 and 2: Latourette, Kenneth Scott, Harper, 1975, 724 pages. The most accurate, detailed account of church history available.

Aspects of Pentecostal-Charismatic Origins: Synan, Vinson. Logos International, Plainfield, NJ 07060 1975. The roots and early history of the Pentecostal-Charismatic movements.

Catholic Pentecostals: Ranaghan, Kevin & Dorothy. Paulist Press, New York, NY 10019, 1969. About the Charismatic Renewal in the Catholic Church.

Daughters of the Church: Tucker, Ruth A. and Liefeld, Walter. Zondervan, 1987. How GOD used women throughout Church history.

Rees Howells, Intercessor: Grubb, Norman. CLC, 1973. About an intercessor who helped change the world.

The Pilgrim Church: Broadbent, E.H. Gospel Folio Press, Port Colborne, Ontario, Canada. Traces simple, New Testament churches through the Centuries.

The Search for the Twelve Apostles: McBirnie, William Steuart. Tyndale, 1973. The life and travels of the twelve original apostles.

The Torch of the Testimony: Kennedy, John W. Christian Books, Goleta, CA 1965. About the many Christian church groups that have been outside of the Catholic and Protestant groupings.

They Marched to Heaven's Drumbeat: Finsaas, Clarence. Creation House, 1985. Brief biographies of twenty-two pioneers throughout Church history.

21

New Testament Church Life

Brethren, Hang Together: Girard, Robert C.   Zondervan, 1979. Restructuring the church for relationships.

Destined for the Throne: Billheimer, Paul E. CLC, 1975. The church as GOD's instrument of intercession.

Handbook on Deliverance: Meade, Russell.   Creation House, 1973. Excellent on the subject of deliverance from demons.

Like a Cleansing Fire: Hagee, John C. Revell, 1974. Visions of the end-time church.

Spiritual Leadership: Sanders, Oswald J.   Moody, 1967.   About the character qualifications needed for spiritual leadership.

The Gifts of the Spirit: Horton, Harold.   Assemblies of God Publishing House, London, England, 1934. The classic on the 1 Corinthians 12:4-11 gifts of the Spirit.

The Normal Christian Church Life: Nee, Watchman. Tyndale, 1969. A very important book on GOD's plan for His church.

The Problem of Wine Skins: Snyder, Howard, Intervarsity, 1975. A fresh look at church structure.

There Are Other Gifts Than Tongues: Grossman, Siegfried. Tyndale, 1971. A very practical, balanced book on the gifts of the Spirit.

Evangelism, Revival, and Missions

Evangelism

A Lost Secret of the Early Church: Bethybridge, WJ. Bethany. The importance and practics of home Bible study groups.

Every-Member Evangelism: Conant, J.E. Harper, 1922. A classic that calls every believer to the task of soul winning.

Exploring Evangelism: Taylor, Mendell. Nazarene Publishing House, Kansas City, MO, 1964. An overview of the theology, history, and methods of evangelism.

Goal-Oriented Evangelism-in-Depth: In-Depth Evangelism Association, Miami, FL 33157, 1972. Biblical principles on which community evangelism should be based.

Great Personal Workers: Whitesell, Faris Daniel. Moody, 1956. About some great soul winners.

New Testament Follow-Up: Moore, Waylon B. Eerdmans, 1963. A classic on the practical nurture of new believers.

Soul-Winning Made Easy: Lovett, C.S. Personal Christianity, Covina, CA, 1959. A simple plan for leading a person to Christ.

The Kingdom of the Cults: Martin, Walter R. Zondervan, 1965. A classic on Christian cult groups.

The Master Plan of Evangelism: Coleman, Robert E. Revell, 1963. Jesus' strategy for reaching the world by discipling a few.

The Unshakable Kingdom and the Unchanging Person: Jones, E. Stanley. Abingdon Press, Nashville, TN, 1972. Applying the Kingdom of GOD to all of life.

Revival
A Christian Manifesto: Schaeffer, Francis A. Crossway Books, Westchester, IL, 60153, 1981. Schaeffer's classic call for the church and society to return to biblical truth and the Lordship of Christ in all of life.

Another Wave of Revival: Bartleman, Frank. Whitaker House, Springdale, PA 15144, 1962. About the Azusa Street revival of 1905.

Heart-Cry for Revival: Olford, Stephen F. Revell, Old Tappan, NJ 07675, 1962. The challenge of needed revival.

Herald of His Coming: a monthly newspaper. Challenging information on prayer and revival.

Like a Mighty Wind: Tari, Mel. New Leaf Press, Harrison, AR 72601, 1971. The miracles of the New Testament seen in modern times in Indonesia.

Rain From Heaven: Wallis, Arthur. Hodder and Stoughton Limited, London, England, 1979, 125 pages. A treatise on the coming, last, great, end-time revival.

The Calvary Road: Hession, Roy. CLC, 1950. The life of brokenness and humility, the keys to revival.

The many writings of J. Edwin Orr.

The Vision: Wilkerson, David. Revell, 1974. Coming end-time events.

Why Revival Tarries: Ravenhill, Leonard. Bethany, 1959. A very stirring book on why we don't see revival.

Missions

A Global View of Christian Missions: Kane, J. Herbert. Baker, 1977, 590 pages. Tells how the Gospel came, nation-by-nation.

From Jerusalem to Irian Jaya: Tucker, Ruth A. Zondervan, 1983, 511 pages. A biographical history of Christian missions.

Let the World Hear His Voice: World Wide Publications, Minneapolis, MN 55438, 1975. A comprehensive reference volume on world evangelization.

Operation World: Johnstone, P.J. Zondervan. How to pray for every nation - updated occasionally.

Perspectives on the World Christian Movement: Edited by Winter, Ralph D. and Hawthorne, Steven C. William Carey Library, Pasadena, CA 91104, 1981, 846 pages. Biblical, historical, cultural, and strategic perspectives by world mission leaders.

What Do You Say to a Hungry World?: Mooneyham, Stanley. Word Books, Waco, TX 76700, 1973. About the world's food shortage and what to do about it.

America's Christian History

America: God Shed His Grace on Thee: Flood, Robert. Moody, 1975. The Christian history of America.

America: To Pray or Not to Pray?: Barton, David. Wallbuilder Press, Aledo, TX 76008, 1988. A look at what has happened since prayer was taken out of the public schools.

America's Dates With Destiny: Robertson, Pat. Thomas Nelson, Nashville, TN, 1986. The spiritual turning points in America's history.

Celebrations of a Nation: Johnston, Lucile. Biword Publications, Willman, MN, 1987. The Christian origins of our major national holidays.

The Essential American: A Patriot's Resource: Cushman, Jackie Gingrich. Regnery Publishing, One Massachusetts Avenue, NW, Washington, DC 20001, 2010. Twenty-five important documents and speeches from our history.

God's Signature Over the Nation's Capitol: Millard, Catherine. SonRise Publications, New Wilmington, PA 16142, 1985. Evidence of our Christian heritage in the architecture of Washington, DC.

One Nation Under God: Walton, Rus. Third Century Publishers, Washington, DC 20013, 1975. The Christian approach to government.

The Conscience of a Conservative: Goldwater, Barry. Macfadden Books, New York, NY 10017, 1960. A call for limited government.

The Light and the Glory: Marshall, Peter, and Manuel, David. Revell, 1977. The history of America from a Christian perspective.

Miscellaneous

Economics in One Lesson: Hazlitt, Henry. Harper, 1946. A primer on economics.

Go Natural!: Virkler, Mark & Patti. Destiny Image, Shippensburg, PA 17257, 1994. How to eat and live properly.

Inflation: The Ultimate Graven Image: Ferris, James Jay. New Leaf Press, Harrison, AR, 72601, 1982. The history of money from Genesis to Revelation, from gold to the mark of the beast.

Prescription for Nutritional Healing: Balch, James F. & Phyllis A. Avery Publishing Group, Garden City Park, NY, 1933.

The Day the Dollar Dies: Cantelon, Willard. Logos, 1973. An excellent picture of the coming cashless society.

APPENDIX 5 - BOOKS and BOOKLETS WRITTEN by NATE and JOANNE
(Nate wrote all of these books except
Woman, which was written by Joanne.)

You Can be a Soul Winner - Here's How, 1962. A here's-how manual on personal evangelism. It went through several editions by various publishers. Over 60,000 copies in print. It has been translated into several other languages.

Bible Studies for Soul Winners, 1962. A Bible study booklet on the subject of evangelism. It has gone through several editions by various publishers. Over 30,000 copies in print.

A World to Win, Bethany Fellowship, Minneapolis, MN, 1966, with foreword by Clyde Taylor. Secrets of New Testament Evangelism. Out of print.

Soul Winning Laymen, Beacon Hill Press, Kansas City, MO, 1972. Nate Krupp gathered the biographical material for this book - Evelyn Stenbock did the actual writing. These are stories of contemporary lay witnesses. Out of print.

The Way to GOD, Preparing the Way Publishers, 1973, revised 2012. This 16-page booklet presents the way of salvation.

The Omega Generation, New Leaf Press, Harrison, AR, 1977. About current world conditions and coming persecution. Out of print.

The Church Triumphant at the End of the Age, Destiny Image, Shippensburg, PA, 1984. This book tells about the end-time Church characterized by revival, restoration, unity, world evangelization, and persecution. A second edition was co-written with Janice Woodrum and published by Preparing the Way Publishers in 2010.

Fulfilling the Great Commission by A.D. 2000
New Wine Skins
Characteristics of the New Testament Church
These three booklets were published in 1990 and printed by Orval Johnston's printing company in Detroit, MI, but are no longer in print.

New Wine Skins - the Church in Transition, Preparing the Way Publishers, 1990. Fifteen ways God is changing His Church today. It has been translated into German.

God's Simple Plan for His Church - and Your Place in It, first edition by Solid Rock Books, 1993; second edition by Preparing the Way Publishers, 2003. A manual for house churches. It has been translated into several other languages, including Spanish and Telugu, a language in India.

Leadership-Servanthood in the Church - as found in the New Testament, Preparing the Way Publishers, 1994.

Woman - God's Plan, not Man's Tradition, Joanne Krupp, Preparing the Way Publishers, 1999. This book examines every major passage in the Bible on the subject of God's plan for women. It refutes the traditional teaching of husbands having authority over their wives and of a limited role for women in the church. It biblically releases women to become all that God intends them to be as equal partners in the home and the church. It has been translated into Arabic and Urdu. A Workbook is also available.

Fostoria, Ohio - as told by Paul H. Krupp, Volume 1, Arcadia Publishing, Chicago, IL, 2001. Historical stories about Fostoria, Ohio, edited by Nate Krupp.

Fostoria, Ohio - as told by Paul H. Krupp, Volume 2, Arcadia Publishing, Chicago, IL, 2002. Historical stories about Fostoria, Ohio, edited by Nate Krupp.

Knowing GOD Series This Series consists of five study books. Each one takes you deeper in your knowledge of GOD's Word and in your relationship with Him. You do not need to do the series in the given order (1-5), but you may find that helpful.

#1 - Basic Bible Studies   ISBN 1-929451-02-4   80 pages $11.95

A question-and-answer type, foundational Bible study book about the Christian faith and life. Chapters include:

1   Is There a God?
2   The Issue of Sin
3   What Provision Did God Make For Man's Sin?
4   How Should Man Respond to God's Provision?
5   Abiding in Christ
6   The Christian and God's Word
7   The Christian and Prayer
8   The Christian and the Holy Spirit
9   The Christian and Warfare
10   The Christian and Witnessing
11   The Christian and the Home
12   The Christian and the Church
13   The Christian and Business Affairs
14   The Christian and Discipleship
15   The Christian and Service
16   The Christian and the Return of Christ

(This is a combination of three earlier booklets, New Life Through Christ, Bible Studies for New Christians, and Bible Studies in Christian Discipleship.) It has been translated into Hindi, the major language of India.

#2 - New Testament Survey Course   ISBN1-929451-03-2
234 pages $19.95

This is a very unique 47-lesson Bible study survey of the New Testament.
-        It covers every verse of the New testament.
-        It leads you in an in-depth study of each book. You will read the entire New Testament and either answer summarizing questions or summarize the book, a paragraph at a time.
-        It harmonizes the Gospels so that you study Jesus' life in a single, chronological narrative.
-        It places the letters in the order in which they were actually written.
-        You will apply each book to your own life situation.
-        You will have a basic understanding of the New Testament when you have finished this study.

#3 - Mastering the Word of God - and Letting It Master You!
ISBN 1-929451-04-0   46 pages $6.95
This book is about various methods of in-depth Bible intake: how to hear, read, study, memorize, and meditate on the Word of God. With this book you will learn how to study the Bible. You will be able to develop a life-long plan of in-depth Bible study - mastering God's Word, and letting It master you.
Workbook   A helpful Workbook for **Mastering** is also available.
ISBN 1-929451-09-1   34 pages $5.95
Bible Outlines   Outlines every book, title for every chapter.
ISBN 1-929451-10-5   62 pages $9.95

#4 - Getting to Know GOD   ISBN 1-929451-05-9   288 pages $23.95
A devotional Bible study book on 57 aspects of GOD's Person, Character, and Attributes: His love, His mercy, His faithfulness, His goodness, etc. For each attribute, you will read an introduction, prayerfully read three or four pages of appropriate Scripture verses, answer study questions, do research, meditate on and apply the lesson to your life, memorize verses of your choice, and pray a closing prayer. An actual Bible study group wrote this book. This study will change your life!

#5 - Qualities GOD is Looking for in Us   ISBN 1-929451-06-7
384 pages $29.95
A 53-week Bible study, devotional book on the qualities God is looking for in us: abiding in Christ, boldness, contentment, diligence, discipline, early riser, forgiving, generous, holy, honest, humble, obedient, praiser, prayer, servant, wise, zealous, etc.   For each quality, you will read an introduction, prayerfully read three or four pages of appropriate Scripture verses, answer study questions, do research, meditate on and apply the lesson to your life, memorize verses of your choice, and pray a closing prayer. An actual Bible study group wrote this book. This study will greatly challenge you!

All of these books are available through -
Preparing the Way Publishers, Chehalis, WA 98532.
Phone (360) 262-3027, Website - ptwpublish.com,
E-mail - ptwpublish@q.com

APPENDIX 6 - BOOKS PUBLISHED BY PTWP

The following books, in addition to their writings, were published by Preparing the Way Publishers while the Krupps had it, 1999-2007. More have been published since the Woodrums took it over in October 2007.

Restoring the Vision of the End-times Church, Vern Kuenzi, 2000. A visionary look at the victorious end-times Church walking as Jesus walked.

God's Word Puts the Wind in My Sail, Joanne Bachran, 2001. A devotional guide to knowing GOD and His Word.

The Church in the House - a Return to Simplicity, Robert Fitts, 2001. Fulfilling the Great Commission by multiplying house churches around the world.

Foundations for the Christian Life, John G. Gill, 2002. Gives the foundation stones for the Christian life listed in Hebrews 6:1-3.

Richness in Christ, Chuck Tooman, 2006. The simplicity and richness of living in a loving relationship with Jesus.

Calling Forth the Remnant - by Way of the Cross, Stella Paterson, 2006. A treatise about the need to die to the flesh, return to the Cross, and become a Beautiful Bride for our Lord Jesus. Very radical!

All of these books are available through -
Preparing the Way Publishers, Chehalis, WA 98532.
Phone (360) 262-3027, Website - ptwpublish.com,
E-mail - ptwpublish@q.com

APPENDIX 7 - TEACHING ON CD/DVD

The following messages by Nate and Joanne are available on video, DVD, or CD.

By Joanne
WOMAN: God's Plan, not Man's Tradition. An overview of her book by the same title. 45 minutes.

By Nate
1 The Great Commission. What it is all about, the success of the Early Church, why they had that success, how we can fulfill the GC today. 60 minutes.

2 How to Present the Gospel. How to present the Gospel to an individual and lead them to Christ - from his book *You Can be a Soul Winner - Here's How.* 45 minutes.

3 Mastering the Word of GOD - and Letting It Master You! The importance of GOD's Word and how to take it in - hear, read, study, memorize, and meditate. 60 minutes.

4 GOD's Simple Plan for His Church. An overview of his book by the same title. 45 minutes.

5 The Church Triumphant at the End of the Age - Characterized by Revival, Restoration, Unity, World Evangelization, and Persecution. An overview of his book by the same title. 45 minutes.

For further details and/or to order, contact -
Preparing the Way Publishers
411 Zandecki Rd.
Chehalis, WA 98532
Phone: (360) 262-3027
E-mail: ptwpublish@q.com
Website: ptwpublish.com

APPENDIX 8 - CHRISTIAN LEADERSHIP UNIVERSITY

(The following courses by Nate and Joanne are offered by CLU. THE 207 is Joanne's - the rest are Nate's.)

BIB 109 - New Testament Survey. In this course you will study the entire New Testament, verse by verse, using a study guide written by Nate Krupp. You will apply all of this to your everyday life. You will memorize various passages of Scripture. You will have a basic understanding of the New Testament when you are finished.

BIB 110 - Mastering the Word of GOD. This course will take a look at the five major ways to master GOD's Word - hear, read, study, memorize, and meditate. You will learn how to do these methods by actually doing them. You will also learn how to allow the Word of God to master you. As part of the course you will develop a plan of lifelong Bible intake.

EVA 210 - Personal Evangelism. This course is a study of the Biblical role of, and practical approaches to, personal evangelism. It includes learning how to initiate the conversation with someone, present the Gospel to them, and lead them to Christ if they are ready. The course includes spending twenty hours in actual, practical, personal evangelism.

REN 110 - Qualities GOD is Looking For in Us. In this course you will study fifty-three disciplines and character traits that GOD is looking for in us including such things as fearing GOD, waiting on GOD, walking with GOD, Spirit-led, fully surrendered to the Lordship of Jesus Christ, a person of prayer, forgiving, content, joyous, watchful, self-controlled, diligent, humble, disciplined, teachable, integrity, enduring, servant, etc., as found in the Bible.

REN 220 - What GOD Is Saying to the Church Today. This course will take an overview look at the Church throughout history and a look at what GOD is saying to and doing in the Church today. It will look at the five basic areas of revival, restoration, unity, world evangelization, and end-time persecution. The book *The Church Triumphant at the End of the Age*, by Nate Krupp, will be used as the basic text.

THE 103 - Foundational Studies About the Christian Faith. This course is a study of what the Bible says about the basic truths of the Christian faith and life. It is a question-and-answer type study. You will discover what the Bible has to say about these basic areas of truth by looking up and studying the key passages on each subject and answering questions that are asked in the text. You will also apply each area of truth to your own life. There are also verses to be memorized in connection with each study.

THE 207 - GOD's Release of Women. This course will take a look at GOD's true plan for women: a plan of equality and release, in the home and in the Church. All the major portions of Scripture dealing with the role of woman will be carefully studied. The book *WOMAN: God's Plan, not Man's Tradition*, by Joanne Krupp, *will* be used as the basic text. You will also study other contemporary material on the subject. This course is for men as well as women. Until men have a revelation of the truths of this course, we will not see God's plan for women realized in the fullest.

THE 210 - Getting to Know GOD. In this course you will study fifty-seven aspects of the Person, character, and attributes of GOD - His mercy, His grace, His faithfulness, His glory, etc., as found in the Bible. For each attribute you will read an introduction, prayerfully read three or four pages of appropriate Scriptures, answer study questions, and do some additional research. You will also apply all of this to your everyday life and memorize various passages of Scripture. You will know GOD much better when you have finished this course.

THE 331 - House Church. This course will take a look at GOD's original plan for His Church, a plan that was very simple and easily reproducible. Many believers today are being led to try to recapture the simplicity of this early Church. This course will look at what the Scriptures teach about the Church as compared with the many traditions of men that have developed through the centuries. The course will include how to start and conduct a house church. It will emphasize how to evangelize the world today by a multiplication of simple house churches.

THE 332 - Leadership-Servanthood in the Church. This course will take a look at GOD's plan for leadership in His Church. Every major passage of Scripture dealing with the subject will be carefully studied.

These courses have been taken by more than 150 students, have changed lives, and are being reproduced around the world. A lady missionary taking Nate's course on House Church is now planting house churches throughout a Muslim nation. A young man who took the course on Personal Evangelism is now training soul winners in Hong Kong. Joanne's course has changed the lives of many women. Many courses are being re-taught in local churches by those who have completed them.

APPENDIX 9 - FULFILLING THE GREAT COMMISSION

(This message is the core of my life and ministry. - NK)

I. The Great Commission
   1. Jesus gave the Great Commission –
      Mt. 28:18-20, Mark 16:14-20, Luke 24:45-49, John 20:21-22, Acts 1:8
   2. It is a Commission to GO! A Commission to GO and take the Good News to every nation, every people group, every language, and every person.
   3. It is a personal command from Jesus to each of us - to go to our personal world and share the Good News with all.
   4. Much of the Church today has the Great Commission backwards. We devise all sorts of programs to get the lost to come to us to hear the Gospel. They are not to come to us - we are to GO to them!

II. Success of the Early Church
   1. They had converts daily - Acts 2:47, 16:5.
   2. They touched the whole known world
      - Acts 17:6.
   3. They totally evangelized some areas
      - Acts 19:10, 1 Thess. 1:8.
   4. All without the printing press, radio, TV, modern means of transportation, etc., etc.

III. Why did they have such success?
   1. They understood and exercised their <u>authority</u> - the right to proclaim the Gospel - Mt. 28:18.
   2. They ministered with the Holy Spirit's <u>power</u> - Luke 24:49, Acts 1:8, 4:29-31

3. Their pattern of evangelism -
   a. Everybody shared the Gospel - Mt. 4:19, John 15:16.
   b. Everywhere they went - Mark 16:15, 20.
   c. Every day - Acts 5:42.
4. They multiplied - 2 Tim. 2:2.
5. GOD attested to their work with miracles - Mark 16:20, Acts 4:30, etc.
6. Their Church life was very simple and easily reproducible.

IV. Can we have that success today? - and fulfill the Great Commission?
1. How? By returning to New Testament evangelism.
2. What are YOU going to do?

APPENDIX 10 - PROPHETIC PRAYER OF REPENTANCE FOR USA

(Given to Nate Krupp by the Holy Spirit on Sunday afternoon, September 15, 1996, and prayed at the Prayer Convocation in Jerusalem, Israel, that evening.)

A. **1 Peter 4:17 - GOD judges the Church first - then the nation.** The nation is a reflection of the condition of the Church. The U. S. condition is not good - the Church must not be what it should be.

B. **We repent:**
1. We must not have fulfilled the conditions of 2 Chronicles 7:14 because our land is not healed. **Please forgive us.**
2. For our superficial Christianity, lack of holiness, lack of unity, please **forgive us.**
3. For building our own Kingdoms rather than Your Kingdom, **please forgive us.**
4. For our spiritual pride, **please forgive us.**
5. For our idolatry - buildings, traditions, theologies, programs. We have wasted billions on our buildings and programs - money that could have been used to evangelize and feed the world. **Please forgive us.**
6. The Church has not been a prophetic voice to our nation - we have wanted the world's approval rather than preaching to the sins of our society. **Please forgive us.**
7. We have not fed the poor, clothed the naked, etc. - and have by default turned most of it over to the government. **Please forgive us.**
8. We have preached a watered-down Gospel and have not called men to repent. **Please forgive us.**
9. We have stayed in our comfortable meeting places rather than going out and evangelizing the lost. **Please forgive us.**

10. As leaders we have all too often "used" GOD's people rather than laying our lives down for them. We have used their money, time, and gifts to fulfill our vision - rather than releasing them to follow their vision.

We have often controlled and manipulated the people of GOD.

We have not released the women to fulfill their destiny in GOD.

We have not understood and released the apostles and prophets.

We have been CEO's rather than broken servants. **Please forgive us.**

11. We have exported -

- theologies and books - rather than the life of Christ.

- American churchianity and expected mission churches to accept that - rather than exporting New Testament Christianity. **Please forgive us.**

C. May this night be the beginning of truly meeting the conditions of 2 Chr. 7:14

- that genuine revival might break forth.

- that the Church will be fully restored to all that GOD intended.

- So that we will see - the world evangelized, a beautiful Bride prepared, and society impacted.

APPENDIX 11 - WHAT GOD IS AFTER IN HIS CHURCH

(Nate Krupp gave this teaching at a House Church Conference in Salem, Oregon, on April 22, 2007.)

1   He is after a Church where Jesus Christ is Lord of all. He is after a Church that is led and controlled by Him, not men.   Throughout Church history, GOD has often initiated something and then man soon takes it over; tries to organize it and control it; and GOD leaves the scene.

2   He is after a Church that gets people out of religion and programs - and challenges them to develop a deep, personal, intimate relationship with GOD.

3   He is after a Church that will be built on GOD-ordained relationships - and all needs (parenting children, evangelism, discipling converts, caring for the elderly, etc., etc.) are met through GOD-ordained relationships, not programs.

4   He is after a Church that will release all believers into their wholeness, giftings, ministries, and destiny.

5   He is after a Church that will recognize and enhance the GOD-ordained importance of the family.

6   He is after a Church that will work under any circumstances - urban, suburb, rural, free society, Communism, Islam, etc.

7   He is after a "new wineskin" that can catch and preserve the "new wine" that GOD is pouring out around the world.

8   He is after a Church that is so simple, easily reproducible, and GOD-led that it can grow, divide, multiply, and cover the earth. He is after something that will result in the Gospel being taken to every nation, language, people group, neighborhood, family, and individual on the face of the earth.

9   He is after a Church that will be a glorious, beautiful Bride, prepared for His Return.

APPENDIX 12 – A PROPHETIC WORD

(Nate Krupp gave this prophetic word at a house church group in Salem, Oregon, on November 13, 2010.)

Read Mark 8:34-38; Luke 14:26-27, 33-35; Ephesians 4:11-16.

"The Lord would say to each of us:
It is time to grow up -
- It is time to get out of whatever ditch you are in
- It is time to repent of your sins
- It is time to get healed of whatever hurts from the past still plague you
- It is time to quit getting offended - Ps. 119 - 'great peace have they which love Thy Law, and nothing shall offend them'
- It is time to get to know GOD - and become serious with Him - and love Him with all your heart - and your neighbor as yourself.
- It is time to humble ourselves and learn to submit to one another
- It is time to 'lift up your eyes on the fields and see that they are ripe already for harvest'
- It is time to find out what your gifts and ministries are - and begin to do the will of GOD
- It is time to turn away from the world - and give your life to extending the Kingdom of GOD
- It is time to become a soldier, yes, a warrior, for Jesus Christ.

Today is your day of decision - choose you this day whom you will serve - your immature, carnal, selfish desires - or the Living GOD."

APPENDIX 13
TOTAL MOBILIZATION
FOR TOTAL EVANGELIZATION
AND TRANSFORMATION

Introduction: As the world continues to fall apart the Church of Jesus Christ needs to mobilize for total evangelization. This plan was written for a major U.S. city and can be adapted for any city.

I. Preparation
A. Unity
1. Spiritual leaders (men and women) of the city (pastors and all other spiritual leaders, including some Christian businessmen) begin to meet monthly for fellowship, sharing, and prayer.
2. Spiritual leaders and their spouses meet annually for a meal, fellowship, sharing, and prayer.
3. The believers in every neighborhood, regardless of church affiliation, begin to meet a minimum of four times a year and a maximum of every other month - to get acquainted, share, pray, and become the Body of Christ in that neighborhood, meeting the neighborhood's spiritual and practical needs.

B. Revival
1. All local churches, neighborhood groups, other ministries, and other small groups begin praying for personal revival and an outpouring of GOD's Spirit upon the city.

C. Organization
1. Appoint an oversight committee to oversee this "Total Mobilization for Total Evangelization and Transformation" Project.

2. Every church appoint:

a. A prayer coordinator to coordinate a growing prayer emphasis.

b. An evangelism coordinator to coordinate the growing evangelism activity.

c. A mission coordinator to coordinate a greater overseas outreach.

d. A transform (name of city) coordinator to coordinate all of the church's transform (city) activities.

II. Mobilization

1. All believers trained for witnessing and soul winning - either in the local churches or in a citywide seminar.

2. The city divided so that every home is the responsibility of a nearby local church.

III. Evangelization

1. All believers continually encouraged to witness and give out Gospel literature as they go through the day.

2. Each church set aside one evening a week for visitation evangelism, where trained soul winners will go in teams of two to homes to present the Gospel.

3. Each church spend one Saturday a month going door-to-door in their area to meet people, leave Christian literature, and make appointments for a return visit with those who express interest in talking further.

4. The men of the church go to the taverns one Friday or Saturday evening a month to hand out literature and talk with those who are open to talking.

5. Other evangelization efforts can be undertaken as the Holy Spirit might direct.

6. Begin to transform the city physically, neighborhood by neighborhood, cleaning up the area, repairing homes, mowing the lawn, etc.

7. Continue to multiply the neighborhood groups for the benefit of the new believers.

8. The spiritual leaders will spend some of their monthly time together sharing the results of the evangelization efforts and encouraging one another in this great effort to evangelize and transform the city.

As this plan is implemented it should result in the growth of believers, a spiritual awakening coming to the city, the Gospel taken to every person in the city, new believers discipled, and the Great Commission fulfilled.
To GOD be the glory!

APPENDIX 14 - REPORTS
FROM AROUND THE WORLD

"Joanne's book was an eye opener." - wife of a house-church planter, Pampanga, Philippines

"You have impacted my life in many ways . . . I remember you giving out tracts on the streets of Tonga in 1979."
- Carol Preston. **USA**

"I took your course on Personal Evangelism from CLU. Your books *Bible Studies for Soul Winners* and *You Can be a Soul Winner - Here's How!* have impacted me in a profound way! I have never known fishing can be so fun. I am teaching others how to win souls."
- Jick Keng Foo, **Malaysia**

"Thank you for the book *God's Simple Plan*. I have read this book thrice. Can you come to teach us in 1997? I need your help." - National church planter, Kenya**, East Africa**

"I sent your book *God's Simple Plan* to my friend in Seoul. He wants to translate your book into Korean." - Young missionary, (from **North Korea**) now in Jerusalem

"We are a new house church here in Portugal and it was helpful reading *God's Simple Plan*." - **Portugal**

"It is miracle for me to have this kind of material. We now have nine home churches." - **Philippines** leader

"I'm returning to Russia with strong plans to do this work in my country, to renew the Church in the Spirit of Christ. I know I'm not alone in this job, because of your book (*God's Simple Plan*)."
- Professor in **Moscow, Russia**

"Thank you so much for sending your book *God's Simple Plan for His Church*. I like it very much. It is Biblical teaching. It will help me, I am sure, in my future ministry in **Myanmar** (formerly Burma)."
- Student, Union Theological Seminary, Philippines

"I have finished reading your book (*God's Simple Plan*) three days ago. I must confess that the contents have deeply sunk into me. I have never had such an experience in my life. I have never had such a spirit of revival taken place in me. There is hope! The world can be won for the Lord!"
- National leader, Ghana, **West Africa**

"I am very happy to tell you that the message in your book *God's Simple Plan for His Church* has greatly changed God's Church and has challenged me. We are now having ten house churches . . . and the expenses on big prayer houses and fat salaries for pastors are being reduced."
- National leader, Malawi, **Central Africa**

"I am very glad and grateful to state that I have received the book *God's Simple Plan for His Church*. The house churches concept is not a new phenomenon, but, because the Church universal for hundreds of years has deviated from this simplicity, many of us are seeing it a gigantic challenge. It is my humble, but fervent, prayer that the Holy Spirit will bring this to the utmost attention of Church leaders worldwide to speed the fulfilling of the Great Commission. As a church planter and the General Overseer of the Frontline Gospel Church International, I consider your book as an important tool in my ministry." - Church leader, Ghana, **West Africa**

Regarding the book **The Church Triumphant at the End of the Age,** (which was Nate Krupp's thesis for a master's degree from YWAM's University of the Nations) -

"The author has effectively raised the clarion call for 'revival' for the Christian movement of our day."
- Dr. O. D. Emery, General Superintendent, The Wesleyan Church

"Nate Krupp has done the Christian world a valuable service in documenting renewal and revival throughout Church history. His earnest burden to help the Church recover its New Testament fervor and format appears on almost every page." - Dr. Raymond L. Cox, Pastor and Historian, The International Church of the Foursquare Gospel

"Few books have dared to document so fully the incredible ways in which God has been working in His Church as we approach the year 2000. Should be required reading for any world Christian."
- Jay Gary, *World Christian* magazine

"This book will enlighten and inspire your vision and prayer and faith for 'revival in our time.' " - Armin Gesswein

"Nate has convinced me with both facts and the Word of the Lord that completion of the Great Commission will only come as the Church pays the price in desperate prayer for a might end-time revival." - Graham Kerr

"I do not know any other one source where I could obtain so much information on the subject of revival so quickly."
- Ray E. Smith, General Superintendent, Open Bible Standard Church

"Nate Krupp has produced a major work which, if used as a text, can provide superb training for the harvesters when God calls. This book is informative, stimulating, and highly motivational. It is a timely work, which has substantially advanced the fulfillment of the Great Commission." - Dr. C. Peter Wagner

"*The Church Triumphant* has been twenty-five years in the making. In these pages, Nate shares the things God has poured into his life in the areas of revival, restoration of the Church, and world evangelism. May God use this book to encourage His Church to do great exploits and triumphantly bring back the King!" - Loren Cunningham, founder, Youth With A Mission

"Two underlying theses of this book are: (1) We may expect a major, worldwide revival in coming years, which will immediately precede Christ's Second Coming, and (2) God has been progressively restoring the Church to the New Testament model. The comprehensiveness, sensitivity, and essentially Biblical concept of the Church evident in these pages make this a useful study book for all careful, prayerful Christians."
- Dr. Howard A. Snyder

"Nate Krupp's book, *The Church Triumphant*, has proven over the years to be the most informative, formative, and destiny-provoking book I have ever read - next to my Bible. As a missionary for over twenty years, no other influence has been more significant to instruct and prepare me for the ministry God has ordained for me and my husband. The concise histories of the Church, revivals and reformations through the centuries, and development of the world mission movements have proven to be the most vital information I have needed for my work in world missions. And this book is an integral component for over twenty Bible schools we have started in Asia and Africa. I believe it will continue to echo loudly throughout the Christian world until the return of Jesus Christ."
- Janice Woodrum

APPENDIX 15 - SHARED AT MOAA

Chaplain Nate Krupp shared
the following items at MOAA meetings.

Month	Theme	Shared
December 2010	Christmas	Luke 2:8-11.

January 2011	New Year	2 Timothy 4:7-8 - "keep the faith."
February	(Chaplain was sick.)	
March		Lincoln's Gettysburg Address.
April	Easter	Matthew 28:1-6, John 3:16 - What does it mean to believe.
May	(Group on a cruise - I did not share.)	
June		The miracle of Dunkirk.
July	(The Chaplain was out of town.)	
August	Read portions of the Declaration of Independence.	
September	9/11 - End times	Matthew 24:3-8.
October Convention	Invocation	Invite GOD to be part of your life.
	Luncheon	Portions of Deuteronomy 8.
	Banquet	Joshua 24:15 - serve the Lord.
	Closing	Sang *GOD Bless America*.
November	Thanksgiving	Pilgrim story.
December	Pearl Harbor, Christmas	Roosevelt's address
.		

January 2012	Importance of daily Bible reading.	
February	Presidents	Lincoln's 2nd Inaugural.
March	My visit to the Battleship Missouri.	
April	Mayor's visit	Romans 13, Big government.
May	Mother's Day	Proverbs 31, Joanne prayed.
June	(The Chaplain was out of town.)	
July	(No meeting.)	
August	The spiritual life of General Douglas MacArthur.	
September	More about MacArthur.	
October	Elections	Elections.
November	Veterans' Day	Isa. 40:28-31 - wounded warriors.
December	Christmas	Portions of Isaiah 53.

Month	Theme	Shared
January 2013		Importance of daily Bible reading (repeat).
February	Presidents	Sang *America* from new songbook.
March	Easter	John 14:1-7 - Jesus is the way.
April	Boston massacre	End times - Mt. 24:3-7, 11-14.
May		Men and women - Joanne's book.
June		Mem'l Day, Flag Day - Sing, "You're a Grand Old Flag."
July	4th	Patrick Henry
August		Freedom to do GOD's will.
September		George Patton's prayer life.
October		GOD's love and goodness - Ps. 86:5, 10,13,15.

APPENDIX 16 - NATE'S
TRIBUTE TO JOANNE

(Written on their 50th Wedding Anniversary, September 16, 2011.)

*It was my honor and privilege to marry
Joanne Elizabeth Sheets Brannon 50 years ago today on
Saturday, September 16, 1961, in Marion, Indiana.*

*We had met at the College Wesleyan Methodist Church in
August 1960; and had a Coke date after the Sunday evening
church service in October. On December 7, GOD spoke to me
through Genesis 24:7, and 27, that she was "the one," so we
began dating in January 1961; engaged in March;
announced it in May and married September 16, 1961.
GOD had clearly brought us together.*

*Joanne was surely GOD's perfect choice for me. She has been
my partner in life and ministry; my wonderful sweetheart;
my best friend; my chief counselor, critic, and adviser;
our secretary and treasurer; and an excellent mother,
grandmother, and great-grandmother.*

*She pretty much raised the children as I was out holding
Lay Evangelism Crusades across the U.S. and Canada;
and later, teaching in Youth With A Mission
missionary training schools around the world.*

*Her book on GOD's releasing plan for women has gone around
the world - and she has been a friend and counselor to many.*

I have learned so much from her and am so extremely grateful to GOD for bringing us together. I don't know what I would ever do without her!

APPENDIX 17 - FAMILY PHOTOS

"I'm Back in the Saddle Again"

Christmas with Mom and Dad

Family photo during high school

Student Body President at Purdue

Purdue University grad – June 1957

U.S. Navy Civil Engineer Corps officer - 1957-59

**Recent photos of the two men who
led me to Christ on March 17, 1957**

Nate Scharff

Abraham Zion David

Our wedding on September 16, 1961

At our home in Chicago in 1968: Nate, Jo, Gerry, Bethie.

With Youth With a Mission in Hawaii in 1979: Nate, Jo, Beth, Gerry

Teaching principles of personal evangelism.

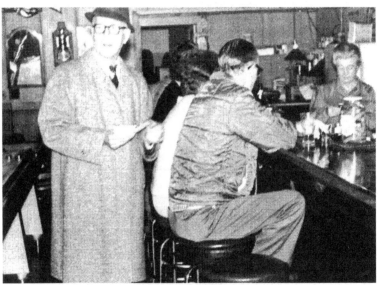

One of the Lay Evangelism participants passes
out Christian literature in a tavern.

At Christ's empty tomb in Jerusalem in 1996.

Our team and participants at New Wine Skins
Conference in Ghana, Africa, in 1999.

Family Reunion and 50th Wedding Anniversary Celebration June 2012 at Oceanside, California.

Back row (L to R): Andrew (Jamie's husband), Cameron (Kelly's fiancé), Greg (Beth's husband), Dan (Beth's son), Geoffrey (Gerry's oldest), Gerry (our son), Alex (Gerry's twin), Wenda (Gerry's wife).

Middle: Kelly (Beth's daughter).

Front row (L to R): Aaron (Jamie's son), Jamie (Beth's daughter), Beth (our daughter), Audra (Jamie's daughter), Nate, Jo, Allison (Gerry's twin).

My beautiful, wonderful wife:
Joanne Elizabeth (Sheets) Krupp.

Joanne and Nate

Our home and offices in Salem, Oregon.

My favorite pastime.

My little boat at a lake in the Cascade Mountains.

Oregon scenery: Pacific Ocean and Mt. Hood.

NOTES

TO OBTAIN COPIES OF THIS BOOK

Available from Amazon.com, CreateSpace.com, and other retail outlets.

To contact the author, e-mail him at kruppnj@comcast.net.

Made in the USA
Columbia, SC
01 November 2021

47953693R00261